1000
Motorbikes
History · Classics · Technology

© Naumann & Göbel Verlagsgesellschaft mbH, a subsidiary of
VEMAG Verlags- und Medien Aktiengesellschaft, Cologne
www.apollo-intermedia.de

Author: Carsten Heil
Complete production: Naumann & Göbel Verlagsgesellschaft mbH, Cologne
Printed in Poland

1000
Motorbikes
History • Classics • Technology

CONTENTS

The history of the motorbike and of the people who made it

The starter's gun which heralded a new era was fired about 100 years ago. The dynamics introduced by the introduction of mechanical power carried mankind into the age of mobility and shortened distances. What kind of developments will motorcyclists witness in the future? What discoveries and obstacles have marked the way, what turning points determined the course of the history of the motorbike? And what innovations are taking us faster into the future? Naturally there are hundreds of factors which have played a part, involving thousands of discoveries, inventions and developments. In addition, every individual will consider particular things to be the most important. Yet the enthusiasm for one technical solution or another often blurs our vision of the essential. Fundamentally, the motorcycle is a motor-driven single-track (i.e. two-wheeled) vehicle whose most important component is the rider. If it is not moving or if there is no rider, it simply falls over. The condition of movement is essential in a motorcycle since it is otherwise unstable, and the rider represents about one-third of the weight of the motorbike. When this ratio is not correct, the motorbike may be damaged or destroyed and the rider injured. This has consequences which affect static equilibrium, dynamics and ergonomics. Whether a motorcycle has one cylinder or eight, a 2-stroke or a 4-stroke engine, or a chassis made from wood or carbon fibre, is of only secondary importance.

In the beginning was the motorbike

The motorbike was a development of the bicycle combined with the steam engine. The first self-propelled bicycle was built in 1869 by the French bicycle makers Ernest and Pierre Michaux using a small steam engine under the saddle which drove the rear wheel through two leather belts. The contraption conceived by the steam engine manufacturer Sylvester Roper was even crazier. Because even in those days everything was larger in America, he chose a 2-cylinder steam engine with a capacity of 600 cc which was remarkably practical, being fuelled by charcoal. Roper had also designed the very first, forward-placed footrests in the Easy Rider style, extending on both sides of the front wheel axle. The problem with steam drive for two-wheel vehicles is obvious: the rider is engulfed by steam and flames whenever it falls over.

Otto's achievement

By 1874 Nikolaus August Otto had developed the first internal combustion engine ready for production. Two years later he patented the 4-stroke engine, an achievement which is still important today since it is used in the vast majority of cars and many motorbikes. Otto's engineer Gottlieb Daimler was very enthusiastic about the new development and he joined forces with his colleague Wilhelm Maybach to set up their own workshop in Cannstadt, near Stuttgart, manufacturing internal combustion engines. On 10 November 1885, ten years or so after Otto's invention, the two engineers fitted a lighter and more powerful internal combustion engine to a wooden bicycle. According to the account of Daimler's son Paul, the first ride was made to Untertürkheim nearby with Wilhelm Maybach. Gottlieb Daimler did not trust the stability of the two-wheeler so he had installed two lateral stabilisers to prevent it toppling; yet even so he registered a patent for a two-wheeled vehicle. It is indeed normally accepted that his vehicle, known as a 'riding machine', was the origin of all motorbikes. However, for us motorcyclists it was his partner Wilhelm Maybach who was the more important of the two. This was not only because he later built motorbikes in his factory at Friedrichshafen but more significantly because he also invented the principle of the spray carburettor with an enclosed float chamber which is still used today. The system which was common at the time was known as a 'surface vaporiser', where air was drawn over liquid fuel or a fuel-soaked wick; these were horrendous devices for motorbikes. We have already mentioned the problem of the bike falling over and the

9

Daimler riding vehicle (1885)
The first motorcycle. This reproduction of the first motorcycle, powered by a petrol engine and built by Gottlieb Daimler and Wilhelm Maybach, is on display at the German Bicycle Museum in Neckarsulm. The single-cylinder 4-stroke engine had a capacity of 264 cc and developed half a horsepower.

consequent conflagration, and a puddle of petrol burns better than any steam engine.

For the same reason, the importance of the invention of high tension magneto ignition with spark plugs cannot be over-estimated. In 1902 Robert Bosch finally succeeded in bringing the ignition of the fuel under control. Admittedly the first high tension magneto ignition had been used in France since 1898, yet Count Albert de Dion still used the contact-breaker ignition system when building his motorised three-wheeled vehicle. The count imitated Daimler's engine but he made it lighter by using an aluminium casing, and he also combined the flywheel with the crankshaft and the ignition control with the camshaft. This light, compact engine was ideal for two-wheeled vehicles so that De Dion and shortly afterwards Peugeot engines were sold successfully all over the world, by Pope in the USA and Norton in England among others.

Mass production

At the end of the 19th century and the beginning of the 20th, many factories specialising in very varied fields became interested in two-wheeled vehicles. Most of them, such as Bianchi in Italy (from 1897), Adler in Germany, Norton in England and Peugeot in France (all from 1899 onwards), were already producing bicycles. But others just wanted a share of this flourishing new market because their existing markets were stagnating. These included the Neckarsulm knitting machine factory (NSU, 1901) and Birmingham Small Arms (BSA, 1903). Others again were completely convinced of the future of the motorbike from the very beginning.

Such were the brothers Wilhelm and Heinrich Hildebrand with their partner Alois Wolfmüller in Munich and the Russian Michel Werner, living in exile in Paris, with his brother Eugène. All can claim to have contributed more or less at the same time to the spread of the word 'motorcycle'. The Werner 'motocyclette' officially went into production in 1896 while in 1897, the last year of production, Hildebrand & Wolfmüller patented their 'motorcycle'. The Munich company had already launched its prototype for commercial production in 1894 so their vehicle can be considered the first mass-produced

Hildebrand & Wolfmüller (1894)
The first mass-produced motorbike in the world was also made in Germany. Wilhelm and Heinrich Hildebrand and their partner Alois Wolfmüller patented the word 'motorcycle'. The 2-cylinder 4-stroke engine with hot-tube ignition and water-cooling had a capacity of just under 1.5 litres and was capable of developing 2.5 bhp. The total number of Hildebrand & Wolfmüller motorbikes produced was about 2,000.

motorbike in the world. Although it was technically already lagging behind its competitors with its rubber piston-return belts, about 1,000 were sold in three years. On the other hand, after experiments with the engine operating the front wheel, by 1900 Werner's motorcycle had acquired its standard appearance as we know it today: a compact engine in the lower part of the frame, with a transmission conveying power to the rear wheel and a fuel tank between the saddle and handlebars. The idea of placing the engine in this position came from Václav Laurin, who together with his business partner Václav Klement, built a frame with a Werner engine inside it.

The pioneers who paved the way for the motorbike were Nikolaus August Otto, Wilhelm Maybach, Count Albert de Dion, Michel Werner, Václav Laurin and Robert Bosch.

The policy for the future

As gregarious animals, human beings organise themselves hierarchically and as hunters they value speed. Nothing had changed in this New Age: the person who was in the lead was best. People were already racing in 1899, as is shown by a poster advertising the first 'Racing for motorbikes' in Exelberg in Austria . The development of speed and of speed-lovers soon highlighted a serious problem: at high speed it was difficult for riders to keep their hands on the handlebars, let alone to operate the numerous control levers. In 1904 in Dourdan the 2-cylinder Peugeot reached the dizzying speed of 123 km/h (76 mph) on a very wet surface – a world record! While riding the bike the rider had not only to accelerate using the twist grip and move the ignition timing lever; he also had to take one hand off the handlebars to pump the oil or petrol. The thin wheel forks were now strengthened by parallel construction but they were still unsprung.

A suspension was therefore indispensable. It is difficult to establish exactly when this was first fitted to a motorbike. The French Griffon is thought to have already had one in 1903. What is certain is that in 1904 Peugeot with the Truffault fork produced one of the most modern motorbikes of the time. In 1905 Bianchi developed a swinging fork and then Norton's victory in the first Tourist Trophy in 1907 with a coil-sprung trapezoid fork marked a breakthrough. Until the First World War all larger motorbikes were based on this principle for the front wheel suspension. The swinging arm and the parallelogram spring fork (Harley-Davidson 1909) were some of the early systems which are still being used today. The trapezoid fork was abandoned for a while and then rediscovered 80 years later by the Englishman Norman Hossack. At the same time, the first rear-wheel suspension was being produced. Although it made riding more comfortable, it was not used in racing because it made the motorbike more unstable at higher speeds.

It was in this period that Indian, a make founded by George M. Hendee and Carl Oscar Hedstrom in 1901, came to prominence in the world of motorbikes. In 1907 it won the Reliability Trials, known today as the Scottish Six Day Trials, and in 1911 the Tourist Trophy. The victory in the Trials was clearly the result of the chain drive to the rear wheel which the Nuremberg-based Victoria AG had been using for two years to replace the traditional drive belts. The first three places in the Tourist Trophy were won by Indians, a disaster for the English. A third of their bikes had a

Suspension (1909)
At the beginning of the 20th century motorbike manufacturers experimented with a wide range of front-wheel suspensions. Harley-Davidson used the so-called 'spring fork' system for the first time in 1909 and even today models with this type of suspension system are still produced in Milwaukee.

gear ratio appropriate for the hilly stretches, while the rest had to stop before starting on steep climbs in order to move the drive belt onto a larger gearwheel. Hestrom had developed a reliable gear transmission with two gears which could be switched by means of a clutch while driving. In combination with the non-slip chain transmission, this proved to be a superior concept. To be fair, it should be mentioned that in 1913 England's presentation racing bike by Rudge was fitted with an adjustable belt pulley which made 21 ratios possible. This helped the bike to finish in second place in the Senior TT of that year and Rudge would play an increasingly important part in the history of the motorbike. The pioneers we single out in this period are the brothers Jean-Pierre and Jean-Frédéric Peugeot, George M. Hendee and Carl Oscar Hedstrom.

Technical developments

After the First World War innovations developed for military purposes could now be used for civilian ones. Engine technology had made enormous progress as a result of the advances in aviation. This progress had been vital because originally more pilots were lost through failures in mechanical technology than through being shot down. The effects on the engine of centrifugal force when looping, of increasingly thin air at high altitude and of icy temperatures all created new problems which had to be solved. Then as now, aeronautics were synonymous with technological progress, and aviation contributed to the development of vibration-resistant materials and clever innovations such as twin ignition and camshafts driven by vertical drive shafts. The link between the aeroplane and the motorbike was underlined by the blue and white propeller symbol of BMW and the eagle of Moto Guzzi. It was no coincidence that the first models produced by these makers had another point in common: in 1921, two years after Carlo Guzzi's C2C came out, air pioneer Max Friz's BMW R32 had a direct connection linking the steering head and rear axle. These were the first two motorbikes which moved away from the traditional motorbike chassis, now taking static equilibrium into account.

Also making a name for himself was Ernest Neumann, who later added 'Neander' to his name. Originally a graphic artist, he had designed bodywork for Austro-Daimler before the First World War but in the Roaring Twenties he displayed a revolutionary approach to design. Having joined Allright-Werke in Cologne, he built his first motorbike in 1924, which was also the first to have an aluminium frame. Today sports bikes are made entirely from seamless tubes of lightweight materials. Always a puzzle freak and a practical person, he was more interested in ideas than in money. Interchangeable wheels and engines secured only by a central bolt, fuel tanks welded rather than bolted in place and comfortable seats with air cushions were but a few of the innovations introduced by Ernest Neumann. The greatest coup for this otherwise financially unfortunate man was the sale of the licence for his chassis design to Opel in 1928. He was particularly keen on smaller front and rear wheels which were later fitted to enduro and chopper bikes. Another of his inventions was the fully-floating axle. More local and therefore also more successful were the Danes Jörgen Skafte Rasmussen and Hugo Ruppe in Zschopau, Germany. The abbreviation of Rasmussen's 'Dampfkraftwagen' ('steam-driven vehicle') survived in the name of the motorbike marque: DKW. Instead of steam

BMW R32 (1923)
Farewell to the bicycle frame. The BMW R32 and Moto Guzzi C2V were the first motorbikes with a direct link between the steering head and rear axle. The much-improved frame geometry which resulted from this made the handling of the motorbike very much simpler.

drive, and unlike almost all the competition which used 4-stroke engines, DKW switched to using 2-stroke engines in 1917. Until then only Scott in England had been able to demonstrate the efficiency of this system, as reflected in its TT victories in 1912 and 1913. From its first 30-cc auxiliary bicycle engine to the water-cooled 500-cc 2-cylinder engine developed at the end of the 20th century, DKW contributed to the breakthrough of the 2-stroke engine with only three moving parts. In France, Motobécane was very successful with such engines and it still produces very quick little powerplants. In Italy, under the management of the young Rudolf Carraciola, Garelli – the first company to make motorbikes with twin-piston engines – easily overhauled the Guzzis and Gileras. But not only did DKW put Germany on two wheels: it also exported its bikes all over the world. The first assembly-line production of motorbikes in 1926 was the logical conclusion. The heroes of this era include the names of Max Friz, Ernst Neumann-Neander, Jörgen Rasmussen and Hugo Ruppe.

Economics and new materials

The world economic slump in the late 1920s marked the end for many innovative small companies, including that of Neumann-Neander. But it also saw the closure of the noble Tornax company of Wuppertal because it was no longer allowed to buy English JAP engines: this was one of Hitler's bans which seriously affected technical development, since success in

DKW advertising (1949):

By the end of the 1920s DKW had become the largest motorbike manufacturer in the world. As the pioneer of 2-strokes, DKW built bikes with engines ranging from 125 to 500 cc. After the war DKW in Zschopau became VEB Motorradwerk Zschopau or MZ for short. DKW started building motorbikes in Ingolstadt in 1949.

motorcycle racing had become a matter of prestige for several nations. British, German and Italian riders would compete regularly to beat the world speed record. For experts to exchange information as they had in the past would now be considered treason. On the other hand, there was the attraction of financial gain. Most motorbike makers did not care about politics. This was the case with the young Italian engineers Carlo Gianni and Pietro Remor. As early as 1924 Remor had already had the idea of mounting a 4-cylinder engine transversely on a motorbike, instead of lengthways as in cars. Together with Count Bonmartini of the Italian National Aeronautics Cooperative, he developed the GRB with air-cooled 4-cylinder engine. Then the prosperous Giuseppe Gilera bought the idea and employed Remor. From then on the Gilera Rondine with Piero Taruffi competed against Eric Fernihough's Brough Superior and Ernst Henne's supercharged BMW. Italian, British and German engineers also contributed to further developments in the moving parts of the motorbike. 1935 marked the breakthrough of rear-wheel suspension, fitted for instance on the Moto Guzzi which won the Junior and Senior TT. In the same year BMW introduced hydraulically damped telescopic forks which today is still the system most commonly used. Two years later Edward Turner was successful with his twin engine, barely larger than a single-cylinder one but with a higher performance. Parallel twins, based on this principle, set the tone for the next 40 years. Completely new materials were used to meet the new performance expectations. Light metals such as aluminium, electron and magnesium had made their appearance some time earlier. Bakelite marked the first technical application of a synthetic material and was used for headlight casings, switches and light gear wheels in dynamo drives. 'Vorsprung durch Technik' ('Progress through technology'), was promised by DKW/Auto-Union in 1939, and so it was that complete motorbike frames, consisting of three moulded parts glued together, were constructed from synthetic materials. Engineers under Dr. Richard Bruhn recognised that these materials required different shapes from metal to ensure strength and rigidity: in spite of having the usual 2-stroke engine, the object patented looked rather absurd. It was never produced because the world's war lords had decided to reduce the world to rubble. Some names to remember from these years are Dr. Richard Bruhn, Carlo Guzzi, Pietro Remor, Rudolf Schleicher and Edward Turner.

Biedermeier and Rock 'n' Roll

In the 1950s Corrado d'Ascanio pulled off the coup of the century with his Vespa, with its one-sided suspension and in particular the swing-arm drive train which are still used today. This little motor-scooter became one of the world's best-sellers. Tiny motorbikes were also produced by other companies such as Moto-bécane, which launched its Mobylette, and NSU which produced the Quickly. This moped headed the sales charts and was popular throughout the world. Small

Moto Guzzi Bialbero (1954):
Moto Guzzi won many World Championship titles in the Grand Prix calendar with its 350 and 500-cc Bialbero Racers in the course of the 1950s. Some of the technical features of these bikes are still used today, such as their double ignition and the tubular space frame made of steel.

2-stroke engines experienced a revival. DKW returned to the scene on both sides of the newly-erected Berlin Wall: the 125, built at Ingolstadt and Zschopau, served as a model for BSA, Harley-Davidson and Suzuki.

Sea mammals became increasingly popular. The bikes with which NSU and Moto Guzzi won their victories were streamlined with fairings in dolphin-like shapes. Using its wind tunnel built in 1950, the Mandello-based maker was able to carry out important pioneering work on the aerodynamics of the motorcycle. In the 1980s, tests in the VW wind tunnel confirmed that the Moto Guzzi 1000SP had approximately 50% less lifting force on the front wheel than the BMW K100RS or the Yamaha FJ1100.

With Albert Roder, NSU too set standards in the drawing office. 'Baumm's lounger', designed by Gustav Adolf Baumm, had only one-eighth of the air resistance of a non-streamlined bike and rider. Subsequently all cigar-shaped record-breaking motorbikes have followed Roder's concept.

Wind tunnel (1951):
Moto Guzzi and NSU were the first motorbike manufacturers who, in the 1950s, developed aerodynamically streamlined full fairing with the aid of extensive wind tunnel testing. Their pioneering work in wind tunnels was rewarded by great success in racing.

At first the fairings of racing bikes were hammered by hand from aluminium but soon this was replaced by synthetic materials. The development of synthetics such as fibreglass (glass-reinforced plastic or GRP) took off on a large scale during the war because they were not visible to radar. Malicious gossip has it that US customisers had also developed the material for their hot rods. But the fact is that Major Kenneth Brooks, who worked for boat builder William Tritt, was the first to mount a fibreglass body on a Jeep in 1950. The Chevrolet Corvette was the first mass-produced car with a fibreglass body while the Vincent Series D, launched in 1954, was the first motorbike.

'Put your ass in fiberglass' was the

NSU Baumm record-breaking vehicle (1954):
It was with this record-breaking vehicle that H.P. Müller set a total of 36 motorcycle world records on the Bonneville Salt Flats (USA) in 1956. The 50-cc single cylinder Quickly engine was fitted with a rotary piston supercharger. The 10-bhp 2-stroke power unit enabled the vehicle to reach a speed of 196 km/h (121.8 mph). Fitted with the 125 cc 4-stroke engine of the NSU Rennfox, 'Baumm's lounger' could reach a top speed of 243 km/h (151 mph) with a mere 20 bhp.

American motto of all DIY mechanics who could now easily make the parts themselves. Further developments in the technique made triumphant progress, culminating in the carbon fibre and Kevlar of the present day. The 1950s saw the introduction of telescopic forks, the rear wheel swing-arm, the foot-operated gear-change and the hand-operated clutch. So far as construction was concerned, there was now hardly any difference between mass-produced bikes and sports bikes. But racing bikes were unstoppable: Gilera's 4-cylinder was followed by Moto Guzzi's V8 designed by Giulio Cesare Carcano. But Carcano, who loved heavyweight bikes, recognised that such monsters were not made for the street. All his life he remained of the opinion that up to 500 cc one cylinder was enough, and over that, two. To be honest: is a Honda Hornet really more roadworthy on a country road than a KTM Duke? Walter Kaaden, Giulio Cesare Carcano, Albert Roder and, indirectly, William Tritt all played a major part in the development of the ordinary road motorbike.

A coup overturns the system

At the end of the decade, a new trend emerged in Czechoslovakia: special bikes were offered for sale. In 1957 ESO built the first bikes with extras designed for moto-cross. Jaroslav Simandl had been building his special engines for speedway racing since 1948. Until then sports bikes always had their mass-produced equivalent, a perfect example being the BSA Goldstar, but specialisation started in the 1960s. Companies such as Bultaco emerged as a result of this; Francisco Bulto was obsessed with competition. Others such as Maico or Zündapp survived the decline in the motorbike market as a result of this specialisation. The requirements of racing led to specific technical features: a trial bike no longer had anything in common with a road bike. But these technical features were later incorporated in mass-produced bikes, such as the moto-cross single suspension. The motorcycle market changed completely. Soishiro Honda drew the right conclusions from the situation and perhaps even contributed to its development. He manufactured mass-produced motorbikes which as well as their performance and reliability were technically astonishing. It had been said that over-sophisticated, complicated motorbikes were hard to sell, but the CB 450 and CB 750 proved this not to be the case. From now on, Japanese production philosophy set the course of the new technology. By the end of the 1960s no one wanted a sensible all-rounder bike that would simply take its owner to work. The system went into reverse: engineers no longer designed bikes which the manufacturer would then seek buyers for, but instead they designed bikes which they knew buyers wanted. The characters who played a major part in this revolution were Jaroslav Simandl, Francisco Bulto and Soishiro Honda.

The Stuyvesant Generation

Specialisation and individualisation in the 1970s led more to a broadening of the range than to new technology. Even in 1976 an expensive high-tech motorbike such as the Van Veen OCR still had a frame made from steel tubes, telescopic forks and swing-arm, with twin suspension struts. Meanwhile there were also technical innovations such as hydraulic disc brakes (Honda 1968), electronic ignition (Maico 1971) and gear-driven toothed-belt camshaft (Morini 1973) whose importance should not be underestimated. But on the whole for 20 years the basic construction of motorbikes hardly changed. The boom led to new phenomena which had certain consequences later. Enthusiasts who produced parts and motorbikes specially to order for their customers started their own companies and exported their ranges all over the world. One of the most successful was the Californian Arlen Ness with his chopper bikes. He had started in 1970 and had already made café racing bikes for the Rickmann brothers and Paul Dunstall in Britain.

Arlen Ness:
The Californian Arlen Ness was one of the first professional 'customisers' who in the 1970s started converting motorbikes according to the clients' wishes. The trend towards individualisation is still very much alive today.

The New Zealand Wave

The trend towards diversity accelerated in the 1980s almost to the degree of confusion, with existing categories being further subdivided. There were tourer enduros, sports tourers, full dressers and super sportsman bikes. Nothing was spectacularly new, yet every model was praised as if it was the invention of the wheel. Bikers liked variety but they also liked convention, so for instance the innovative Yamaha TR1 with air inlet integrated in the monocoque frame had in the end to be sold off at a loss. Meanwhile, at the other end of the world a DIY man broke with all tradition. The New Zealander John Britten's first motorbike, launched in 1977, was so improved during the decade that it eventually beat the other superbikes. The engine had an unusually narrow valve angle and formed part of the frame, while the fork with adjustable triangular steering combined old knowledge and new possibilities. Its engine served more or less as a model for all modern sports V-twins. In mass-production bikes the development of technology was already playing a part behind the scenes and computer technology and micro-electronics became commonplace in the 1990s.

Techno parade

Miniaturisation opened up new possibilities both in the field of engine technology and the chassis frame. There is very little space for equipment in a motorcycle, so for example the mechanical anti-lock braking systems (ABS) which Dunlop and Girling had developed in the 1960s could only be fitted in cars. Ironically, this system was particularly desirable for motorbikes because of the ease with which they can skid and crash. It was only electronic control systems which made it possible to use it in bikes, BMW introducing ABS in the K1 series In 1989, as well as a computer-controlled engine management system and catalytic converter. The Japanese concentrated more on engine optimisation and in particular on top-class performance as reflected

BMW C1 (2000):

The C1 cabin-scooter was BMW's attempt to combine the features of the car and motorbike, thus creating a new vehicle concept. Nimble, economical and providing very good protection against wind and rain, this unusual vehicle nevertheless failed to find sufficient buyers and production was discontinued after four years.

in ram-air systems and variable inlet and outlet port sections. More recently light-weight construction, using aluminium and synthetic materials, has at last reduced the weight to a more tolerable level.

The end of the 20th century was marked by two main trends. Motorised two-wheeled vehicle once again become a significant means of transport with automatic bikes such as the sophisticated BMW C1. And emotion is playing a more important part than ever, whether reflected in the passion for a Ducati 996 or the nostalgia of a Kawasaki W 650.

Science fiction

Individualisation and miniaturisation will become even more important in the future. The module motorbikes are already getting on their marks, whether enduros, classics or tourers. Following light-sensitive and temperature-dependent paints, some computer-controlled variable paints are already being developed – today a red bike, tomorrow a green one. Apart from these amusing details, the development of new materials is paving the way for further significant progress. Foamed metal and powdered metal will contribute to further weight reduction while providing the same or even greater rigidity. Composite materials made of metal and ceramics have higher heat resistance, which could lead to engines needing no lubrication. Teflon coating already makes this possible for many components. Adhesives in general which bind either chemically or mechanically are now commonly used and are already making life easier, since less thread-cutting and fewer bolts are now needed. More efficient conversion of energy, 'intelligent' lighting and a chassis structure which can be adjusted to the height of the rider are sensible improvements. But rationalism alone is no fun. This is why there are also 8-cylinder super-bikes and 'dirty fighters', which admittedly are by no means milestones in the development of the motorbike, but they are crazy, enjoyable machines.

Kawa ZZR-X (2004):

This is how Kawasaki sees the ultimate high-speed tourer of the future. A system for setting different operating modes enables the rider to select the riding position and behaviour of the bike for a particular purpose and to meet the personal requirements of the rider. The brake discs attached to the wheel rim are cone-shaped to provide efficient cooling while variable flaps, adjusted automatically according to the speed of the bike, provide wind protection. Other interesting additional features are a silencer integrated into the fairing and a large storage space in front of the seat. Single-armed wheel suspensions – at the rear with integrated shaft drive – combine the functionality of a sports tourer with the aggressive design of a supersport bike. This concept model never went into series production in this form.

The Great Motorbike Marques from A to Z

Adler – A pause of 40 years

When he founded the Adler motorcycle factory in 1886, Heinrich Kleyer laid the foundations of one of Europe's largest office machine manufacturers. The first motorised two-wheelers, fitted with a De Dion engine, left the Frankfurt factory in 1901. In 1903 the company started producing its own motorcycle engines, but in 1907 the management decided to concentrate on the production of cars and bicycles. For 40 years the company stopped making motorbikes, and it was only in 1949 that it resumed its production once more. The first post-war model, with a small 98-cc single cylinder 2-stroke engine, was just right for the time. When the demand for motorbikes with higher performance emerged in the early 1950s, Adler launched 2-cylinder models with capacities of 200 and 250 cc. The modern technology of these motorbikes boosted sales and in 1955 Adler produced 90,000 bikes. But in spite of their excellent performance, Adler's motorbike production ceased in 1957 because of the slump in sales. Adler was then taken over by Grundig. Because of its original pioneering construction, the 2-cylinder bike proved to be a model design widely copied by foreign maufacturers.

Adler V2

In the pioneering days of Adler, motorbike production continued for only six years. This motorcycle combination powered by a twin-cylinder engine dates from this time. The power of the slide valve engine without gears was delivered to the rear wheel directly by a belt. With its well-sprung sidecar with a leather seat attached, the Adler was a striking vehicle.

Model:	V2
Year:	1902
Power:	5 bhp
Capacity:	576 cc
Type:	V-twin, 4-stroke

Adler 3.5 PS

The first motorbikes produced by the Adler company, which until then had made bicycles and cars, were initially fitted with the French De Dion engine. This single-cylinder model developed a power of 3.5 bhp which was transferred to the rear wheel by a direct belt drive. Minimal braking was provided by a simple band brake on the front wheel. From 1903 the company began manufacturing its own engines.

Model:	3.5 bhp
Year:	1902
Power:	2.5 bhp
Capacity:	370 cc
Type:	Single-cylinder, 4-stroke

Adler M 200

In autumn 1951, the Adler factory in Frankfurt launched its new twin-cylinder 2-stroke motorbike. As well as its competitive performance, the twin-cylinder engine was remarkable for its outstandingly smooth performance. However the chassis with direct suspension for the rear wheel and short suspension travel with friction damping for the front wheel could not keep up with the performance of modern engines.

Model:	M 200
Year:	1952
Power:	9.3 bhp
Capacity:	195 cc
Type:	2-cylinder, 2-stroke

Adler M 250

Enlarging the capacity of the M 200 by boring out the cylinders seemed to be a logical step. So in 1953 Adler launched a high-performance 250 with a remarkable maximum speed of 116 km/h (72 mph), compared to the 95 km/h (59 mph) of its smaller sibling.

Model:	M 250
Year:	1953
Power:	12 bhp
Capacity:	248 cc
Type:	2-cylinder, 2-stroke

Adler 250 GS

Although Adler was taken over by Grundig in 1957 and motorbike production was discontinued, Dieter Falk won the German Championship on an Adler in the following year. Then in the 1970s the racing mechanic Willy Klee continued to build racing bikes for enthusiasts which were recognised as providing serious competition for the Yamahas.

Model:	250 GS
Year:	1953
Power:	17 bhp
Capacity:	247 cc
Type:	2-cylinder, 2-stroke

Adler MB 200

Only with the MB models did the Adler chassis equal the standard of the famous engine. Like its predecessors, the MB twins had delicate 16-inch wheels. With the 200 cc engine, there were two different variaitons in the Adler model range: the MB 201 with a single-cylinder 2-stroke engine and the MB 200 with a twin 2-stroke.

Model:	MB 200
Year:	1954
Power:	11.4 bhp
Capacity:	195 cc
Type:	2-cylinder, 2-stroke

Adler MB 250

In contrast to the M250 of 1954, the MB 250 was presented with a new chassis. Its slide valve 2-cylinder 2-stroke engine was capable of remarkable performance and made the machine one of the sportiest in its class. Its lively tractive power, remarkable lack of vibration and exceptional engine note attracted the progressive rider, at the expense of the production of the M250.

Model:	MB 250
Year:	1955
Power:	16 bhp
Capacity:	248 cc
Type:	2-cylinder, 2-stroke

Aermacchi – Racing and Harley-Davidson branches

As an aircraft manufacturer, Aeronautica Macchi (Aermacchi) felt the need to find a new sphere of activity after the Second World War. This is how this company from Schiranna in Varese came to produce first of all little three-wheeler transport vehicles and then in 1951 2-stroke motor scooters and motorbikes as well. In 1956 the company launched the Chimera, its first 4-stroke motorcycle. After Aermacchi was bought by the American company Harley-Davidson, the north-Italian factory also produced models sold under the name of its parent company in North America. But the European models continued to be included in its range. In the following years the sporty single-cylinder proved extremely successful in competition. In the 1970s the maker tried to resist the invasion of Japanese brands with comfortable 350 cc models but in this it was only moderately successful. As a result Harley-Davidson sold off the Italian company in 1978 and concentrated on its V-twin motorbikes. Production was resumed in 1979 under the name Cagiva.

Aermacchi Chimera

As the maker's first 4-stroke, the Chimera first saw the light of day at the 1956 Milan Salon. The extensive use of sheet metal for the fairings revealed that the manufacturer was a former aicraft manufacturer. Nevertheless, the showy design was not particularly successful with the public. The sportier models which succeeded it sold much better.

Model:	Chimera 175
Year:	1958
Power:	10 bhp
Capacity:	172 cc
Type:	Single-cylinder, 4-stroke

Aermacchi-Harley-Davidson Sprint

The Sprint was the first model exported to the USA under the Harley label. In its light 'Americanised' form with high handlebars and teardrop-shaped fuel tank, it was known as the 'Baby Sporty' and was particularly popular with young people on the far side of the Atlantic. It was also offered in various scrambler versions until the 1970s, and from 1969 with an engine capacity of 350 cc.

Model:	Sprint 250
Year:	1961
Power:	18 bhp
Capacity:	247 cc
Type:	Single-cylinder, 4-stroke

Aermacchi Ala Verde

Although the single-cylinder Aermacchi did not have an overhead camshaft, it proved extremely successful in circuit racing. Its low weight, small frontal area and balanced centre of gravity position were supplemented by the legendary reliability of the engine which was fitted horizontally. In particular, the models with five-speed gearboxes were sought after for rebuilding in the style of the Ala d'Oro racing bike.

Model:	Ala Verde Corsa
Year:	1966
Power:	22 bhp
Capacity:	247 cc
Type:	Single-cylinder, 4-stroke

Aermacchi Ala d'Oro 350 dohc

Uncertain as to whether the future of motorbike racing would belong to 4-stroke or 2-stroke engines, in 1968 Aermacchi developed in both directions. From the earlier 250 and 350 ohv engine, faster-revving twin-cam engines were developed, but these were never used in series production. The time had passed for 4-stroke engines in the smaller categories, and the 2-stroke twin-cylinder engines developed in parallel proved so superior that Aermacchi put its money on this type and allowed the 4-stroke to vanish from the scene.

Model:	Ala d'Oro 350 dohc
Year:	1968
Power:	46 bhp
Capacity:	348 cc
Type:	Horizontal dohc Single-cylinder, 4-stroke

Aermacchi 350 GTS

The 350 GTS was marketed in the North America in virtually the same form as the Harley-Davidson Sprint SS 350. In fact both versions were manufactured in Varese, Italy. The perennial powerful ohv single-cylinder engine was common to both bikes. The bike's centre of gravity was very low as a result of the low-mounted engine with its cylinder arranged horizontally.

Model:	350 GTS
Year:	1972
Power:	25 bhp
Capacity:	344 cc
Type:	Single-cylinder, 4-stroke

23

AJS – Hand in hand with Matchless

The history of the English Stevens Screw company started in 1897 with the production of a 4-stroke engine. The four Stevens brothers had developed the right product at the right time and the water-cooled single-cylinder engine was used by many motorbike manufacturers as a bought-in engine. In 1909 Jack Stevens founded the AJS company because he wanted to build a complete motorbike. The first motorbike he built had a 300-cc side-valve engine. The Wolverhampton-based maker became popular as a result of its triumph in the 1914 Tourist Trophy. Further spectacular victories in a series of competitions followed in the course of the 1920s. AJS extended its range of road motorbikes but it over-extended itself when it began producing small cars, radios and other products. In 1931 the company was bought by Matchless and the production of motorbikes then took place in the Matchless factory in London. AJS caused a sensation when it launched a spectacular racing motorbike with 500 cc V-4 engine which was fitted with a supercharger shortly before the outbreak of the Second World War. In 1956 Norton also became part of the Associated Motorcycles (AMC) group. Gradually AMC removed most models with the AJS logo from its range. 1967 saw the final exit of the traditional AJS 4-stroke motorbike. A final attempt was made to revive the AJS make at the end of the 1960s.

AJS 7R

Overall, the AJS 7R stands out as one of the best-known British motorbikes. The elegant 350-cc racing bike was similar to the Matchless G50, the latter however having a 500-cc engine. Admittedly, neither won World Championship honours, but both played an important role in the hands of the talented private entrants of the post-war racing scene. Thanks to its magnesium engine casing, aluminium fuel and oil tanks and consequent light weight, the 'Boy Racer' was smaller than most of its competitors. A chain-driven overhead camshaft meant that this single-cylinder engine was very powerful and reliable at speed.

Model:	7R
Year:	1961
Power:	41 bhp
Capacity:	348 cc
Type:	Single-cylinder, 4-stroke

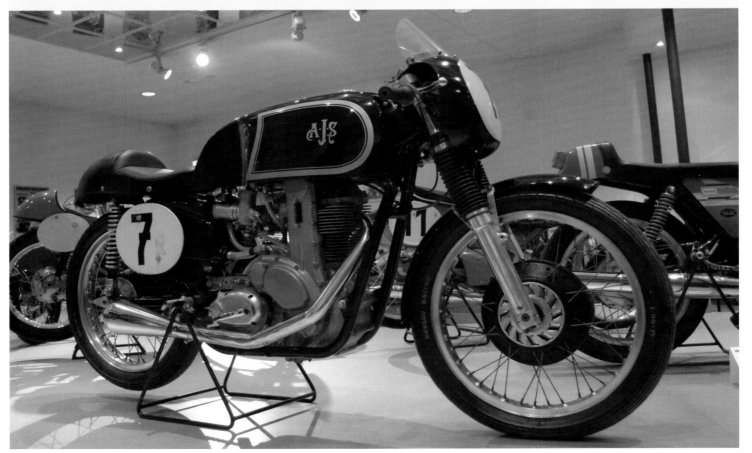

AJS 18

Technically the post-war single-cylinder models were based on the models of the 1930s. Although they were brought up-to-date so far as lights were concerned, and had a twin-loop frame as well as battery coil ignition, they were still conservative motorcycles. The range included 350 and 500-cc variants as well as scrambler and trials bikes.

Model:	18
Year:	1961
Power:	25 bhp
Capacity:	497 cc
Type:	Single-cylinder, 4-stroke

AJS 33

After the takeover of AJS and Matchless by Norton, strange hybrids appeared under the logos of the respective makers, in which parts from the different manufacturers were mixed. So the AJS 33 was inspired by a Norton Dominator twin, the chassis and tank came from the AJS 20 Twin, while on the other hand the forks and wheels came from the Norton Regal. The Matchless model was called the G 15 and the comparable Norton the N 15. With the ending of this confusing variety of types and brands in 1968, the era of the AJS 4-stroke came to an end.

Model:	33
Year:	1965
Power:	55 bhp
Capacity:	745 cc
Type:	2-cylinder, 4-stroke

AJS Double T Racer

The Norton-Villiers company revived the AJS name in 1967 with a 2-stroke series. A single-cylinder Villiers Starmaker engine of 250 and later 350 cc powered these little sports motorbikes. The models presented were the Double T Racer and the Alamos Scrambler. In 1969 these were replaced with updated models (Starmaker and Y4), the first implementation of the last motorbikes from the AJS make with its wealth of tradition.

Model:	Double T Racer
Year:	1967
Power:	32 bhp
Capacity:	247 cc
Type:	Single-cylinder, 2-stroke

Aprilia – The Italian racing spirit

In 1946 Alberto Beggio founded a motorbike factory in a small location near Venice. His son Ivano, a motor sports enthusiast, worked as a mechanic in the factory and dreamt that one day the company would also produce cross-country motorbikes. Business was good and so Ivano was eventually able to persuade his father to produce such motorised two-wheelers. At first the two men concentrated on development and bought most parts from suppliers. The first 'proper' motorbikes appeared in the mid-1980s. But the first major breakthrough came at the beginning of the 1990s when Aprilia launched its cheeky motor scooter on the market. In 1992 Aprilia entered into a contract with BMW to produce the BMW F 650 as well as the Pegaso, the successors of which are still in the catalogue today. The company's reputation was further boosted by the victories of Max Biaggi and Valentino Rossi in numerous World Championship races. Encouraged by these successes, Beggio decided to do things properly and at the end of 1998 he presented the RSV Mille at the IFMA show. With this model Aprilia finally became a member of the club of serious motorbike manufacturers. Everything seemed to be going perfectly and in the year 2000 the company even bought the ailing makers Laverda and Moto Guzzi. But as the scooter market was collapsing in Italy, Aprilia, Laverda and Moto Guzzi were all taken over by the Piaggio group.

Aprilia RSV 250

Active in motor sport from the beginning, Aprilia concentrated first on moto-cross and trials bikes, and it also sent works teams to Grand Prix events. Even in the first season the newcomer Loris Reggiani succeeded in taking podium places with the machine and the Italian maker established itself behind the experienced teams of Honda and Yamaha. In the course of the 1990s, the rotary-valve 2-strokes came to achieve real

success in the 125 and 250-cc classes. The champions Max Biaggi and Valentino Rossi won their first titles riding for Aprilia, and many other riders also put their faith in the bikes from Noale, Italy. With its production racing bikes, Aprilia made fully competive bikes available to private entrants and from its sales it was able to finance its own three works teams in the three most extensive solo categories. Up to now, Aprilia has won a total of 23 World Championship titles.

Model: Aprilia RSV 250
Year: 1985
Power: 75 bhp
Capacity: 249 cc
Type: Tandem-V-Twin,
                2-stroke

Aprilia Moto 6.5

This design statement on two wheels designed by Philippe Starck was unfortunately a complete flop. In spite of its undisputed qualities, the Aprilia went down like a lead balloon with the dealers. The heart of the Moto 6.5 was its water-cooled Rotax engine, as used in the BMW F650. However in the Aprilia it had only a single carburettor. On the other hand, the BMW had four valves while the Moto 6.5 had five to do the same job. For engineers, the valvegear is a treat: all the valve shafts are centrally drilled longitudinally.

Model: Moto 6.5
Year: 1999
Power: 42 bhp
Capacity: 649 cc
Type: Single-cylinder, 4-stroke

Aprilia RS 250

The RS 250 is a hi-tech 2-stroke racing bike which has won several World Championships for the Italian maker. It was only logical that Aprilia should make commercial use of these successes, and the early 1990s saw the appearance on the market of a replica of the World Championship bike. The technical solutions which led to Aprilia's predominance in the 250-cc category of the World Championship also went into the development of the RS 250. Precise handling was ensured by the exceptionally rigid chassis, made of an alloy of aluminium and magnesium, and the high-quality suspension components used. The watercooled V-twin 2-stroke engihne came from Suzuki and was first used in the RGV 250.

Model:	RS 250
Year:	2001
Power:	56 bhp
Capacity:	249 cc
Type:	V-twin, 2-stroke

Aprilia RSV Mille

With this model Aprilia set out on the journey to be treated as a serious motorbike manufacturer. Initially developing 118 bhp, the top version of 2005 achieved an output of 141 bhp. The picture shows the 2001 model, when performance had already risen to 128 bhp. But even more impressive than the Rotax V2 engine was the logical sports arrangement of the machine. Its racing performance was not far behind the Ducati racers or the Japanese supersport bikes. The sturdy aluminium chassis frame and the use of high-quality suspension components made the RSV Mille an accurately handling sports bike for real racing enthusiasts.

Model:	RSV Mille
Year:	2001
Power:	128 bhp
Capacity:	998 cc
Type:	V-twin, 4-stroke

Aprilia Blue Marlin

At the EICMA motorbike show in Milan in September 2001, Aprilia presented a spectacular new design in the shape of the Blue Marlin which unfortunately never went into production. This was a pity, because the concept bike with its 60° Rotax V2 engine designed by the French company Boxer Design was well received by the public. The conical, upward-pointing silencers which fit the rear frame so perfectly were wonderul to look at. Noble too were the rear wheel off-centred swing-arms, and the wheels were true works of art. The chrome-molybdenum twin frame combined a high degree of rigidity with low weight. A nice detail was that the oil tank was integrated into the frame. The instrument panel was a mixture of traditional round instruments and digital read-outs. The long, extended fuel tank and the ends of the stub handlebars sticking outwards and downwards suggested a sporting, perhaps even uncomfortable, riding position. The seat was in fact for only one person. This raw sports bike with the retro look of the 1960s and 1970s did not go into production.

Model:	Blue Marlin
Year:	2001
Power:	130 bhp
Capacity:	998 cc
Type:	V-twin, 4-stroke

Aprilia ETV 1000 Mana

At the Bologna show in December 2001, April-ia presented the ETV 1000 Mana. 'Mana' means 'so much' as well as 'energy' and 'strength' in the language of the Maoris of New Zealand. The name may have been carefully chosen but the bike never went into series production. This muscular fun-bike created by Aprilia's young designers was based on the ETV Caponord touring-enduro bikes, with a practical aluminium frame. Exclusive components were combined to good effect, such as the single swing-arm of the RST Futura sports touring bikes and the individual design of the front with its two aggressive headlights.

Model:	ETV 1000 Mana
Year:	2001
Power:	125 bhp
Capacity:	998 cc
Type:	V-twin, 4-stroke

Aprilia RST 1000 Futura

With the futuristically-styled Futura, Aprilia wanted to provide a suitable bike for touring. In this it succeeded perfectly: the fairing provided excellent protection from wind and bad weather, the seat position was relaxed and sporty, the engine provided ample performance and the Futura was also very competitively priced. However it was a slow seller and was eventually removed from the range in 2004. Perhaps customers were put off by its unconventional design or the harsh sound of the Rotax V2 engine at low revs.

Model:	RST 1000 Futura
Year:	2003
Power:	113 bhp
Capacity:	998 cc
Type:	V-twin, 4-stroke

Aprilia ETV Caponord

The Aprilia Caponord was the first production bike suitable for off-road use with an aluminium frame, but it was apparent that its off-road suitability was a slight exaggeration. In spite of its aluminium frame, the large sports-tourer with its all-in weight of about 250 kg (551 lb) was too heavy. Forest, field and meadow tracks passed smoothly beneath the rider but larger jumps were out of the question because of its great weight. It was powered by the well-known strengthened V2 engine from the RSV Mille, specially tuned to develop an insurance-friendly 98 bhp and plenty of torque. Although it was a V engine which works more smoothly at low revolutions, the Rotax unit in the Caponord revved up quick-ly. It would reach a speed of 220 km/h (137 mph) on the track, at least with a little following wind. The sitting position could be unusually upright because the windshield was effective even for people over 1.80 m (5 ft 11 in). Even when moving fast the fairings were remarkably effective in protecting the clothes from being soaked. As well as eating up the miles on motorways and country roads, the Caponord was also suitable for reliable touring without any compluslion to achieve the fastest times. The suspension was undoubtedly tuned too much in favour of comfort. The Honda Varadero and even more the Suzuki V-Strom or the Triumph Tiger was clearly much more direct and precise round fast corners. But both driver and passenger would sit more comfortably on the Caponord than on any any of these.

Model:	ETV Caponord
Year:	2003
Power:	98 bhp
Capacity:	998 cc
Type:	V-twin, 4-stroke

Aprilia RSV 1000 Tuono

There are some motorbikes which arouse the deepest desire just by looking at them. Although Aprilia's contribution to the street-fighter market did not really look bad, the Tuono did not immediately turn heads completely. But it stole the mind and inspired the senses as soon as one sat astride it. On mounting the bike, the rider was in an almost heroic sitting position. Admittedly the attitude was one of leaning forward in a sports riding position, but it was a completely relaxed and confident one. Thanks to the high superbike handlebars, the bull could be grabbed by the horns extremely well. The finely-tuned Aprilia chassis responded impressively quickly and directly to the rider's will. This was no surprise since at the end of the day this was a stripped-down version of the RSV Mille and the equipment used was correspondingly excellent.

Model:	RSV 1000 Tuono
Year:	2003
Power:	125 bhp
Capacity:	998 cc
Type:	V-twin, 4-stroke

Aprilia Pegaso 650 i.e.

The Pegaso was the 'jogger' of the Aprilia model range. Developed in cooperation with BMW in 1992, from being a sporty off-roader it has over the years undergone various model improvements and become an all-round machine with particularly good riding qualities. Like the BMW F 650, the Pegaso was powered by a modern five-valve single-cylinder engine manufactured by Rotax. In 2001, the engine was brought to the forefront of current technology by the application of electronic fuel injection. The Pegaso and its BMW sibling are both assembled by Aprilia and have similar qualities.

Model:	Aprilia Pegaso 650 i.e.
Year:	2004
Power:	48 bhp
Capacity:	652 cc
Type:	Single-cylinder, 4-stroke

Aprilia ETV Caponord Rally Raid

The Caponord Rally Raid was the 'adventure' version of the 'normal' Caponord. With aluminium bodywork, off-road tyres, longer spring travel, engine protection and roll-over bar, central stand, optional top case and headlight protection, it was also practical for long trips as well as for off-road use. However, the long-legged Aprilia with a weight of barely 270 kg (600 lb) was not the ideal vehicle for cross-country use in the desert. The Rally Raid was best suited for extended holiday touring on tarmac roads.

Model:	ETV Caponord Rally Raid
Year:	2004
Power:	98 bhp
Capacity:	998 cc
Type:	V-twin, 4-stroke

Aprilia RSV 1000 Tuono Racing

The Tuono Racing was the exclusive sister-model of the 'normal' Tuono. It was more expensive as a result of having fully-adjustable Öhlins suspension as well as from the use of weight-saving components such as titanium silencers, carbon fibre fairings and light metal forged wheels from the celebrated wheel manufacturer OZ. The Mille V2 engine had been largely untouched, but with new air-inlets and different electronics it developed more torque.

Model:	RSV 1000 Tuono Racing
Year:	2004
Power:	126 bhp
Capacity:	998 cc
Type:	V-twin, 4-stroke

Aprilia Pegaso 650 i.e. Tuscany Tibet

For the 2004 season Aprilia presented a touring version of the 650 Pegaso with the name Tuscany Tibet. The name was explained by the globetrotter capability indicated by the top case, taller windshield and longer suspension travel of the remodelled single-cylinder enduro bike. The desert look of the paint scheme indicated the direction in which the touring Pegaso was headed.

Model:	Pegaso 650 i.e.
	Tuscany Tibet
Year:	2004
Power:	49 bhp
Capacity:	652 cc
Type:	Single-cylinder, 4-stroke

Aprilia 1000 R Nera

In the 2004 season Aprilia delighted its sports enthusiasts with a new Mille generation consisting of three different versions: R, R Factory and R Nera. The last of these was a noble edition of the RSV 1000 R, limited to 200 examples. The fairings made entirely of carbon fibre, the matt-finished frame, the magnesium wheels as standard, the titanium exhaust system with catalytic converter and titanium screws, as well as the optimised Mille V2 engine, resulted in a combination which was 10 kg (22 lb) lighter and a good 2 bhp more powerful compared to the factory version which was already very powerful and light in weight. This was the material of which motorbike dreams are made. With its high price it was truly no bargain, but a fabulous sports bike which left nothing to be desired. This was also the case with the more reasonably priced versions.

Model:	1000 R Nera
Year:	2004
Power:	141 bhp
Capacity:	998 cc
Type:	V-twin, 4-stroke

Aprilia RSV 1000 R Factory

The Factory was the top model of the 2005 RSV Mille generation. Visually, it is hard to distinguish from its sister model without the Factory designation. Nor were there any differences in the engine department: the Rotax delivered 139 bhp from its 1000-cc capacity, compared with the relatively modest 118 bhp of the first Mille. The Factory version had Öhlins suspension components and was very attractive with its lightweight OZ forged aluminium wheels. It also cost more than the R-version.

Model:	RSV 1000 R Factory
Year:	2005
Power:	139 bhp
Capacity:	998 cc
Type:	V-twin, 4-stroke

Aprilia Pegaso 650 Strada

The Aprilia Pegaso 650 Strada was all things to all men, since it felt at home on practically every kind of terrain. In principle it was a fast city bike with medium seat height and short suspension travel, but it could also negotiate winding roads with ease and could even be used for moderate off-road terrain. Compared to the standard Pegaso, the Strada had ABS, a neat windshield integrated with the fuel tank and a lockable storage compartment which opened automatically when the engine was running. The engine came from the Yamaha XT 660, but in the Aprilia it developed an additional 2 bhp.

Model:	Pegaso 650 Strada
Year:	2005
Power:	50 bhp
Capacity:	659 cc
Type:	Single-cylinder, 4-stroke

Ariel – Tradition and extravagance

The British company Ariel was one of the pioneers in the history of the motorcycle. In 1898 the first motorised vehicle left the workshop in Selly Oak, Birmingham. In 1902, after experimenting with vehicles powered by French De Dion engines, the company made motorbikes with modern bought-in engines produced by Kerry. In the mid-1920s Ariel used single-cylinder power units developed by the constructor Val Page. But the real sensation was the Square Four touring motorbike which was fitted with a compact 4-cylinder engine. This square engine with two crankshafts had been designed by Edward Turner. In the mid-1950s a bolder move forward was made in the shape of the 250 cc Leader. This parallel-twin-cylinder 2-stroke engine was very progressive compared to the more conservative models produced by the competition. But in the early 1960s sales suddenly dropped dramatically and even stringent economy measures could not prevent the decline of the company.

Ariel Red Hunter

The series of single-cylinder Ariels had a reputation for robustness and efficiency. Both the 350 and the 500-cc variants sold well before the Second World War and they were also outstanding export successes. After the war the Red Hunter models were made more powerful, but they continued to use the overhead-valve engine which had been developed by Val Page.

Model:	VH Red Hunter
Year:	1938
Power:	24 bhp
Capacity:	497 cc
Type:	Single-cylinder, 4-stroke

Ariel Square Four

The unique Ariel Square Four was the controversial solution to an insoluble problem: how could a 4-cylinder engine be made as compact as a single cylinder? This solution appeared in the 1930s when the 500-cc 4-cylinder engine with its overhead camshaft was presented in the frame of an Ariel Single. After the Second World War this 1000-cc square four experienced a renaissance. The Ariel bike was brought up to date after the takeover by BSA in 1947.

Model:	Square 4 Mk II
Year:	1959
Power:	42 bhp
Capacity:	995 cc
Type:	Square four, 4-stroke

Ariel Square Four/Stoye

With its powerful 4-cylinder engine, the Ariel Square Four 1000 was particularly suitable for driving a sidecar. Developing a power of 36 to 40 bhp, the whole family could be transported comfortably, together with their luggage. Shown here is the large Ariel combined with a slim sidecar made by the Stoye company with a single seat in its enclosed cockpit.

Model:	Square Four 1000
Year:	1956
Power:	36 bhp
Capacity:	995 cc
Type:	Square four, 4-stroke

Ariel Super Sports Arrow

In the 1960s Ariel discontinued production of the traditional 4-stroke, replacing it with a twin-cylinder 2-stroke engine and an individual pressed-steel chassis. The sports variant of the Arrow was given its nickname 'Golden Arrow' because of its striking appearance. With a larger carburettor than the Standard Arrow, flat sports handlebars and a windshield as standard, this nimble 250-cc motorbike had a top speed of 130 km/h (81 mph).

Model:	Arrow
Year:	1961
Power:	18 bhp
Capacity:	247 cc
Type:	2-cylinder, 2-stroke

AWO/Simson – Solid meat from the GDR

The AWO was in fact a Simson, and the Simson factory in Suhl in Thuringia, part of the German Democratic Republic, operated under the direction of the Soviet military administration. The AWO was certainly no copy of a western model. The first series which left the Simson factory in 1950 was a completely novel interpretation of a motorbike. The adaptation of the BMW single-cylinder engine was born of need. In the socialist planned economy of the post-war years the country was short of everything. Timing chains were expensively smuggled in from the West and driving chains were almost non-existent. This is why the manufacturers used shaft-operated drive and valvegear rather than chains and tappets. Therefore it was sensible to mount the engine lengthways. Unlike the BMW engine, hairpin springs and valve rockers on needle bearings were located at the front. In 1960 only the clatter of 2-stroke engines was heard in the DDR .

AWO 425 T

The so-called AWO Tourer was the workhorse of the marque. With a low compression ratio of 6.7:1 and developing just 12 bhp, the maximum speed of 100 km/h (62 mph) was the butter on the bread. It was popular as a sidecar machine, but the name was misleading since in the German Democratic Republic no one went on long-distance 'tours'. Nearly 125,000 examples of this model were manufactured.

Model:	425 T
Year:	1950
Power:	12 bhp
Capacity:	250 cc
Type:	Single-cylinder, 4-stroke

AWO 425 S

The compression ratio of the AWO Sport's thermally efficient cylinder head was 8.3:1. It developed 14 bhp and gave a maximum speed of 110 km/h (68 mph). The chassis was fitted with proper suspension to justify the 'Sport' name. About 85,000 examples of the 425 S were built between 1956 and 1961.

Model:	425 S
Year:	1956
Power:	14 bhp
Capacity:	250 cc
Type:	Single-cylinder, 4-stroke

Simson E 350

Based on the 250-cc single-cylinder, this 350-cc model was designed to be an escort bike for the Berlin Guards' regiment. A disguised civilian design had already been under preparation in the research and development department at Suhl. But this proved to be the swan-song of the 'Construction and Testing Department' since from then on only the constructionally simpler 2-stroke was made in the GDR.

Model:	E 350, prototype
Year:	1960
Power:	20 bhp
Capacity:	350 cc
Type:	Single-cylinder, 4-stroke

Doppeltes Lottchen ('Double Ender')

Only after the fall of the Berlin Wall did this one-off bike fall into the eager hands of eastern enthusiasts. The strange construction actually worked, although it was not as fast as had been anticipated. Two engines developing 14 bhp each did not deliver 28 bhp when combined, a fact which must have disappointed the builders at the time.

Model:	Single example
Year:	1996
Power:	about 20 bhp
Capacity:	2 x 250 cc
Type:	2 x single-cylinder, 4-stroke

Benelli – The comeback of a legend

The birth of Benelli in 1911 was a perfect example and illustration of the typical Italian family business. The company was founded by the widowed Teresa Boni Benelli who was looking for work for her six sons Giuseppe, Giovanni, Francesco, Filippo, Domenico and Antonio. She sold land and bought machinery which she put in a wing of the family home in Pesaro: the Officina Meccanica Benelli was born. Ten years after the company was set up it launched its first motorbike on the market. Encouraged by their success, the Benelli brothers decided to take part in racing, which was an expensive activity and one which required an efficient 4-stroke power unit. This 175-cc engine had an overhead camshaft driven by spur gears, a very modern arrangement. In 1927, in the first year of its life, the motorbike carried Benelli to victory in the Italian Championship. The mass-produced 175 Grand Sport, derived from the racing bike, was launched in 1931, while a dohc engine was developed for racing purposes. After the Second World War Dario Ambrosini won the 250-cc World Championship title with a dohc engine and in 1969 the title went to Pesaro again with Cel Carruthers. But the small quantities of mass-produced motorbikes were unable to finance the expensive sport of racing and in 1972 the Italian-Argentinian Alejandro de Tomaso took over the company. The launch of the Benelli 750 Sei, the first mass-produced 6-cylinder motorbike, caused a real sensation. But the growing impact of the Japanese brands on the market seriously affected Benelli, which only managed to survive through partial closure. In 1995 the company experienced a revival in the hands of the industrialist Andrea Merloni and since 2002, when the powerful dohc 3-cylinder Tornado made its debut, Benelli has made a comeback.

Benelli 175 Grand Sport

This production model with overhead camshaft driven by spur gears on the right-hand side of the engine was based on the 4-stroke racing bikes produced between 1927 and 1931. The external rotating flywheel was typical of the time and the bike had a three-speed gearbox and chain drive. With only the rear wheel sprung, the maximum speed of this motorbike was about 80 km/h (50 mph).

Model:	175 Grand Sport
Year:	1932
Power:	5 bhp
Capacity:	173 cc
Type:	Single-cylinder, 4-stroke

Benelli/Motobi B 115

Giuseppe Benelli left the family business in 1949 over differences of opinion and established his own motorcycle works. His first machines were sold under the names 'Moto B Pesaro' and then 'Motobi'. The first model was this original 2-stroke with rotary valve induction, the engine being fitted within a pressed-steel frame. There was a 98-cc version with a single seat and from 1952 onwards a 115-cc model which could have two seats.

Model:	B 115
Year:	1952
Power:	5 bhp
Capacity:	115 cc
Type:	Single-cylinder, 2-stroke

Benelli/Motobi B 200 Spring Lasting

The Spring Lasting model with its backbone frame first appeared in 1952 and it set the pattern for the Motobi bikes which followed, with the oval-shaped engines which became characteristic of the maker. Also with rotary inlet valves, the two-cylinder engine had a three-speed gearbox and from 1953 a four-speed one. The 250-cc Grand Sport and Grand Sport Special designed for long distance events such as the Milan-Taranto Tour were based on it.

Model:	B 200 Spring Lasting
Year:	1953
Power:	8.5 bhp
Capacity:	195 cc
Type:	2-cylinder, 2-stroke

Benelli 175 Sport

Compared with the earlier, costly overhead camshaft engine, this post-war 175-cc model had simpler push-rod valve operation which was less expensive to produce, thus resembling the models of other makers. The obligatory sports version had an open carburettor intake and double-wall silencer on the right-hand side as well as aluminium wheels. In spite of all its sports qualities, the needs of everyday life were acknowledged by the air pump attached to the frame.

Model:	175 Sport
Year:	1957
Power:	9 bhp
Capacity:	172 cc
Type:	Single-cylinder, 4-stroke

Benelli Catria Lusso

From 1956 Giuseppe Benelli devoted himself to overhead-valve 4-stroke engines, but still with the familiar oval shape. First he made a 125-cc model, then the 175-cc model illustrated which was eventually bored out to 203 cc. The sports version of the Catria competed successfully in road races in Italy, and the Swiss Werner Maltry even combined two of these engines in a 500-cc twin.

Model:	Catria Lusso
Year:	1957
Power:	12 bhp
Capacity:	172 cc
Type:	Single-cylinder, 4-stroke

Benelli 175 Normale

For years models such as the Benelli 175 Normale embodied the most typical features of Italian motorcycle design. The low, sporty lines were characteristic: even the standard version had features such as low handlebars, friction steering damper and quick-release filler cap for the ergonomically designed fuel tank. Compared to the sports version, it had slightly inferior performance, an air filter and a simpler silencer. In the 1960s about 300 bikes of this type left the production line in Pesaro.

Model:	175 Normale
Year:	1959
Power:	8 bhp
Capacity:	172 cc
Type:	Single-cylinder, 4-stroke

Benelli 250 Sport Speciale

After the death of Giuseppe Benelli in 1957, his sons at first continued with the Motobi factory, but in 1962 it merged with the Benelli company again. Until 1972, bikes from both makers were sold under both brand names. A typical example was the Benelli/Motobi Sport Special which, ridden by Eugenio Lazzarini, won over a dozen Italian championships.

Model:	250 Sport Speciale
Year:	1968
Power:	16 bhp
Capacity:	245 cc
Type:	Single-cylinder, 4-stroke

Benelli Leoncino 125 Scrambler

At the end of the 1960s, the Benelli range started with these little 50 and 125-cc 2-strokes. Made specially for export to the USA, these so-called 'Scrambler' versions differed from the normal models in having a single seat, a smaller tank, higher handlebars, protected engine and somewhat longer suspension travel. Clearly visible in the picture are the two alternative rear sprockets, for road or cross-country conditions.

Model:	Leoncino 125 Scrambler
Year:	1969
Power:	10 bhp
Capacity:	124 cc
Type:	Single-cylinder, 2-stroke

Benelli Tornado 650 S

The large sales of British brands in the United States encouraged Benelli to create this parallel twin in 1969. The short-stroke engine was supplied with fuel by two 29-mm Dell'Orto carburettors. In spite of its sports performance and suspension, the Italian bike failed to match the success of the British bikes.

Model:	Tornado 650 S
Year:	1969
Power:	50 bhp
Capacity:	643 cc
Type:	parallel-twin, 4-stroke

Benelli 250 GP

From 1960 Benelli developed the 4-cylinder racing bike for the 250-cc World Championship. Starting in 1962, it was first ridden by Silvio Grasetti and then by Renzo Pasolini, who later died in an accident at Monza. Eventually the Australian Kel Carruthers won his second World Championship title in 1969 at the controls of this bike. The outstandingly well-built engine with gear-driven double overhead camshafts was mounted in a chassis which was very good for the time. Today, this World Championship bike capable of 230 km/h (143 mph) is used for demonstration runs.

Model:	250 Grand-Prix
Year:	1969
Power:	52 bhp
Capacity:	246 cc
Type:	4-cylinder in-line, 4-stroke

Benelli 350 GP

As a development of the 250-cc model, from 1967 onwards Benelli created competition bikes on the same lines for the 350 and 500-cc classes. The picture shows the 350-cc version, as ridden in 1973 by Walter Villa. In spite of some successes, including among others a win at Modena, the new company management decided to withdraw from the expensive business of racing at the end of the season. Since then the bike has been part of the Willie Marewski collection in Frankfurt and it is seen from time to time at classic events.

Model:	350 Grand Prix racer
Year:	1973
Power:	60 bhp
Capacity:	343 cc
Type:	4-cylinder in-line, 4-stroke

Benelli 750 Sei

After Benelli merged with Moto Guzzi and was taken over by the Tomaso group, together with the Maserati, Ghia and Vignale car companies, the new head of the company entered the struggle with the Japanese makers. Inspired by the Honda CB 500, two cylinders were added to create the world's first 6-cylinder bike. On the occasion of the 200-mile race at Imola in 1973, the former Benelli works rider Tarquinio Provini rode a couple of laps in front of the enthusiastic crowds. This was a coup, since when the plans of Honda and Kawasaki were leaked the Benelli 6-cylinder was already running. With a lower capacity compared to the Japanese bikes which appeared later, the Benelli could clearly score points for weight and handling. The unique six exhaust pipes of this exclusive bike were dispensed with in the 900-cc version, which remained in the range until 1989.

Model:	750 Sei	Capacity:	748 cc
Year:	1977	Type:	6-cylinder in-line, 4-stroke
Power:	75 bhp		

Benelli Tornado 900 Limited Edition

Benelli began its comeback in 2000 with the Tornado L.E., limited to 150 examples, which turned the motorbike world upside-down. However, more than two years passed between its first presentation at a motorbike show and the date on which this unusual 3-cylinder sports bike went into production. The Tornado L.E. was admittedly extremely expensive, but it used only the best components from Öhlins, Brembo and other exclusive manufacturers.

Model:	Tornado L.E.
Year:	2001
Power:	144 bhp
Capacity:	898 cc
Type:	3-cylinder in-line, 4-stroke

Benelli Tornado 900 Tre

Not only technology nuts rave about this sculptural motorbike – and not just because of the twin cooling fans of the rear-mounted cooling system. The Tornado is the only motorbike with the cooling system under the seat, a revolutionary solution which enabled the frontal area of the bike to be drastically reduced. With the removal of the radiator to the back, the aerodynamics of the narrower front were very efficient. But the Tornado was not lacking in other technical highlights: from the organically shaped banana swing-arm mounted on the very rigid chassis structure (in which the solid light metal swing-arm assembly was firmly attached to the interlaced tubular steel frame) to the 3-cylinder engine with cassette gearbox and anti-hop clutch, everything combined to make the racing enthusiast's heart beat faster. 2003 was the year in which the more affordable production version of the 'Novecento Tre' went into production, having been preceded only by the very exclusive 'Limited Edition'.

Model:	Tornado 900 Tre
Year:	2003
Power:	136 bhp
Capacity:	898 cc
Type:	3-cylinder in-line, 4-stroke

Benelli Tornado RS

After the limited edition Tornado L.E. and the Tornado Tre, in 2004 the Benelli Tornado RS appeared. Based on the 2003 Tornado Tre, it was fitted with light OZ rims, Brembo radial brake calipers, new forks and telescopic dampers with high and low-speed compression adjustments combined with a more powerful engine of 143 bhp. Other features completing the RS package were the milled fork bridges, black-painted frame and swing-arm, a new instrument panel design and other pleasing touches.

Model:	Tornado RS
Year:	2004
Power:	143 bhp
Capacity:	898 cc
Type:	3-cylinder in-line, 4-stroke

Benelli Goddard Replica

On 24 June 2001 Benelli made its comeback in the World Superbikes Championship at Missano with the Tornado 900 and the rider Peter Goddard. After two World Championships, won in 1950 and 1969, the return to racing marked the completion of the first phase of the programme announced by the head of Benelli in 1997 when the company was taken over by Pesaro. The homologation model for the superbike racer had high quality components with forged aluminium wheels, racing forks and racing telescopic arms by Öhlins, magnesium engine casing, adjustable steering head and swing-arm pivot as well as visible carbon fibre fairings and a titanium exhaust system compared with the Standard Tornado.

Model:	Tornado L.E. Goddard Replica
Year:	2004
Power:	146 bhp
Capacity:	898 cc
Type:	3-cylinder in-line, 4-stroke

Benelli TNT 1130

Trinitrotoluene, known by the abbreviation 'TNT', is one of the most powerful explosives in the world. This is probably why Benelli gave this name to its first streetfighter machine, an extremely powerful, completely exaggerated motorbike. Its aggressive shape and sensual curves were combined with exceptional mechanics. Visually the TNT was a naked bike while its chassis and suspension were those of a supersport. It provided close to record-breaking sprint performance, giving a surprising adrenalin rush. With its enormous torque and even power curve it was also very suitable for touring. For the TNT, Morini developed the three-cylinder engine from the Tornado, boring it out to 1131 cc and setting it up it to give complete priority to torque. The experience of the inferno (in both senses) began almost from idling speed. The 3-cylinder engine pulled away with an ease and insistence that was a joy to the heart. This explosion of power was accompanied by a blood-curdling roar which rivalled that of a straight four.

Model:	TNT 1130	Year:	2004	Power:	137 bhp
Capacity:	1131 cc	Type:	3-cylinder in-line, 4-stroke		

Benelli TNT 1130 Café Racer

With the TNT Benelli created a milestone in motorbike construction. The torque-monster was undoubtedly the highlight of the 2004 season and sold very well in spite of its magnificent price. It was therefore no surprise that in 2005 the Italians brought many and varied offshoots of the TNT to the market. The Café Racer version was popular with riders who preferred a bent-down driving position provided by the sports-style cranked aluminium handlebars. This model also attracted those of an egoistical nature since the tail fairing made it impossible to carry a companion.

Model:	TNT 1130 Café Racer	Year:	2005	Power:	137 bhp
Capacity:	1131 cc	Type:	3-cylinder in-line, 4-stroke		

Benelli TNT 1130 Titanium

By using a titanium exhaust system and forged aluminium wheels, the Titanium model of the TNT saved several kilos in weight compared with the standard model, which was in any case too heavy. The radial brake calipers and dry clutch were reminiscent of the racing version of the TNT, and in 2005 all versions had an adjustable engine management system. An inconspicuous button on the instrument panel enabled the rider to choose between very stormy or almost hurricane-like performance from the hefty 3-cylinder engine.

Model:	TNT 1130 Titanium	Year:	2005	Power:	137 bhp
Capacity:	1131 cc	Type:	3-cylinder in-line, 4-stroke		

Benelli TNT 1130 Sport

It was not only the red finish of the frame of this TNT derivative which justified its Sport designation. With fully adjustable Marzocchi inverted forks and bolted-on Brembo radial callipers, this sports version gave ambitious racing riders the opportunity of enjoying the unbelievable performance of the TNT to the full.

Model:	TNT 1130 Sport
Year:	2005
Power:	137 bhp
Capacity:	1131 cc
Type:	3-cylinder in-line, 4-stroke

Betamotor – Trials specialist from Tuscany

In 2004 Betamotor celebrated its 100th anniversary and it is therefore the oldest surviving motorcycle manufacturer in Italy. At first the company produced motor-assisted bicycles. In 1972 the company opened a new factory in Rignano sull'Arno. Here, in the beautiful Tuscan hills, the company produces 20,000 bikes a year. After winning seven World Championship titles in trials racing, the old traditional motorbike manufacturer had made a name for itself in the world of motorcycling. The successful Beta racing bikes were fitted with engines developed and built by the company itself. The introduction of the aluminium bridge-type frame of the best-seller Rev3, illustrated here, was a pioneering development which enabled it to win numerous World Championship events. The scooter programme has three ranges of models including mini-cross machines, enduros and supermoto bikes as well as two roadsters.

Betamotor 125 SG

Having committed itself to cross-country sports bikes in the 1960s, a new model range with 50, 100 and 125 cc engines was introduced in the 1970s. Shown here is the enduro created by the Italian factory in 1975 with the encouragement of Berliner Motor Corporation, the large American motorcycle importer.

Model:	125 SG
Year:	1975
Power:	20 bhp
Capacity:	124 cc
Type:	Single-cylinder, 2-stroke

Betamotor 125 CR

Initially Beta had its own works drivers and scored points in many national and international competitions. In this way it became Italian Moto-Cross champion in 1977 with this and other machines. With front and rear suspension travel of over 250 mm (10 inches) and a weight of only 85 kg (188 lb) it was far superior to the competition.

Model:	125 CR
Year:	1977
Power:	24 bhp
Capacity:	124 cc
Type:	Single-cylinder, 2-stroke

Betamotor Alp

Beta's Alp series does not attempt to compete with the hardcore mania of today. The Alp models are staightforward, everyday vehicles, robustly built, with 200 and 350-cc 4-stroke Suzuki engines of comparatively modest performance enclosed in a simple steel frame.

Model:	Alp 4.0
Year:	2004
Power:	27 bhp
Capacity:	349 cc
Type:	Single-cylinder, 4-stroke

Betamotor Jonathan

With the twin Euro and Jonathan models, Betamotor had two scrambler roadster bikes with 350-cc Suzuki engines in its range. The elegant siblings differed primarily in their appearance and equipment. Thus, the Jonathan is a purist black while the Euro has stylish two-colour paintwork. With their low weight and low seat height, the Beta cruisers were particularly appealing for beginners who are attracted by outstanding handling and period design.

Model:	Jonathan 350
Year:	2002
Power:	27 bhp
Capacity:	349 cc
Type:	Single-cylinder, 4-stroke

Bianchi – Italian motorbike pioneer

Bianchi was one one of the greatest pioneers of the history of the motorcycle. Edoardo Bianchi had his own motorcycle workshop at the tender age of 18. A mere five years later he already had to move into larger premises and in 1897 together with Gian Fernando Tomaselli he built his first two-wheeler with engine. In 1903 Bianchi positioned the engine so that the centre of gravity was as low as possible by fitting the single-cylinder 4-stroke engine at the lowest point of intersection of the triangular frame, thus ensuring safer performance for the bike. In 1912 the new 500-cc Bianchi was the first motorbike to have a three-speed gearbox. In addition it also had two brakes which worked independently of one another. When the 350-cc Freccia Celeste made its debut in 1924, it remained the fastest racing bike in the world for many years and with it the famous rider Tazio Nuvolari won the Prize of Nations race at Monza on four occasions. In the early 1930s Bianchi launched several models with overhead camshaft which were all inspired by the 350-cc Freccia Celeste. Edoardo Bianchi died in 1946 and therefore did not live to see the revival of his company with a mass-produced 250-cc bike designed before the war. In 1957, after launching several successful bikes, Bianchi returned to the world of competition, setting several speed records with an entirely faired bike designed by Sandro Colombo. In spite of this success the company fell into difficulties and Bianchi disappeared as a motorbike manufacturer in 1967.

Bianchi 250 ES

The first post-war motorbike from the Milanese maker was identical to the 250-cc sports bike of the 1930s, which already had direct rear-wheel suspension before many other manufacturers had introduced it. Also remarkable was the overhead camshaft drive used in the sports Bianchis, traditional with the company since the vertical drive shaft of the 1924 Freccia Celeste. Another characteristic of the maker since its earliest days was the brilliant colour scheme in light blue or turquoise.

| Model: | 250 ES | Year: | 1937 | Power: | 10 bhp |
| Capacity: | 249 cc | Type: | Single-cylinder, 4-stroke | | |

Bianchi 250 Dolomiti

Bianchi liked to name its motorbike models after mountains, as in the case of this Dolomiti of 1948. While the first version still had a three-speed gearbox and trapezoid front forks, this was succeeded by a modernised version with telescopic forks and four-speed gearbox, called the Stelvio. In other respects it was technically identical and the 250-cc engine with a compression ratio of only 5.5:1 was above all a robust, economical motorbike for post-war Italy.

| Model: | Dolomiti 250 | Year: | 1948 | Power: | 9 bhp |
| Capacity: | 249 cc | Type: | Single-cylinder, 4-stroke | | |

Bianchi 175 Tonale

The highest-selling Bianchi model of the 1950s was the 175 Tonale, which was even exported to countries such as Great Britain. Its modern engine had a chain-driven overhead camshaft and was known for its economy. The road bike also enjoyed a good reputation and the sports version of the Tonale with a capacity of 203 cc was entered successfully in races such as the Motogiro d'Italia and the Milan-Taranto Tour.

Model:	175 Tonale
Year:	1956
Power:	9 bhp
Capacity:	175 cc
Type:	Single-cylinder, 4-stroke

Bimota – Exclusive bikes from Italy

Valerio Bianchi, Giuseppe Morri and Massimo Tamburini named the Bimota company by stringing together the first two letters of their names and they made it a sucess with their amazing energy. Having originally set up as a company specialising in heating systems, the three founders gave in to their private passion in 1970 and became motorbike manufacturers. To start with, Tamburini produced conversions of MV Agusta and Honda CB 750 bikes. Then a year later the recently founded company moved entirely to building motorcycles. In 1975 Johnny Cecotto gave the company some excellent publicity in the World Championship. Designed for public roads, the KB 1 was a commercial success, while the SB 2 was sensational with its fuel tank placed under the engine. In 1982 the company launched the futuristic Tesi with a Honda engine, as a road motorbike with king-pin steering. The company tried to increase its share of the market and in 1994 it launched a 'touring' Bimota: the extravagant Mantra with oval frame. But in the late 1990s the quality of the Japanese mass-produced motorbikes plunged the company into serious financial problems and eventually led to its bankruptcy. But the name retained its attraction and soon new life was breathed into the old factory.

Bimota KB 1

Bimota had its first big commercial success with the KB 1. The good-looking bike of high technical quality with the Kawasaki Z 900 or Z 1000 engine fitted to an excellent Italian chassis was an unqualified success. Between 1978 and 1982 over 800 examples were sold, making the KB 1 the best-selling Bimota after the SB 6.

Model:	KB 1
Year:	1978
Power:	94 bhp
Capacity:	1016 cc
Type:	4-cylinder in-line, 4-stroke

Bimota Mantra

Bimota's Mantra qualifies as one of the most unusually styled motorbikes of all. With this model, the Italian maker wanted to appeal to the developing streetfighter community of the late 1990s. The design was probably too daring for competition because the Mantra did not become a race winner, although for a Bimota the price was relatively affordable. The Bimota engineers fitted a Ducati engine tuned for higher performance within the the light alloy bar frame.

Model:	Mantra
Year:	1998
Power:	85 bhp
Capacity:	904 cc
Type:	V-twin, 4-stroke

Bimota SB 6R

As successor to the SB 6, the SB 6R was one of the most powerfully performing bikes of all. Descended from the Suzuki GSX-R 100, the engine was significanty modified for this new role. The SB 6 models were the best-selling bikes in the Bimota range.

Model:	SB 6R
Year:	1998
Power:	156 bhp
Capacity:	1074 cc
Type:	4-cylinder in-line, 4-stroke

Bimota DB 4

In 1999 another model appeared with Ducati's twin-valved engine. The tubular bar frame, skilfully formed from aluminium with an oval profile was similar to that of the Mantra which was already in production. As was typical of Bimota, the other chassis components were the finest from Öhlins and Brembo.

Model:	DB 4
Year:	1999
Power:	90 bhp
Capacity:	904 cc
Type:	V-twin, 4-stroke

Bimota YB 11 Nuda

The former German importer ZTK was reluctant to accept the vacuum between 2000 and 2004 when no new models appeared, so it created this fashionable streetfighter based on the Bimota SB 6R and YB11 models with a weight of 200 kg (440 lb).

Model:	YB 11 Nuda
Year:	2001
Power:	145 bhp
Capacity:	1002 cc
Type:	4-cylinder in-line, 4-stroke

Bimota SB 8K

Bimota's resurrection began with the SB 8K, which was already in the model programme before the bankruptcy of 2000. Driven by Suzuki's powerful 1000-cc V-twin engine, this model was available as the Gobert Replica and the Santamonica. The latter had lighter wheels and bolted on radial brake callipers.

Model:	SB 8K Gobert Replica
Year:	2004
Power:	143 bhp
Capacity:	996 cc
Type:	V-twin, 4-stroke

Bimota DB 5

With the DB 5 the engineers of Bimota demonstrated that they were indeed serious. Rarely has so skilfully-shaped a motorbike been created. The design of the openwork frame consructed of oval-shaped metal bars is continued in the openwork suspensions made of the same oval material. The truncated fairing and the sexy rear end with the same tail light as the Benelli Tornado could not be more beautiful. It is surprising that the Italian public held back from this remarkable sports bike with a twin-valved V-twin Ducati engine developing 'only' a little over 90 bhp.

Model:	DB 5
Year:	2005
Power:	92 bhp
Capacity :	992 cc
Type:	V-twin, 4-stroke

Bimota Tesi 2D

The extremely futuristic Tesi 2D astonishes the eyes of all who behold it with its fully detached wheels and its many-fretted light metal frame, and its front-facing exhaust system mounted beneath it. Weighing about 170 kg (375 lb) fully loaded, the Tesi is extremely light.

Model:	Tesi 2D
Year:	2005
Power:	86 bhp
Capacity:	992 cc
Type:	V-twin, 4-stroke

BMW - A German success story

There are several examples of aircraft manufacturers and airline companies which have turned to manufacturing motorbikes, but few have been as successful as BMW. The First World War came to an end with the surrender of Germany and the peace treaty prohibited any involvement in aeronautics and aviation. In effect this made it impossible for the Bayerische Motoren-Werke to remain in business because until then it had produced excellent aircraft engines which had become deservedly celebrated. Inevitably the company had to find a new field of activity. At the end of 1919 the chairman Franz-Josef Popp asked his head designer Max Friz to design a motorbike engine. Friz developed and built a twin-cylinder boxer engine which had many revolutionary design features. At first the engine was offered to other motorbike manufacturers to be fitted to their bikes and in this it proved very successful. But then the newly-founded Bayerische Motorenwerke AG decided to go into the production of two-wheeled vehicles itself and in 1923 it presented its first model. The R 32 already displayed many of the design and constructional features which continue to distinguish the BMW boxers of today. The R 32 was a remarkable success and the company quickly produced more models. Soon BMW also became involved in competition where it won many successes. This was excellent publicity which led to further increases in sales. By the beginning of the Second World War, the maker with the propeller emblem had become an internationally successful and renowned company, and soon after the war BMW was able to resume business. Things were quite difficult in the 1960s when the motorbike market was at its lowest ebb and at that time the company seriously considered ceasing motorbike production. But BMW decided to carry on and moved its production to Berlin-Spandau. Although BMW motorbikes often appear conservative, the manufacturer has in fact always been interested in revolutionary innovation and for ten years has been a trendsetter in the motorbike design. For years BMW has been leading the registration league tables in all the most important markets. There is still no end in sight for Friz's success story.

BMW R 32

The ingredients were not new but nonetheless the results were close to revolutionary. The R 32 and its large 500-cc engine, with side valves and enclosed inlet manifold, had a very modern pressure lubrication system. It developed a power of 8.5 bhp which was delivered through a single-disc dry-plate clutch to the three-speed gearbox with hand-operated gear change and from there to a low-maintenance drive shaft leading to the rear wheel. Weighing only 120 kg (265 lb), the machine was very smooth-running and durable and it worked well as a whole. Also, with its relatively efficient leaf-spring front suspension it was comfortable to ride.

Model:	R 32
Year:	1923 to 1926
Power:	8.5 bhp at 3300 rpm
Capacity:	494 cc
Type:	2-cylinder boxer, 4-stroke

BMW R 37

BMW's first sports model was developed by Rudolf Schleicher. The R 37 was based on the R 32, but it had fully-enclosed overhead valves and developed 16 bhp. It could reach a speed of 115 km/h (71 mph). The twin-loop tubular frame of the R 32 was strong enough to handle this power.

Model:	R 37
Year:	1925–1926
Power:	16 bhp at 4,000 rpm
Capacity:	494 cc
Type:	2-cylinder boxer, 4-stroke

BMW R 39

BMW's first single-cylinder machine was not a beginner's model but a 250-cc sports bike. The square engine block was made entirely of aluminium. For the first time, an external brake operated on the rear shaft drive. However, because of its high price it did not sell very well.

Model:	R 39
Year:	1925 to 1927
Power:	6.5 bhp at 4,000 rpm
Capacity:	247 cc
Type:	Single-cylinder, 4-stroke

BMW R 47

The successor of the sensational R 37 sports model was improved in a number of details, being 2 bhp more powerful and 4 kg (9 lb) lighter. The overhead-valve 500 reached a maximum speed of 110 km/h (68 mph), far faster than most of the roads of the time allowed.

Model:	R 47
Year:	1927 to 1928
Power:	18 bhp at 4,000 rpm
Capacity:	494 cc
Type:	2-cylinder boxer, 4-stroke

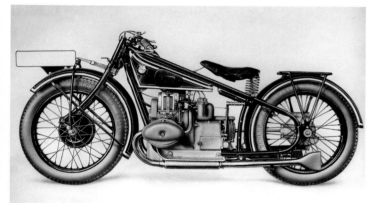

BMW R 63

In 1928 BMW introduced a completely new programme which included the sturdy R 63 with its short stroke 750-cc engine. For the first time this motorbike had a drum brake at the front, which was needed in view of its high performance.

Model:	R 63
Year:	1928 to 1929
Power:	24 bhp at 4,000 rpm
Capacity:	735 cc
Type:	2-cylinder boxer, 4-stroke

BMW R 11

In 1929 BMW turned its back on tubular frames and presented its first model with a pressed-steel frame riveted and bolted together. The engine was adapted from the earlier R 62 (side-valve) and R 63 (overhead-valve) engines.

Model:	R 11
Year:	1929 to 1934
Power:	18 bhp at 3,400 rpm
Capacity:	745 cc
Type:	2-cylinder boxer, 4-stroke

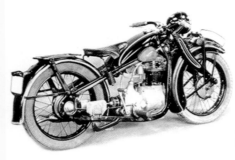

BMW R 2

From April 1928 new regulations in BMW's home market allowed motorbikes with a capacity of under 200 cc to be ridden without incurring tax. As a result the company launched its first real high-volume model, the single-cylinder R 2 which was a great success in spite of the world economic crisis and its fairly high price.

Model:	R 2
Year:	1931 to 1936
Power:	6 bhp at 3,500 rpm
Capacity:	198 cc
Type:	Single-cylinder, 4-stroke

BMW R 4

With the R 4, in 1932 BMW finally filled the middle ground between the R 2 and the 750 Boxer. The single-cylinder R 4 was admittedly heavy and somewhat nose-heavy but it was also virtually indestructible, which made it very popular with authorities such as the police.

Model:	R 4
Year:	1932 to 1937
Power:	12 bhp at 3500 rpm
Capacity:	398 cc
Type:	Single-cylinder, 4-stroke

BMW R 17

The successor of the R 17 now had telescopic front forks instead of the pressed steel leaf spring suspension used until then. The 750-cc overhead valve engine had increased in performance over the years, but now, with its horizontally divided engine casing, it made its distinctive final appearance.

Model :	R 17
Year:	1935 to 1937
Power:	33 bhp at 5,000 rpm
Capacity:	735 cc
Type:	2-cylinder boxer, 4-stroke

BMW R 5

With the stylish R 5, BMW, turned for the first time to a welded tubular frame and sports rear end, adopting oil-damped telescopic shock absorbers. The machine was an international sensation and the engine appeared again in the post-war R 51/2.

Model:	R 5
Year:	1936 to 1937
Power:	24 bhp at 5,800 rpm
Capacity:	494 cc
Type:	2-cylinder boxer, 4-stroke

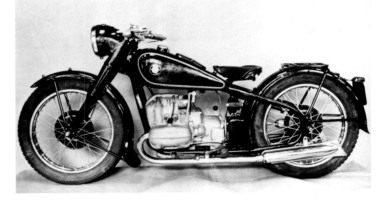

BMW Henne RS 51

After it had put its skills to the test in numerous cross-country and track races, the BMW management concentrated seriously and succesfully on breaking speed records. Its greatest triumph was in 1937 on the Frankfurt–Darmstadt autobahn when a fully streamlined supercharged RS 51 with a 500-cc engine developing 100 bhp reached a speed of 279.5 km/h (173.7 mph). This was its 76th world record and world's best performance, the pinnacle of its career.

Model:	Henne-RS 51
Year:	1937
Power:	100 bhp
Capacity:	494 cc
Type:	2-cylinder boxer, 4-stroke

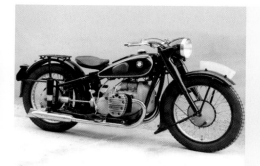
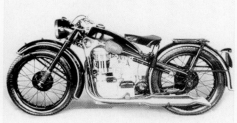

BMW R 71

With the R 5 sports bike BMW had returned to the elegant – and this time progressively curved – tubular frame. Models R 51 (ohv) to R 71 had direct rear-wheel suspension. The side-valve R 71 was designed as a robust touring machine, primarily for use with a sidecar.

Model:	R 71
Year:	1938 to 1941
Power:	22 bhp at 4,600 rpm
Capacity:	745 cc
Type:	2-cylinder boxer, 4-stroke

BMW R 35

Compared to the R5, the single-cylinder R 35 was relatively unadventurous. In fact it was strongly based on the R 4, but with undamped telescopic forks. Many thousand R 35s served in the war. As the EMW (Eisenacher Motorradwerke) R 35 it celebrated a resurrection in the Soviet occupied zone.

Model:	R 35
Year:	1937 to 1940
Power:	14 bhp at 4,500 rpm
Capacity:	342 cc
Type:	Single-cylinder, 4-stroke

BMW R 20

As the successor to the wonderful R 2, in the spring of 1937 BMW launched the R 20 with a newly-designed slim tunnel engine housing and three-speed foot-operated gearbox. The 200-cc engine gave the machine a maximum speed of 195 km/h (121 mph).

Model:	R 20
Year:	1937 to 1938
Power:	8 bhp at 5,400 rpm
Capacity:	192 cc
Type:	Single-cylinder, 4-stroke

BMW R 51 RS

With its characteristic howl, by 1939 the supercharged BMW had already put hundreds of thousands of people under its spell and won dozens of places on the rostrum. The engines were mechanical marvels with overhead camshaft and vertical drive shaft which developed about 60 bhp as a result of being supercharged. In 1939 Schorsch Meier rode it to victory in the notorious Isle of Man Senior TT – so becoming the first foreigner to appear in the list of winners in the 500 cc class.

Model:	R 51 RS
Year:	from 1939
Power:	about 60 bhp
Capacity:	494 cc
Type:	2-cylinder boxer, 4-stroke

BMW R 75

The massive 750-cc bike was completely adapted to military requirements. The frame was bolted together, the four-speed foot-operated gearbox provided extra-slow speeds and reverse gear, and the sidecar wheel was also driven, by means of a shaft connected to the rear wheel. In rough terrain the R 75 was superior to most Jeeps.

Model:	R 75
Year:	1941 to 1944
Power:	26 bhp at 4,000 rpm
Capacity:	745 cc
Type:	2-cylinder boxer, 4-stroke

BMW R 24

BMW production started again in 1948 with the R 24 based on the pre-war R 23 model. The economy production of this model was clearly apparent, with chrome decoration almost completely non-existent. Nevertheless the bike proved to be a success and this only ended two years later when it was superseded by the more sophisticated R 25.

Model:	R 24
Year:	1948 to 1950
Power:	12 bhp at 5,600 rpm
Capacity:	247 cc
Type:	Single-cylinder, 4-stroke

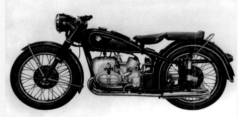

BMW R 51/2

After the Allied occupying powers had raised the limit on capacity to 350 cc, BMW from 1950 onwards once more offered boxer models. However the R 51/2 based on the pre-war R 51 found few buyers because of its high price. The picture shows the side-car version.

Model:	R 51/2
Year:	1950 to 1951
Power:	24 bhp at 5,800 rpm
Capacity:	494 cc
Type:	2-cylinder boxer, 4-stroke

BMW R 68

BMW's first 'hundred-mile-an-hour racer': the R 68 was based on the hefty R 67 but with performance increased by 35 bhp as a result of using a different cylinder head and carburettors. Narrower mudguards underlined the sporting claims of this production racer, which could reach a good 160 km/h (100 mph). Today the R 68 is one of the most sought-after BMWs of all.

Model:	R 68
Year:	1952 to 1954
Power :	35 bhp at 7,000 rpm
Capacity:	594 cc
Type:	2-cylinder boxer, 4-stroke

BMW R 25/3

There was a strong demand for motorbikes in the 1950s and the sturdy BMW R 25/3 fully met the requirements of the public. The entry model with damped telescopic forks was not particularly sporty, but its quality overcame any doubts. Manufactured until 1956, the 250-cc model remained the most successful for a long time. Its successors had to contend with a rapidly diminishing motorbike market.

Model:	R 25/3
Year:	1953 to 1956
Power:	13 bhp at 5800 rpm
Capacity:	247 cc
Type:	Single-cylinder, 4-stroke

BMW R 25/3-Gespann (combination)

Since 1924, customers had been able to order complete motorcycle combinations from BMW. The sidecars leaving Munich were supplied by renowned makers such as Royal, Steib and Stoye. This approach had the advantage that matters such as the guarantee and repairs were in the same hands and also that the sidecar wheel and those of the motorbike were often identical and could be interchanged. The picture shows an R 25/3 with a Standard-Steib sidecar.

Model:	R 25/3
Year:	1953 to 1956
Power:	13 bhp at 5,800 rpm
Capacity:	247 cc
Type:	Single-cylinder, 4-stroke

BMW R 51/3

BMW's first new design after the war was a success from the start. The new engine with only a single spur-gear-driven overhead crankshaft was regarded as economical, steady at speed and extremely long-lasting. No expense was spared with this BMW, as the ignition system showed. Although it had a powerful dynamo the machine had no battery but magneto ignition. As a bike for pulling a sidecar, BMW offered the technically identical R 67 with a 600-cc engine developing 26 bhp.

Model:	R 51/3
Year:	1951 to 1954
Power:	24 bhp at 5,800 rpm
Capacity:	494 cc
Type:	2-cylinder boxer, 4-stroke

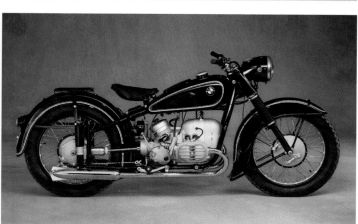

BMW R 50

The new swinging fork frame established a hitherto unknown standard of comfort because the long-travel suspension of the front forks and tapered roller bearing had usually been reserved for the race track. The engine was a more refined version of the previous models. In Britain and the United States the range soon acquired the reputation of the Rolls-Royce of motorbikes.

Model:	R 50
Year:	1955 to 1969
Power:	26 bhp at 5,800 rpm
Capacity:	494 cc
Type:	2-cylinder boxer, 4-stroke

BMW R 26

There was a delay of a year before the comfortable, secure swinging fork suspension of the boxer made its appearance in the R 26, although in a severely shrinking motorbike market this delay proved not to matter. The engine used by BMW was largely unchanged from the successful R 25/3, with a larger 26-mm carburettor and a bigger air-filter housing together providing two additional horsepower.

Model:	R 26
Year:	1956 to 1960
Power:	15 bhp at 6,400 rpm
Capacity:	247 cc
Type:	Single-cylinder, 4-stroke

BMW R 69 S

The S stands for 'sport'. The R 69 S was the top model of the range and with special pistons, cylinder heads and carburettors, BMW increased the performance of the 600-cc engine to 42 bhp. At prolonged high speeds the crankshaft sometimes broke, so BMW soon fitted the engine with a crankshaft vibration damper. 'S' models are particularly sought-after in collectors' circles.

Model:	R 69 S
Year:	1960 to 1969
Power:	42 bhp at 7,000 rpm
Capacity:	594 cc
Type:	2-cylinder boxer, 4-stroke

BMW R 50 S

The R 50 S, the smaller sibling of the Supersport BMW R 69 S, only survived for two years in BMW's programme. The 500-cc engine developed 35 bhp and was just as powerful as the R 69 with 600 cc.

Model:	R 50 S
Year:	1960 to 1962
Power:	35 bhp at 7,650 rpm
Capacity:	494 cc
Type:	2-cylinder boxer, 4-stroke

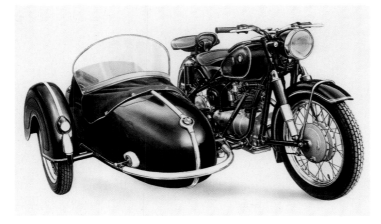

BMW R 27

The motorbike market was in severe decline when BMW launched the final development of the single-cylinder series with the R 27. Little was changed for the practical motorcycle-combination version. The engine was to a large extent based on its predecessors, except that the swinging fork suspension was mounted in rubber. In 1966 BMW's single-cylinder production ceased for many years, when it was revived with the F 650.

Model:	R 27
Year:	1960 to 1966
Power:	18 bhp at 7,400 rpm
Capacity:	247 cc
Type:	Single-cylinder, 4-stroke

BMW R 75/5

With the appearance of the 1969 model BMW introduced a completely new series to its range. The rigid distortion-free frame was inspired by Norton's famous Featherbed frame, but it was no longer suitable for a sidecar. The new engines with fluid film bearings used parts from motor-car engines. Built for the first time in Berlin-Spandau, demand already exceeded production in 1971. The motorcycle quickly acquired a reputation for robustness.

Model:	R 75/5
Year:	1969 to 1973
Power:	50 bhp at 6,200 rpm
Capacity:	745 cc
Type:	2-cylinder boxer, 4-stroke

BMW R 90 S

Painted in a glaring Daytona orange, with handlebar-mounted front fairing, stylish tail fairing, twin disc brakes and an instrument panel with four instruments, the fast R 90 S perfectly met the tastes of the new motor-cycling generation. The engine had a higher compression ratio and Dell'Orto carburettor which improved performance so that it was capable of 200 km/h (124 mph). This rapid machine was BMW's first superbike.

Model:	R 90 S
Year:	1973 to 1976
Power:	67 bhp at 7,000 rpm
Capacity:	898 cc
Type:	2-cylinder boxer, 4-stroke

BMW R 90/6

In parallel with its well-known R 90 S sports bike, BMW offered the R 90/6 touring model, which with its unusual Bing constant vacuum carburettor and lower compression ratio developed only 60 bhp. It had a single disc brake at the front.

Model:	R 90/6
Year:	1973 to 1976
Power:	60 bhp at 6,500 rpm
Capacity:	898 cc
Type:	2-cylinder boxer, 4-stroke

BMW R 100 RS

In 1976 BMW went for a capacity of a full litre and replaced the 900-cc engine with a power unit of 1000 cc. This outstanding model was the R 100 RS, the first production motorbike to have fairings completely designed in a wind tunnel. However, while its streamlined fair-ing was reasonably effective, the R 100 RS with a speed of 200 km/h (124 mph) was actu-ally no faster than the R 100 S with handle-bar fairing which developed 5 bhp less.

Model:	R 100 RS
Year:	1976 to 1984
Power:	70 bhp at 7,250 rpm
Capacity:	980 cc
Type:	2-cylinder boxer, 4-stroke

BMW R 100/7

At the same time as its futuristic R 100 RS, enthusiasts who preferred the more traditional 'naked' bikes could order the R 100/7. This was the standard model in the 1-litre class and with its spoked wheels was still strongly reminiscent of its predecessors the /5 and the /6. It remained in the range for only two years.

Model:	R 100/7
Year:	1976 to 1978
Power:	60 bhp at 6,500 rpm
Capacity:	980 cc
Type:	2-cylinder boxer, 4-stroke

BMW R 100 RT

Two years after the appearance of the RS the R 100 RT came out. Sim-ilar in appearance, this was a fully-faired tourer which provided out-standing weather protection and an adjustable windshield. Comfort-loving riders quickly found that the RT was an excellent long-distance touring bike.

Model:	R 100 RT
Year:	1978 to 1984
Power:	70 bhp at 7,250 rpm
Capacity:	980 cc
Type:	2-cylinder boxer, 4-stroke

BMW R 45

After the R 50/5 was withdrawn in 1973, BMW no longer had any model in the 500-cc category; henceforth the entry-level model was 600 cc. This situation only changed in 1978 with the launch of the R 45. With a boxer engine developing 27 bhp (or optionally 35 bhp) and single disc brake in front, this was the new entry-level machine for joining the world of BMW.

Model: R 45   Year: 1978 to 1985   Power: 27 bhp at 6,500 rpm
Capacity: 473 cc   Type: 2-cylinder boxer, 4-stroke

BMW R 80 G/S

This model became a great success and justified the new type of large enduro-tourer bikes, but at first the R 80 G/S was welcomed somewhat hesitantly with its individual styling and single swing-arm which however considerably simplified the construction of the suspension. But because it was convenient, comfortable and reliable, it was not long before people flocked to buy it.

Model:	R 80 G/S
Year:	1980 to 1987
Power:	50 bhp at 6,500 rpm
Capacity:	797 cc
Type:	2-cylinder boxer, 4-stroke

BMW R 65 LS

The R 45 and R 65 were intended to round off the bottom end of the BMW range. The R 65 enjoyed some popularity among sports riders, particularly after the launch in 1981 of the RS version which also had a futuristic sports design.

Model:	R 65 LS
Year:	1981 to 1985
Power:	45 bhp at 7,250 rpm
Capacity:	649 cc
Type:	2-cylinder boxer, 4-stroke

BMW R 80 ST

The current judgement of both road testers and motorbike riders is that the R 80 G/S was 'the best street motorbike which BMW has ever made'. The company reacted to this praise with the R 80 ST (for 'street') which appeared in 1982, a version of the G/S with shorter spring travel and road tyres.

Model:	R 80 ST
Year:	1982 to 1984
Power:	50 bhp at 6,500 rpm
Capacity:	797 cc
Type:	2-cylinder boxer, 4-stroke

BMW K 100

With its first 4-stroke motorcycle, BMW stunned both fans and experts alike with its concentration of innovations, including the long engine fitted on its side for a low centre of gravity, and Bosch digital electronic fuel injection and ignition control which were at that time characteristic of high-end automobile practice. In 1988 the K 100 Premiere came out, the first motorbike with an ABS braking system, and later the machine could be ordered with a computer-controlled catalytic converter. Initial misgivings concerning the concentration of new technology were quickly set to rest by this reliable and long-lived motorbike.

Model:	K 100
Year:	1983 to 1990
Power:	90 bhp at 8,000 rpm
Capacity:	987 cc
Type:	4-cylinder in-line, 4-stroke

BMW K 100 RT

The 4-cylinder range was rapidly developed and from 1984 touring enthusiasts could also enjoy the reliable low-maintenance engine in the form of the RT with touring bodywork. In the hands of such enthusiasts, many of these bikes accumulated astonishingly long total distances of over 500,000 km (300,000 miles).

Model: K 100 RT	Year: 1984 to 1989	Power: 90 bhp at 8,000 rpm
Capacity: 987 cc	Type: 4-cylinder in-line, 4-stroke	

Paris-Dakar-Werksmaschine

At the beginning of the 1980s, a new form of rally competition came more and more into public consciousness: long-distance cross-country events in Africa. For this kind of high-speed marathon, the G/S models from BMW with their robust, powerful boxer engines had recently been developed. Hubert Auriol had already been spectacularly successful in 1981 and 1983 with a modified G/S bike fitted with a powerful 100-cc engine of 70 bhp. In 1984 the Belgian moto-cross champion Gaston Rahier joined the works team and promptly won the rally. He repeated his success in 1985 with the 1043-cc machine seen here, which developed a power of 80 bhp.

Model:	R 100 G/S Paris-Dakar
Year:	1985
Power:	about 80 bhp
Capacity:	1043 cc
Type:	2-cylinder boxer, 4-stroke

BMW K 75 C

Three years after the appearance of the 4-cylinder K 100, it was followed by the K-75 series with a 3-cylinder in-line engine; both types of engine had been developed in parallel. The K 75 C with small cockpit fairing was the first model of the new series to come on the market and it had an excellent reception with authorities such as the police.

Model:	K 75 C
Year:	1985 to 1990
Power:	75 bhp at 8,500 rpm
Capacity:	740 cc
Type:	3-cylinder in-line, 4-stroke

BMW K 100 LT

Launched in 1986 as the RT with 'another spoonful of butter', the K 100 LT luxury tourer had the same technology as its predecessors, but it also had all kinds of features such as heated hand-grips, a radio and a large top case with back rest, making it a comfortable touring bike.

Model: K 100 LT	Year: 1986 to 1991	Power: 90 bhp at 8,000 rpm
Capacity: 987 cc	Type: 4-cylinder in-line, 4-stroke	

BMW K 75 S

In parallel with the basic K 75 model, the K 75 S appeared in 1986, with an enclosed half-fairing and stiffer suspension. Otherwise this was technically identical with the other model.

Model:	K 75 S
Year:	1986 to 1995
Power:	75 bhp at 8,500 rpm
Capacity:	740 cc
Type:	3-cylinder in-line, 4-stroke

BMW K1

Anyone who had thought of BMW as a maker of rather sober bourgeois motorbikes rubbed their eyes with amazement at the sight of the new K1. Fully enclosed with streamlined fairings also covering the front wheel and the rear of the bike and finished with a spectacular paint scheme, the maker now revealed its definition of a sophisticated sports-tourer. From 1991 the K1 was available with computer-controlled catalytic converter.

Model:	K1
Year:	1989 to 1993
Power:	100 bhp at 8,000 rpm
Capacity:	987 cc
Type:	4-cylinder in-line, 4-stroke

BMW R 100 R

The 'R' stood for 'roadster' and that is precisely what this bike launched in 1991 was. With traditional spoked wheels which nevertheless had modern tubeless tyres, the motorbike had a muscular appearance without fairings, reflecting the spirit of the early 1990s. The power unit was from the GS models while Showa supplied the high-quality suspension elements.

Model:	R 100 R
Year:	1991 to 1996
Power:	60 bhp at 6,500 rpm
Capacity:	980 cc
Type:	2-cylinder boxer, 4-stroke

BMW K 1100 LT

Well-off touring riders could relax on the new 1100-cc version of the LT luxury tourer. This now offered features such as an electrically adjusted windshield which at the push of a button quickly adapted itself to the height of the rider. The high-torque engine dealt easily with the extra weight.

Model:	K 1100 LT
Year:	1991 to 1998
Power:	100 bhp at 7500 rpm
Capacity:	1092 cc
Type:	4-cylinder in-line, 4-stroke

BMW K 1100 RS

Even BMW could not ignore the trend towards larger capacity and it presented the well-known 4-cylinder engine of the K-series in a completely modified form with a capacity of 1100 cc. Combined with a new electronic engine management system and the 4-valve cylinder head of the K1, the engine developed 100 bhp and a maximum torque of 107 Nm .

Model:	K 1100 RS
Year:	1992 to 1996
Power:	100 bhp at 7,500 rpm
Capacity:	1092 cc
Type:	4-cylinder in-line, 4-stroke

BMW R 1100 RS

Seventy years after the appearance of the original BMW R 32, in 1993 BMW presented the new boxer series. The vertically-divided engine casing of the 4-valve aluminium power unit with fuel injection and computer-controlled catalytic converter was so rigid that the wheel suspensions with short supporting frames front and rear were mounted directly on it. Revolutionary as it was, BMW used the so-called telelever suspension system, with a trailing arm spring and shock-absorber and a telescopic fork system for controlling the wheel.

Model:	R 1100 RS
Year:	from 1993
Power:	90 bhp at 7250 rpm
Capacity:	1085 cc
Type:	2-cylinder boxer, 4-stroke

BMW R 80 GS Basic

In 1996 BMW brought the all-white Basic to the market. With the extremely traditional appearance of its predecessors, it was the last representative of the old boxer generation. After 2,995 examples had been manufactured, production of the Basic ended, and with it the construction of the 2-valve boxer engines.

Model:	R 80 GS Basic
Year:	1996
Power:	50 bhp at 6,500 rpm
Capacity:	798 cc
Type:	2-cylinder boxer, 4-stroke

BMW F 650

Twenty-seven years after the R 27 appeared in BMW's showrooms, the single-cyinder F 650 was launched. It was a cosmopolitan 'funduro' bike with a 650-cc Rotax engine from Austria. The bike was manufactured in Italy by Aprilia. Enthusiasts would look in vain for other characteristic BMW features such as shaft drive, since the transmission was by a low-maintenance toothed belt.

Model:	F 650
Year:	from 1993
Power:	48 bhp
Capacity:	652 cc
Type:	Single-cylinder, 4-stroke

BMW R 100 GS Paris-Dakar

In 1988 BMW finally filled out the 1-litre category with the popular best-sellers of the GS range: tourers, everyday bikes and long-distance machines with 1000-cc engines developing 60 bhp were now available. The last was the Paris-Dakar model, directly associated with BMW's successes in that rally. With its fuel tank of 35 litres (7.7 gallons), it was ideal for long-distance riding. In this model the parallel swing arm reduced the lifting effect characteristic of shaft-driven bikes when starting off.

Model:	R 100 GS Paris-Dakar
Year:	1995
Power:	60 bhp at 6,500 rpm
Capacity:	980 cc
Type:	2-cylinder boxer, 4-stroke

BMW R 1100 GS

A year after the appearance of the new boxer generation in the shape of the RS, BMW launched the R 1100 GS as a successor to the popular touring-enduros. The new GS quickly acquired an excellent reputation because of its stability and comfortable suspension and it sold extremely well. That the new model had an extra 50 kg (110 lb) compared to the weight of its predecessor did not affect its popularity on the road.

Model:	R 1100 GS
Year:	1996
Power:	80 bhp at 6,750 rpm
Capacity:	1085 cc
Type:	2-cylinder boxer, 4-stroke

BMW R 1100 RT

In autumn 1995, BMW presented the Tourer R 1100 RT with the new 4-valve boxer engine. With the R 100 RT BMW had launched the first production tourer in the world with fairings developed in a wind tunnel. Over 60,000 examples of the R 100 RT and R 80 RT had been made by the end of the 1995 model year. The R 1100 RT set new standards with regard to modern engines and chassis technology, active safety systems and environmental friendliness. Over 55,000 examples had been made by the end of the year 2000.

Model:	R 1100 RT
Year:	1996
Power:	90 bhp
Capacity:	1085 cc
Type:	2-cylinder boxer, 4-stroke

BMW R 1200 C

BMW goes chopper – this was the shock of 1997 for the maker's many tradition-conscious fans. The reality was that the company had launched a motorbike which had a completely individual appearance in keeping with the Harley boom, but on top of that it had all the traditional BMW virtues. In particular the engine enlarged to 1200 cc provided chopper-like performance with high tractive power at low engine revolutions.

Model:	R 1200 C
Year:	1997
Power:	61 bhp at 5,000 rpm
Capacity:	1170 cc
Type:	2-cylinder boxer, 4-stroke

BMW R 1100 S

In autumn 1998 BMW revived a tradition with the R 1100 S: the use of the letter 'S' in the model designation to indicate the word 'sport', as it had done in the 1960s. Strong emotions were already aroused among BMW enthusiasts by the bike's strange appearance with half-shell fairing, single-seater bench saddle and high-mounted silencers, all indications that the sports talents of the R 1100 S were predominant. The external appearance was not deceptive, because at its heart it had a sports engine which beat even faster and more powerfully than those of its boxer siblings. In fact it was not only the most powerful but also the most controllable and agile of the bikes of the 4-valve boxer generation.

Model:	R 1100 S
Year:	1998
Power:	98 bhp
Capacity:	1085 cc
Type:	2-cylinder boxer, 4-stroke

BMW C1

The objective for the development of the C1 enclosed scooter launched in 2000 was to combine the advantages of motor-driven two-wheelers, mobility and compactness, with the safety aspects of a car. The result had a cage designed for safety, with deformable elements and shoulder restraints as well as two safety belts. It was driven by a 125-cc 4-stroke engine with modern 4-valve technology, electronic engine management system and computer-controlled fuel injection, as well as a computer-controlled three-way catalytic converter. But this innovative vehicle did not win market acceptance. A model with better performance and a capacity of 200 cc failed to change the picture and BMW discontinued production after only four years.

Model:	C1 125	Year:	2000	Power:	15 bhp
Capacity:	125 cc	Type:	Single-cylinder, 4-stroke		

BMW K 1200 LT

At Intermot in Munich in September 1998, BMW launched the K 1200 LT. The new luxury tourer was the logical result of developing a motorbike to be as safe and as comfortable a tourer as possible, with as much attention paid to the comfort of the rider or riders. It had optimal weather protection provided by fairings designed in the wind-tunnel, a large tail section with case and top case, and good manoeuvring qualities with a reverse gear fitted as standard. Sound equipment, Tempomat cruise control, and heated seatings were just a few examples of the bike's extensive range of features.

Model:	K 1200 LT
Year:	2000
Power:	98 bhp
Capacity:	1171 cc
Type:	4-cylinder in-line, 4-stroke

BMW F 650 RR

In 1999 four BMW works bikes started the Paris-Dakar Rally. After 18 days, the winner was Richard Sainct riding the rally version of the F 650. In 2000 the race was from Dakar to Cairo in Egypt. BMW set out with four further improved F 650 RR bikes and, as a surprising addition, two R 900 RR machines, the newly developed rally model of the 4-valve boxer bike. BMW took the first four places.

Model:	F 650 RR
Year:	2001
Power:	over 75 bhp
Capacity:	652 cc
Type:	Single-cylinder, 4-stroke

BMW K1200 RS

In 1996 BMW introduced a new 4-cylinder model in the form of the K 1200 RS. Enlarged to 1171 cc, the engine developed 130 bhp. It was not only the performance of the powerful BMW motorbike which impressed but also the chassis concept, which made it possible to handle the performance of the new sports tourer. The drive assembly was suspended on a vibration-decoupling mounting in a bridge frame of light metal, while the front wheel control was now the first K-model with the unique BMW telelever suspension system.

Model:	K 1200 RS
Year:	2001
Power:	130 bhp
Capacity:	1171
Type:	4-cylinder in-line, 4-stroke

BMW R 1150 GS

After being manufactured for six years, in 1999 the R 1100 GS was replaced by the R 1150 GS. Lighter cylinder heads made of magnesium and a new camshaft with timing adjusted to optimise torque completed the major update of the boxer engine. With a new six-speed gearbox and a facelift to the appearance of the original large adventure and long-distance touring enduros, this machine was well prepared for the 20th year of the succesful history of BMW's cross-country bikes.

Model:	R 1150 GS
Year:	2001
Power:	85 bhp
Capacity:	1130 cc
Type:	2-cylinder boxer, 4-stroke

BMW R 900 RR Paris-Dakar

After the victories of the Frenchman Richard Sainct, BMW entered the 2-cylinder boxer R 900 RR for the 2001 desert marathon. With extensive careful aerodynamic testing in the BMW wind-tunnel, it was found that the windshield could be increased for the rider's benefit while the air-resistance was reduced by about 30%. Weight-saving measures such as the use of titanium springs in the suspension and a magnesium rear axle housing enabled the BMW boxer to reach precisely the minimum weight of 190 kg (419 lb) specified by the regulations. High torque over almost the whole speed range was the mark of the R 900 RR's hefty engine, which was optimised by the engine tuner Helmut Mader of Erding in Munich. However the bike failed to win the event; the highest-placed 900 RR finished only in sixth place.

Model:	R 900 RR Paris-Dakar
Year:	2000
Power:	90 bhp
Capacity:	900 cc
Type:	2-cylinder boxer, 4-stroke

BMW R 1150 GS Adventure

For motorcyclists whose dreams are the most remote spots in the world, in September 2001 BMW introduced the R 1150 GS Adventure. Whether over gravel tracks, rough terrain or long distances, the bike with its increased suspension travel and large luggage capacity was ideal for such purposes. For the first time a BMW motorbike had telescopic arms with varying-response shock absorbers, where the damping increased with the deflection. A larger luggage carrier meant that wider cases with greater capacity could be carried. With a wide range of optional equipment, this cross-country bike could be turned into a long-distance motorbike for every kind of journey.

Model:	R 1150 GS Adventure
Year:	2002
Power:	85 bhp
Capacity:	1130 cc
Type:	2-cylinder boxer, 4-stroke

BMW F 650 CS Scarver

In 2002 BMW followed the funduro F 650 GS with the F 650 CS, a newly designed street motorbike which had only its single-cylinder engine in common with its sibling. The name Scarver stands for agile handling and a peppy engine, and the use of a low-maintenace toothed belt drive to the rear wheel was new. The striking design with its 'must have' appearance represented a conscious departure from conventional ideas.

Model:	F 650 CS
Year:	2002
Power:	50 bhp
Capacity:	652 cc
Type:	Single-cylinder, 4-stroke

BMW Rockster

The engineers at BMW know how to build excellent motorbikes, but unlike the high performance cars made by the company, the motorbikes still have a somewhat conservative image. So the big shots in Munich had to indulge in the enjoyable lack of seriousness of the streetfighter market, and with comparatively modest changes the sensible R 1150 R gave rise to the noisy Rockster. Using chassis components from the 1100 SS, transformed by the use of the asymmetrically-sized twin headlights from the GS, a small front fairing, classic superbike handlebars and a gaudy matt black and brightly coloured paint scheme, a radical bike from Bavaria was created.

Model:	R 1150 R Rockster
Year:	2003
Power:	85 bhp
Capacity:	1130 cc
Type:	2-cylinder boxer, 4-stroke

BMW K 1200 GT

For motorcyclists who put less value on opulent luxury but who do not want to deny themselves good protection from wind and weather and the comfortable upright sitting position of a tourer, BMW has offered the K 1200 GT since 2003. The model designation 'GT' stood for 'Gran Turismo' and was synonymous with refined sports qualities combined with a high level of touring comfort for both rider and passenger. The new K 1200 GT was the third model completing a trio in the classic K series with the K 1200 RSS sports tourer and the K 1200 LT luxury tourer.

Model:	K 1200 GT
Year:	2003
Power:	130 bhp
Capacity:	1171 cc
Type:	4-cylinder in-line, 4-stroke

BMW R 1200 GS

BMW had a big success with the R 1200 GS: once again it surpassed the excellent qualities of its predecessors in all the main areas – more performance and better road-holding with lower weight and reduced fuel consumption. The new boxer power unit now had a balance shaft, which sucessfully reduced the vibration of the engine. The bike had a well-balanced, stable chassis, a front wheel steering assembly with the unique BMW telelever suspension and the newly designed paralever suspension of low weight and optimal geometry at the rear. With the two compact frame elements of lightweight construction, the weight was reduced by virtually 30 kg (66 lb) compared to the previous model.

Model:	R 1200 GS
Year:	2004
Power:	98 bhp
Capacity:	1170 cc
Type:	2-cylinder boxer, 4-stroke

BMW K 1200 S

The long-awaited BMW with a completely new 4-cylinder high-performance engine and revolutionary chassis technology had its world premier at Intermot 2004. The new K 1200 S, the sports motorbike in BMW's K series, did not replace the existing 4-cylinder models but supplemented them. With its engine developing 167 bhp and a weight of 248 kg (547 lb) including fuel, the K 1200 S entered the senior category of high-performance sports motorbikes which had until then been dominated by Japanese manufacturers.

Model:	K 1200 S
Year:	2004
Power:	167 bhp
Capacity:	1157 cc
Type:	4-cylinder in-line, 4-stroke

BMW R 1200 RT

As the second model of the new generation of boxers, BMW introduced the R 1200 RT tourer at the end of 2004. Technically, with the introduction of the R 1200 GS in spring 2004, BMW had developed a new motorbike in all criteria and qualities. The previous model, the R 1150 RT, had acquired a good reputation as a comfortable, reliable touring machine. So far as the basic facts were concerned, the R 1200 RT had 16% more power and about 20 kg (44 lb) less weight, so this sports tourer could confidently be expected to have even better speed and manoeuvrability.

Model:	R 1200 RT
Year:	2005
Power:	110 bhp
Capacity:	1170 cc
Type:	2-cylinder boxer, 4-stroke

BMW R 1200 ST

The R 1200 ST introduced in 2005 was the quintessence of sports tourers. The successor of the R 1150 RS was the third model of the new boxer generation. The foundations for the development of the R 1200 ST were the drive train and innovative chassis elements of the GS. The suffix 'ST' stood for 'sports tourer'. Construction of the R 1200 ST was diverted from the R 1200 RT in December 2004. With 16% more power and weighing under 230 kg (507 lb), this sports tourer was perfect for nimble cornering and very rapid progress in a straight line.

Model:	R 1200 ST
Year:	2005
Power:	110 bhp
Capacity:	1170 cc
Type:	2-cylinder boxer, 4-stroke

BMW K 1200 R

BMW described this streetfighter version of the K 1200 S as a 'high-performance roadster'. This is not surprising, since in this machine BMW had created the most powerful unfaired production motorbike in the world. Even better news was the fact that it showed that the Bavarian maker was concentrating seriously on sports bikes. This strategy in the field of cars has brought considerable success and this injection of new life will do a lot of good to the somewhat stolid, unsophisticated image of BMW in the field of motorbikes. Even less technically-minded enthusiasts will be excited by its techno appearance.

Model:	K 1200 S
Year:	2004
Power:	over 160 bhp
Capacity:	1157 cc
Type:	4-cylinder in-line, 4-stroke

Brough Superior – The best was just about good enough

At the time the motorcycles built by the English maker Brough Superior were considered the Rolls-Royce of motorbikes. The large twin-cylinder engines built in Nottingham stood out both for the quality of their design and the excellence of their finish. George Brough had fallen out with his father, the motorbike designer William 'Bill' Brough, over the design of the latter's motorbikes. The problem was that George wanted to build better motorbikes than his father. In 1920 he produced his first models with a 750-cc engine by Motosacoche and in 1921 he launched models with 980-cc JAP engines, specially produced for him. Even these early bikes displayed the typical tank shape which became the characteristic trademark of Brough motorbikes. Later this ambitious engineer built models with JAP, MAG and Matchless V2 engines as well as 4-cylinder types, for example a combination with a water-cooled 4-cylinder engine by Austin. From 1924 onwards the SS 100 V2-models were supplied with a '100 miles-per-hour' certificate which guaranteed a top speed of 160 km/h (100 mph). But it was not only the road bikes which were fast. Brough won several speed records: for instance in 1929 Bert le Vack reached a top speed of 205 km/h (127 mph) and in 1937 Eric Fernihough achieved a sensational 273 km/h (170 mph). In 1938 Brough presented the Dream model, but this never went into production. Brough ceased production of its distinguished luxury motorbikes in 1940.

Brough Superior SS 80

Even the first vehicles which George Brough developed after leaving his father's workshop were definitely among the fastest motorcycles. He fitted a 980-cc side-valve JAP engine into a chassis he had made himself, creating a bike with a speed of 120 km/h (75 mph), quite considerable for the time.

Model:	SS 80
Year:	1924
Power:	24 bhp
Capacity:	986 cc
Type:	V-twin, 4-stroke

Brough Superior SS 100

There were many famous riders among those who rode the fast motorbikes from Nottingham. Even Lawrence of Arabia was very fond of the noble bikes of George Brough. He had a collection of eight Broughs and every time he wanted to buy a new motorbike he travelled to the factory where he would discuss all the details on the spot. He died in 1935 in a mysterious crash when riding a Brough Superior.

Model:	SS 100
Year:	1929
Power:	45 bhp
Capacity:	996 cc
Type:	V-twin, 4-stroke

Brough Superior Dream

The culmination of George Brough's creativity emerged in 1938 in the form of the sensational Dream; but this gold-coloured luxury motorbike which was presented at the 1938 Earls Court show never progressed beyond the prototype stage. Powered by a 4-cylinder boxer engine with two pairs of horizontally-opposed cylinders and cardan shaft drive, the Dream was a unique bike through and through. It was the last design of the Brough Superior marque.

Model:	Dream
Year:	1939
Power:	n.a.
Capacity:	997 cc
Type:	4-cylinder boxer, 4-stroke

Brough Superior 11.50

The 11.50 motorcycle combination with 1200-cc side-valve engine was an excellent motorbike. On its own it was, like the SS 100 with overhead camshaft JAP engine, one of the fastest motorbikes of the 1930s. But this elegant bike was not only very fast, it was also very comfortable and thanks to its efficient shock-absorbers it was comparatively smooth to handle.

Model:	11.50
Year:	1930
Power:	60 bhp
Capacity:	1096 cc
Type:	V-twin, 4-stroke

BSA – Birmingham Small Arms

Once upon a time they were the greatest – the Beatles and the British motorcycle industry. BSA's first market success was in 1927 with the 500 cc Sloper and soon afterwards it became the country's largest motorbike manufacturer. The models in the BSA range had illustrious names such as Blue Star, Empire Star and Gold Star. After the war the company resumed production of the barely changed single-cylinder motorbike. In 1946 BSA also produced a 500-cc bike, the A7 Star Twin, as its competitor Triumph had done. This BSA was faster than the Indian and more stylish and easier to handle than the BMW. At this time business was thriving for BSA and the company soon became a market leader worldwide. After the home market, the United States was the company's biggest customer. The faster and more powerful the bikes, the better. Gradually the engines were souped up more and more and the bikes were given dramatic names such as Thunderbolt, Firebird, Lightning, Hornet and Spitfire. In principle this could have gone on for ever, but suddenly the Japanese arrived. The Japanese offensive was a rude awakening and BSA reacted by building the BSA A75R Rocket3. It was in vain because in 1973 BSA went into liquidation.

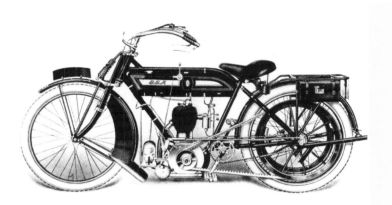

BSA 500

Motorcycle technology was still in its infancy in 1913 and reliability did not exist. So the BSA engineers still equipped their bikes with push-bike pedals to be on the safe side. Admittedly the 500-cc single-cylinder engine was quite substantial, but if the 3.5 bhp 4-stroke engine should give up the ghost, the rider could at least pedal home.

Model:	500
Year:	1913
Power:	3.5 bhp
Capacity:	499 cc
Type:	Single-cylinder, 4-stroke

BSA S 26

BSA made its reputation not least thanks to this sturdy tourer which was a particularly reliable bike. Additional push-bike pedals as provided in the earlier models were therefore no longer necessary. However the performance with its half-litre engine developing 10 bhp was not particularly impressive for the time. A comparable NSU single cylinder was available in the 1920s capable of developing 16 bhp.

Model:	BSA S 26
Year:	1925
Power:	10 bhp
Capacity:	500 cc
Type:	Single-cylinder, 4-stroke

BSA 600 Sloper

Launched in 1927, the new BSA 500 Sloper became a best-seller and trend-setter. The engineers had fitted the single-cylinder engine inclined slightly forward. This sports bike was modelled on the successful TT-racing motorbike of 1921 but the capacity was increased and the performance rose to 20 bhp.

Model:	600 Sloper
Year:	1935
Power:	20 bhp
Capacity:	593 cc
Type:	Single-cylinder, 4-stroke

BSA 1000 G14 Big V-Twin

Like the famous American makers Harley-Davidson and Indian, BSA also produced tourers with large V-twin engines in the 1920s and 1930s. The V-twins existed in different versions ranging from 500 to 1000 cc. The 1000 Big V-Twin launched in 1935 had wide 'highway'-style handlebars, hand gearchange and foot-rests.

Model: 1000 G14 Big V-Twin
Year: 1935
Power: 24 bhp
Capacity: 986 cc
Type: V-twin, 4-stroke

BSA R19 350

Racing has always been very popular in Britain. Amongst BSA's victories in road racing were the Isle of Man TT races and Six Day Endurance races. The forerunners of today's enduros even then had tyres with massive bar treads and the exhaust system was mounted higher up for better ground clearance. The BSA R19 350 was an inexpensive racing bike as well as a road bike which could be used on an everyday basis.

Model: R19 350
Year: 1936
Power: 21 bhp
Capacity: 348 cc
Type: Single-cylinder, 4-stroke

BSA M20

In the Second World War this motorbike acquired the reputation in the British Army of being an indestructible bike. Its many model variations throughout its production until 1963 also pleased thousands of civilian motorbike fans throughout the world, partly because they appreciated the great reliability of the BSA.

Model: M20
Year: 1937
Power: 13 bhp
Capacity: 496 cc
Type: Single-cylinder, 4-stroke

BSA 500 B34 Gold Star Clubman

As early as the 1950s, long before the expression 'café racer' was invented, BSA included in its catalogue a pure-bred road racing motorbike. The ohv single-cylinder engine was capable of developing 40 bhp. The elegant Clubman range was fitted with clip-on foot-rests and a swept-back exhaust system.

Model: 500 B34 Gold Star Clubman
Year: 1954
Power: 40 bhp
Capacity: 499 cc
Type: Single-cylinder, 4-stroke

BSA A10 Road Rocket

The A-10 models were powerful twin-cylinder motorbikes. They were driven by a parallel-twin engine which as well as substantial acceleration also provided an unmistakable sound. The Rocket model sold very well in the United States and was a commercial success for BSA. In addition the Road Rocket was a model which was copied by the emerging Japanese manufacturers, in that countless constructional features of these bikes can be found in, for instance, the Kawasaki W1 of 1965.

Model: A10 Road Rocket
Year: 1955
Power: 40 bhp
Capacity: 650 cc
Type: parallel-twin, 4-stroke

BSA C12 250

Like all well-known manufacturers, BSA also produced 250-cc bikes. These were not exciting motorbikes but bread-and-butter machines for people who could not afford or did not want a larger machine.

Model: C12 250
Year: 1957
Power: 11 bhp
Capacity: 249 cc
Type: Single-cylinder, 4-stroke

BSA 500 A7 Star Twin

Immediately after the war, BSA launched a new 500-cc bike on the market in 1946. The parallel twin developed 26 bhp and was built in the classic English style. The gearbox was behind the engine, and the transmission, dynamo and ignition also had their own housings.

Model: 500 A7 Star Twin
Year: 1961
Power: 26 bhp
Capacity: 497 cc
Type: 2-cylinder, 4-stroke

BSA 650 A10R SuperRocket

Since 1950 BSA had included a 650 in its catalogue in addition to its 500 cc design. BSA could be very happy with the success of the A7 and A10 models but it did not want to rest on its laurels. Soon it launched the 650-cc A10 with 35 bhp. Over the years the twin continued to be developed further and at the beginning of the 1960s it was included in the catalogue under the name of A10R SuperRocket with an amazing 45 bhp and a top speed of over 180 km/h (112 mph).

Model: 650 A10R Super Rocket
Year: 1962
Power: 45 bhp
Capacity: 646 cc
Type: 2-cylinder, 4-stroke

BSA 650 A65 Star Twin

In 1962 BSA in Birmingham started a new generation of motorbikes with the 650 A65 Star Twin. Instead of the traditionally divided engine, the 650-cc top model had a beautiful smooth block engine. After over 30 years the company said goodbye to the A65 model range as it had been and at the same time it also dropped the logo of three crossed rifles which had until then appeared on the timing case. The oval engine casing was extremely compact and construction was simplified, thus cutting production costs by half.

Model:	650 A65 Star Twin
Year:	1962
Power:	38 bhp
Capacity:	654 cc
Type:	2-cylinder, 4-stroke

BSA 650 A65R Rocket

BSA alway built motorbikes for people who knew something about bikes and this type of clientele was continually demanding higher performance. The new A65R Rocket could develop up to 46 bhp and had a 'siamesed' 2-into-1 exhaust system.

Model:	650 A65R Rocket
Year:	1964
Power:	46 bhp
Capacity:	654 cc
Type:	2-cylinder, 4-stroke

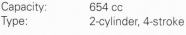

BSA 650 A65L Lightning

The Rocket was a tremendous success when it was launched and it is therefore not surprising that in 1965 it was followed by the next projectile. This time it took the form of the BSA A65 Lightning with an engine developing 52 bhp. A new cylinder head with two Amal monoblock carburettors provided the greater engine power.

Model:	650 A65L Lightning
Year:	1965
Power:	52 bhp
Capacity:	654 cc
Type:	2-cylinder, 4-stroke

BSA 650 A65SS Spitfire MkIV Special

At the beginning of 1968 BSA launched an absolute top model in the A65 range, the A65SS Spitfire MkIV Special. The motorbike's 650-cc engine developed 55 bhp and propelled it at a good 190 km/h (118 mph). At the same time it was the final stage in the development of the A65 range. Anyone who could then afford the high price of the Spitfire Mk IV was the undisputed 'King of the Road', because no other bike, whether Triumph, Norton, Harley or BMW, was faster.

Model:	650 A65SS Spitfire MkIV Special
Year:	1968
Power:	55 bhp
Capacity:	654 cc
Type:	2-cylinder, 4-stroke

BSA 750 A75R Rocket3

BSA produced a genuine sensation in 1968, at least in the eyes of the British. As a final show of strength, BSA launched the 750-cc Rocket3 on the market. But it did so in vain, as the company quickly realised. The end of the 'good old British bike' was unavoidable. Compared to the modern Honda CB750 Four, the brand-new BSA with its 750-cc 3-cylinder engine already looked obsolete. Ironically, today the Rocket3 has become a much sought-after colllector's item. From 1968 until the end of production in 1972 only 5,897 were produced.

Model:	750 A75R Rocket3
Year:	1968
Power:	58 bhp
Capacity:	740 cc
Type:	3-cylinder, 4-stroke

BSA 750 A75R Rocket3
Works racer

For BSA the United States had always been the premier export country. Besides clever advertising, success in competition was also very important to ensure good sales. But a cold wind was blowing from Japan. In 1969 the Honda B-750 Four came onto the American market and as early as 1970 Dick Mann won the 200 Miles of Daytona Beach in Florida on the CB 750 series Honda. Naturally this did not please BSA, but the British motorcycle industry had breathed its last breath. Honda, Yamaha and Kawasaki were the new favourites and this did not change even with Dick Mann's legendary Daytona victory in 1971 on the 750-cc 3-cylinder works BSA. The company went out of business in 1973.

Model:	750 A75R Rocket3
	Works racer
Year:	1971
Power:	85 bhp
Capacity:	740 cc
Type:	3-cylinder, 4-stroke

BSA 650 A65T Thunderbolt

BSA started a new range in 1971 with three models, a series which was described as 'Oil-in-Frame'. The 52-bhp A65L Lightning and the A65FS Firebird Scrambler with 54 bhp were complemented by the A65T Thunderbolt with a comfortable 46 bhp.

Model:	650A65T Thunderbolt
Year:	1971
Power:	46 bhp
Capacity:	654 cc
Type:	2-cylinder, 4-stroke

BSA-Métisse 750 Rocket3 Café Racer

From the 1960s to the beginning of the 1970s the most popular 'in' bikes in England were the so-called 'café racers'. They were home-converted road bikes which looked like real racing bikes. Anyone with plenty of money could buy such an extraordinary bike from a customiser; for instance, a Rickman-Métisse from RGM. Depending on the wishes of the client, there were sports bikes with different engines, either by Triumph, Norton, Royal Enfield or BSA. But Rickman only buiilt 33 chassis kits for the 750-cc 3-cylinder Triumph Trident with a BSA Rocket engine.

Model:	BSA-Métisse 750 Rocket3
Year:	1971
Power:	58 bhp
Capacity:	754 cc
Type:	3-cylinder, 4-stroke

Buell – American sports bike with a Harley heart

It was at the age of 12 that Erik Buell sat on a motorbike for the first time. To pay for his education, he worked in a motorbike shop and was soon promoted from trainee to service manager. During this period he developed his passion for racing. In 1978 Buell achieved the fastest time of any new participant in the Daytona 200 race. Determined to continue working with motorbikes, he was employed as an engineer by the Harley-Davidson Motor Company and developed various motorbike parts. To realise his dream of building his own motorbike, Erik Buell left Harley-Davidson in 1982. The first motorbike which carried his name on the fuel tank was the RW 750. From 1987 onwards he was supported by Harley-Davidson who supplied him with engines for a series of innovative models which enabled him to introduce trailblazing innovations in motorbike production. In 1998 the Buell Motorcycle Company became a subsidiary of Harley-Davidson when the latter bought a 49% share in the company.

Model:	Buell RW 750
Year:	1984
Power:	165 bhp
Capacity:	750 cc
Type:	4-cylinder in-line, 2-stroke

Buell RW 750

The first official Buell was given the designation RW 750. It was a monster 2-stroke with a square 4-cylinder rotary disc-valve engine capable of developing extraordinary power and with a very unusually shaped streamlined fairing. The abbreviation RW stood for Road Warrior. The RW 750 delivered an impressive 165 bhp at the crankshaft and with a weight of only 137 kg (302 lb) could reach a top speed of 285 km/h (177 mph) in tests. The steramlined bodywork was incredibly effective. Erik Buell won several club competitions with this bike but the structural strength of its newly built cylinders, pistons, crankshaft and rotary disc valves was never sufficient for longer competitions. Buell was not going to give up, but just when the RW 750 was about to make its great debut the American Motorcycle Association (AMA) changed its regulations. From one day to the next, there was no longer any market for the RW. This is why only one production model was sold.

Buell RR1000 Battletwin

The second independent Buell model no longer had the temperamental 2-stroke engine and was instead powered by the Harley-Davidson XR1000 engine with rubber mountings, set in a rigid, lightweight frame. The RR1000 must have been the first motorbike which had unusual construction features designed to centralise the weight of the bike as much as possible. These included a central suspension unit, depending on tension, so that the suspension fork was supported against the engine instead of against the frame, thus ensuring that the frame was not affected by vibrations. The location of the shock-absorber under the engine resulted in a short wheelbase and together with the silencer, which was also positioned there, contributed to the centralisation of weight. This was the first typical Buell bike: a completely new type of frame, the radical Formula 1 geometry of the RW, an XR 1000 engine with oscillation damping and an exotic body, which was also inspired by the RW. In the model year 1987/88 some 50 examples of this bike were sold. It won a few victories in races and even a title in a national championship. But yet again the AMA changed its regulations and as a result also cut short the life of this model.

The new Harley-Davidson Evolution 1203-cc engine, presented in 1984, was a very promising starting point for the succeeding model.

The RR 1200 Battletwin road bike using this engine was launched in 1988 and had 65 buyers in the course of the following year.

Model:	RR 1000 Battletwin
Year:	1987
Power:	90 bhp
Capacity:	996 cc
Type:	V2, 4-stroke

Buell Thunderbolt S2

The Thunderbolt S2, launched in 1994, was a milestone in the history of the company. It was the first model to be produced in collaboration with Harley-Davidson. Both customers and the press were full of praise for the new bike and the magazine *Rider* described it as a 'top innovation'. It was successful but it was also a challenge, because with this model Buell was targeting a very special sector of the motorbike market. Its unique styling was more reminiscent of a classic sports car than a motorbike. The strong vibration of the Harley engine was hard on the motorbike so that the tightening of bolts became an on-going task for the machine's owners.

Model:	Thunderbolt S2T
Year:	1996
Power:	68.5 bhp
Capacity:	1203 cc
Type:	V-twin, 4-stroke

Buell Lightning S1

In 1996 Buell presented the Lightning S1, a bike which for the first time gave an idea of the potential of the rustic-style Harley V2 when combined with a sporty frame. With its radical styling and elemental fairing, the Lightning was the first mass-produced streetfighter bike. The White Lightning was a limited edition of the S1, completely in white. Two different shades of white were used on the frame, the wheels and all the add-on parts. The special features of this model were all of a purely visual nature, the engine and chassis being unchanged. The White Lightning has acquired an almost cult status among Buell fans.

Model:	White Lightning S1
Year:	1998
Power:	88 bhp
Capacity:	1199 cc
Type:	V-twin, 4-stroke

Buell M2 Cyclone

The M2 Cyclone produced from 1997 had a shortened S3 frame. Externally, the 'Cyclone' was different with its black steel engine manifold, the absence of a rev counter and the changed windshield of the S1. With its comfortable seats for two people, it became possible to carry a passenger. In the United States the M2 was offered as an alternative to other expensive models with less power. In Europe the M2 was launched with the S1 Lightning of 1996.

Model:	M2 Cyclone
Year:	1999
Power:	88 bhp
Capacity:	1199 cc
Type:	V-twin, 4-stroke

Buell X1 RS 2000

In the style of American muscle cars, the X1 RS 2000 special model appeared in the year 2000. A pair of white lines on the red background running from the front mudguard over the windshield and fuel tank, corresponding with the counterpart on the front spoiler, gave the X1 RS 2000 a decidedly sporty appearance. The black frame and polished light metal wheels provided further stylish accents. The special model had aluminium foot-rests for the rider and passenger as well as a milled tank cover engraved with the serial number of the limited edition.

Model:	X1 RS 2000
Year:	2000
Power:	90 bhp
Capacity:	1199 cc
Type:	V-twin, 4-stroke

Buell Lightning X1

In 1999 the X1 succeeded the S1 in the market. The new frame design made possible a different arrangement for the rear exhaust manifolds, since many S1 riders had suffered from the heat they gave off. Another practical advantage was that it was easier to replace the secondary toothed belt. In the case of the X1 this was behind a bolted-on side frame which made access to the drive belt considerably easier. A no less practical detail of the new frame was that the pillion passenger's foot-rests were bolted onto the frame rather than welded to it. Suspension and shock absorbers now consisted of components from Showa, instead of the White Power parts used at the time of the S1 series. The many large and small modifications made by the American maker to the air-cooled twin were hardly apparent from the outside. They primarily affected the long-term stability of the engine. Among other things, the changes to the internal parts of the engine involved the crankshaft, the toothed wheels of the camshaft, the water pump, the oil pump and circulation, the cylinder liners and the exhaust arrangements. Also new was the fuel supply which was controlled by an electronic fuel injection system.

Model: Lightning X1	Year: 2000	Power: 88 bhp
Capacity: 1199 cc	Type: V-twin, 4-stroke	

Buell Thunderbolt S3T

Shortly after the S1 made its debut in 1996, the S3 appeared. Admittedly at first glance it looked like the S2 but technically it was closer to the S2. The extremely narrow seat of the S3 was not designed for extended touring. The tank was made of plastic and held barely 19 litres (4.2 gallons) of fuel. To achieve further weight saving, the fairings and rear section were made of fibreglass. The power unit was also that of the S1, a performance-enhanced version of the Evolution V2 developing almost 90 bhp. The S3T was the touring version of the S3. The cases designed by the maker were available in two different widths. Very practically, they had optional inside pockets which made loading and unloading the cases very easy, without having to remove them from the vehicle.

Model: Thunderbolt S3T	Year: 2000	Power: 90 bhp
Capacity: 1199 cc	Type: V-twin, 4-stroke	

Buell X1 Ice

As a cool bike for hot summer days, Buell presented this X1 M Ice completely wrapped in silver for the 2000 season. Frame, wheels and manifolds all had the same metal look and even the engine was discreetly silver. The fashionable appearance of the Ice was reinforced by the small but finely executed details of the painting on the tank. The exclusive look was enhanced by the openwork aluminium foot-rests and the cover on the tank engraved with the serial number of the limited edition.

Model:	X1 Ice
Year:	2000
Power:	90 bhp
Capacity:	1199 cc
Type:	V-twin, 4-stroke

Buell Blast

The Blast was specifically built for the United States home market. It was a respectable commercial success for Buell with over 10,000 built in three years, although this was not a large number for an affordable single-cylinder motorbike. The motorbike had a steel frame with bolted-on aluminium components. In spite of its undeniable virtues, the Blast was ridiculed as a delicate riding school motorbike for learners.

Model:	Blast
Year:	2000
Power:	34 bhp
Capacity:	492 cc
Type:	Single-cylinder, 4-stroke

Buell Lightning XB9S

The Lightning XB9S and its sibling model the Firebolt XB9R were among the surprises of the 2002 motorbike season. The three basic constructional principles of the maker's founder Eric Buell were perfectly expressed in these machines: the centralising of weight, the stability of the frame and the reduction of unsprung weight to a minimum. In order to achieve this, some very unusual techniques were employed. The fuel was contained inside the frame itself, and the air filter was located where the fuel tank would normally be. Both models had 375-mm disc brakes at the front with six-piston callipers. The ZTL (Zero Torsional Load) construction transferred the braking force directly to the wheel rim and not, as in normal brakes, first to the wheel spokes – a further contribution to the reduction of unsprung weight. Together with the fundamentally reworked high-powered Harley V2, the bike provided riding enjoyment in a class of its own.

Model:	Lightning XB9S
Year:	2002
Power:	84 bhp
Capacity:	984 cc
Type:	V-twin, 4-stroke

Buell Firebolt XB9R

The Firebolt differed from its 'naked bike' sister, the XB9S, in its decorative mini-dress. It too stored the petrol in the compact bridge-type frame and the oil in the swinging fork. The powerful, curved stainless steel manifold and enormous silencer contributed to noise reduction and performance optimisation in both these models. This made possible free exhaust emission while interference baffles and ram pipes reduced noise levels. The new V2 engines were fired by Dynamic Digital Fuel Injection (DDFI). This created a closed circuit and continuously controlled the operating conditions both inside and outside the engine. The vibrations of the engine which were perceptible in neutral disappeared completely at higher speeds as a result of the patented Uniplanar engine suspension in the frame.

Model: Firebolt XB9R	Year: 2002	Power: 84 bhp
Capacity: 984 cc	Type: V-twin, 4-stroke	

Buell Lightning XB12S

The amazing success of the XB-9 models inspired the Buell engineers to return to the drawing board and further optimise the radical basic concept. To achieve this they helped themselves to the well-stocked engine warehouse of the parent company Harley Davidson and selected the powerful 1200 cc V2 engine for this elegant motorbike. A larger cubic capacity, more torque and over 100 hp – this was what the Buell fans had been waiting for. The 'naked' XB 12S was therefore the most radical mass-produced streetfighter ever built.

Model: Lightning XB12S	Year: 2004	Power: 101 bhp
Capacity: 1203 cc	Type: V-twin, 4-stroke	

Buell City X XB9SX

After the appearance of the XB-12 model with its powerful 1200-cc engine, only a few customers were still interested in the XB9 model; it was obvious that cubic capacity was more important to most people than anything else. As a result, the smaller Firebolt and Lightning versions were replaced by the City X. This is in principle a customised variation of the Lightning XB9S: it is the first motorbike in the world whose coloured parts are no longer conventionally painted but made of a translucent material. This is distinctive and original, looking very modern, and will probably be well-received by lifestyle-oriented customers. Other gimmicks include hand-protectors and handlebars in the moto-cross style.

Model: City X XB9SX	Year: 2005	Power: 84 bhp
Capacity: 984 cc	Type: V-twin, 4-stroke	

Buell Firebolt XB12R

The semi-faired Firebolt boasted a powerful 1200 cc power unit and was the ultimate cornering machine. Its torque-monster of an engine propelled the Firebolt from the lowest revolutions so smoothly that the rider hardly ever had to change gear in spite of all its sports performance. All the XB models had a Kevlar-reinforced toothed belt for its rear-wheel drive because it was lighter, neater and lower in maintenance than any other power transmission system. Its lightness also reduced unsprung weight. The toothed belt had an average life span of about 30,000 km (18,500 miles) and cost no more than a conventional high-quality O-ring chain.

Model:	Lightning XB12R
Year:	2004
Power:	101 bhp
Capacity:	1203 cc
Type:	V-twin, 4-stroke

Bultaco – Everything for sport

When after an argument the Spanish racing enthusiast Francisco Xavier Bulto left the Montesa company which he had co-founded, he decided to set up his own company. But what Don Paco Bulto really wanted was to take part in competitions. In 1958 a small team of engineers started working on the development of the Tralla 101 in Bulto's country house near Barcelona. In fact, the Spanish heralded a new era in trials events. The Sherpa T was the first foreign bike to win the famous Scottish Six Day endurance trial. Bultaco also developed special flat-track competition models for wealthy US customers. Production of the simple but powerful Bultacos continued into the 1980s, but production ceased in 1982 because of financial difficulties.

Bultaco Tralla 101 Gran Turismo

It was in 1958 that Bultaco produced its first model, the Tralla 101 Gran Turismo. Although the 2-stroke bike was built as a reliable utility motorbike, it also boasted considerable sports potential. When presented, the Tralla was the most expensive 125 cc on the Spanish market. Nevertheless it sold extremely well because of its sturdy frame and high-performance engine, thus laying the foundation for the maker's future success.

Model: Tralla 101 Gran Turismo	Year: 1959	Power: 12 bhp
Capacity: 125 cc	Type: Single-cylinder, 2-stroke	

Bultaco TSS

The name Bultaco is closely connected with the world of racing. Its greatest success in road events was with the TSS model, a racing bike with a choice of 125, 175, 250 or 350-cc engines, which everyone could afford. Constant improvements such as a six-speed gear-box and water-cooling (in 1967) made this racer extremely popular for many years. In fact, it was one of the most popular racing bikes of the 1960s both in Europe and South America.

Model:	TSS
Year:	1967
Power:	38 bhp
Capacity:	244 cc
Type:	Single-cylinder, 2-stroke

Bultaco Matador Mk4 SD

The cross-country models produced by Bultaco were called the Matador and the Frontera. The basic concept of the Matador was comparatively simple. The inlet and exhaust manifolds were moved higher up, the ground clearance was increased and the tyres and handlebars were adapted for off-road use. Off-road Bultacos sold extremely well in both Europe and the USA. The addition of 'SD' to the name, which stood for 'Six Days', indicated that the 250-cc Mk4 of 1971 was a pure-bred racing bike.

Model: Matador Mk4 SD	Year: 1971	Power: 23.5 bhp
Capacity: 244 cc	Type: Single-cylinder, 2-stroke	

Bultaco Sherpa 250 T

For many years the Sherpa models were the best-selling trials motorbikes. Specially developed for hill-climbing, these Spanish bikes were the best of their time and they nearly always left their rivals lagging behind. The Sherpa T 250 was the first trials bike with a single tank-seat combination which very soon became a standard feature in motorbikes.

Model: Sherpa 250 T	Year: 1974	Power: 18 bhp
Capacity: 244 cc	Type: Single-cylinder, 2-stroke	

Cagiva – The heritage of the Castiglionis

In 1978 the brothers Gianfranco and Claudio Castiglioni bought the former Aermacchi Motorcycle Company in Varese which had been partly owned by the US motorbike manufacturer Harley-Davidson since 1961, eventually being completely integrated in 1973. Harley-Davidson was in turn incorporated in the American AMF Group. When the latter was disposing of the motorcycle divisions in the group, the Castiglioni brothers jumped at the opportunity of acquiring this company and named it Cagiva after the name of the metalworking factory which had been founded by their father Giovanni in Varese in 1928. Cagiva's road bikes soon became very popular and it also developed moto-cross bikes which won the Italian Moto-Cross Championship in 1981. A year later Gianpaolo Marinoni became the Italian Moto-Cross champion and in 1985 Pekka Vehkoneen won the World Moto-Cross Championship title. Business was good and in 1983 Cagiva bought the ailing Ducati. From 1985 onwards Cagiva took part in the famous Dakar Rally with a 900-cc monster with which Edi Orioli eventually won the event in 1990. Subsequently in 1986 Cagiva absorbed the Swedish enduro manufacturer Husqvarna, then in 1987 it bought Moto Morini and it acquired the right to the name of the racing icon MV Agusta. Between 1986 and 1995 Cagiva competed in 500-cc Grand Prix road races with V4 racing bikes. But gradually Claudio Castiglioni, now wholly responsible for the company, was forced to part with some sections of his empire to help relieve his financial problems. Since the sale of Ducati, Cagiva has used Suzuki engines for its mass-produced motorbikes and Moto Morini has become independent again. In 2004, after some turbulent negotiations, the Asia Proton Group acquired 49% of Cagiva.

Cagiva MRX 250

This moto-cross bike produced in Varese still had many of the distinctive features of the Aermacchi workshop. The air-cooled 2-stroke engine was visually a clear descendant of the power unit used by AMF-Harley-Davidson in the enduro SX 250. Besides this moto-cross version, there was also a cross-country-sport version with which Gianpaolo Marinoni won the Italian Enduro championship in 1981.

Cagiva WMX 125

After Pekka Vehkoneen won the World Moto-Cross Championship in 1985 and Dave Strijbos took the title in 1986, Cagiva produced a replica of the World Championship motorbike for private riders. Compared to the works motorbike of the previous year, the water-cooled engine with six gears developed in-house had an improved Keihin carburetter with a diameter of 36 mm. It was suspended in a twin-cradle frame with aluminium swinging forks and Öhlins single suspension strut.

Cagiva Elefant

Cagiva's most successful model of the 1980s and 1990s was the Elefant. It was first launched on the market with a 650-cc Ducati Pantah-Twin engine in purist enduro style, but there were also a 350 cc and even a 125-cc version. In 1987 Cagiva presented the Elefant 750 cc equipped with the V2 engine of the Ducati 750 SS. After the double Dakar victory of Elefant rider Edi Orioli, a new 900 cc version was launched at the beginning of the 1990s with an engine derived from the Ducati 900SS.

Model:	MRX 250
Year:	1981
Power:	36 bhp
Capacity:	124 cc
Type:	Single-cylinder, 2-stroke

Model:	WMX 125
Year:	1987
Power:	36 bhp
Capacity:	124 cc
Type:	Single-cylinder, 2-stroke

Model:	Elefant 750
Year:	1987
Power:	61 bhp
Capacity:	749 cc
Type:	V-twin, 4-stroke

Cagiva River

The River 500 was an unpretentious motor-bike for everyday use, powered by an air/oil-cooled four-valve single cylinder 500 cc engine. Production of the River came to an end when the 650 cc Raptor was launched. The engine was also used in the 'funduro' Canyon 500 among others.

Model:	River 500
Year:	1999
Power:	34 bhp
Capacity:	498 cc
Type:	Single-cylinder, 4-stroke

Cagiva Navigator

The successor to the Elefant was presented in 1997 and was at first still powered by the Ducati 900 cc Desmo-V2. But with its comparatively measly 68 bhp, the bike which was still known by the name 'Gran Canyon' did not survive for very long, because in 2000 it was fitted with the powerful 1000 cc Suzuki V-engine.

Model:	Navigator
Year:	2000
Power:	98 bhp
Capacity:	998 cc
Type:	V-twin, 4-stroke

Cagiva Raptor 650

In 2001 Cagiva launched its own interpretation of Suzuki's best-selling SV 650. Powered by its famous V-twin but with a completely independent frame and a very attractive appearance, the success of this model was only slightly hampered by the unsatisfactory terms of delivery. It was also available as the V-Raptor with sharply truncated headlight cowling.

Model:	Raptor 650
Year:	2001
Power:	73 bhp
Capacity:	645 cc
Type:	V-twin, 4-stroke

Cagiva V-Raptor 1000

In parallel with the 'naked' Raptor range, Cagiva also launched two very striking 'V' variations with 650 and 1000-cc engines. They still had the same magnificent tubular space frame and the powerful Suzuki V-twin engine but otherwise the two models were very different. Besides the tauter and completely adjustable suspension elements, the 1000-cc was also set apart by its unusually well-designed handlebar fairing which give the Raptor its own very distinctive style. Originally designed as a special model, the Xtra-Raptor shown here replaced the original 1000-cc version in 2004. The increased use of carbon fibre distinguishes the V-Raptor from the Xtra Raptor.

Model:	Xtra-Raptor 1000
Year:	2004
Power:	113 bhp
Capacity:	998 cc
Type:	V-twin, 4-stroke

Cagiva Raptor 1000

The Raptor series celebrated its premier in 2000. As it had in the Navigator, the Suzuki V-twin provided the large Raptor models with breathtaking power. In addition to power and design, the Raptor appealed to fans because of its sturdy, beautiful tubular space frame which, together with first-quality spring elements and excellent brakes, ensured a tremendous riding experience. In 2005 the two Raptors were updated with a new headlight fairing and other improved features.

Model:	Raptor 1000
Year:	2002
Power:	112 bhp
Capacity:	998 cc
Type:	V-twin, 4-stroke

CCM – Clews Competition Machines

In 1971 Alan Clews founded CCM Motorcycles Ltd as a company to satisfy his passion for moto-cross by building motorbikes to his own specifications. From the very start, CCM bikes only used 4-stroke engines – even when all its competitors were using 2-stroke engines. Nevertheless, even in the late 1970s riders such as John Banks were still very successful with 4-strokes. As small-scale manufacturers, CCM produced about one motorbike a week in the early 1990s. Then in 1998 production rose from 50 to at first 1,000 and later even to 5,000 bikes a year. But after this very promising development the small company quickly reached the limits of its resources. The costs resulting from doing business in Europe and the necessary marketing expenditure, together with the dramatic growth in production soon led to financial problems and in 2004 even to insolvency. However the company, in which Superbike legend Carl Fogarty was also involved, found a new investor.

CCM MC 500

Just when 2-stroke engines were dominating the scene in cross-country racing, CCM launched a powerful 4-stroke bike in both moto-cross and enduro versions. Based on the overhead valve power unit of the already discontinued BSA 500 SS launched in 1972, Clews created an engine capable of developing 50 bhp from the 573 cc version.

Model:	MC 500
Year:	1976
Power:	45 bhp
Capacity:	498 cc
Type:	Single-cylinder, 4-stroke

CCM 604 Roadster

The Roadster was an ordinary all-round bike which also provided the basis for the enduro and supermoto models built by CCM. It was better suited to winding its way round corners than racing along straights.

Model:	604 Roadster
Year:	2000
Power:	53 bhp
Capacity:	598 cc
Type:	Single-cylinder, 4-stroke

CCM 644 Dual Sport

The Dual Sport was available in two versions, the Supermoto and the Trial. The two models only differed in the size of the wheels which in the case of the Supermoto measured 17 inches. The two models were based on the Roadster and in 2003 both were fitted with a single-cylinder Suzuki engine, made famous by the Freewind.

Model:	644 Dual Sport Supermoto
Year:	2003
Power:	50 bhp
Capacity:	644 cc
Type:	Single-cylinder, 4-stroke

CCM R 30

In 2003 CCM launched another variation on the Supermoto, based on the Roadster models. Unlike the Dual Sport models, the very distinctive R 30 had swinging forks which had been shortened by 25 mm (1 inch). At first the British drift bike still had to make do with an obsolete Rotax engine and it was only in 2004 that it was fitted with the admittedly less powerful but clearly more sophisticated 644-cc Suzuki engine.

Model:	R 30 Supermoto
Year:	2004
Power:	50 bhp
Capacity:	644 cc
Type:	Single-cylinder, 4-stroke

CZ – Czech people's motorbikes

Initially CZ, founded in 1918, was involved in the production of weapons and gear wheels. In 1935 Ceska Zbrojovka (in English, 'Czech Arms Factory') launched its first motorbike on the market. Soon it was producing larger models with 175, 250 and 350-cc 2-stroke engines. After the war, the company was nationalised in 1945. From 1949 onwards, because of the standardisation in vehicle production ordered by the government, CZ cooperated closely with JAWA, the second-largest Czech motorbike manufacturer. But in spite of working together, CZ retained a certain independence. The export of 125 to 250-cc 2-stroke engines was flourishing in the West and engines were exported to Scandinavia. In 1955 Jawa-CZ became involved in motorbike racing. The Czechs were very successful in cross-country competitions with their moto-cross and GS models . But in the West the old-fashioned 2-stroke engine was no longer selling and the motorcycle had become a fashionable leisure toy. CZ ceased production at the beginning of the 1980s.

CZ 100

Before the Second World War, a workshop in Strakonice built small motorbikes with a divided 98-cc 2-stroke engines. This simple bike had an unsprung rear frame and a hand-operated two-speed gearbox. Compared to the first model, which still very much resembled a bicycle, the models with 76-cc engines already had the appearance of proper motorbikes.

Model:	100
Year:	1935
Power:	2.5 bhp
Capacity:	198 cc
Type:	Single-cylinder, 2-stroke

CZ 350

The top models of the Czech motorcycle factory in the 1930s were a 350-cc 2-stroke single-cylinder bike and a 500-cc with 2-stroke 2-cylinder engine. The pressed sheet-metal frame construction was similar to the German developments of those years, that is, those of Zündapp and BMW. Only a small number of these large 2-strokes were sold.

Model:	350
Year:	1937
Power:	16 bhp
Capacity:	348 cc
Type:	Single-cylinder, 2-stroke

CZ MC 250

The success of the Czech maker in moto-cross racing started in 1964. Although the cross-country motorbikes had a comparatively simple construction, they still managed to win many national and international victories. They continued to be improved over the years but in spite of this they were unable to stand up against the competition in the 1970s.

Model:	MC 250
Year:	1964
Power:	24 bhp
Capacity:	246 cc
Type:	Single-cylinder, 2-stroke

CZ MC 250

The Czech maker's success in cross-country racing was enormous. CZ won the international Six Day Endurance Trial as early as 1947 and repeated this triumph a further nine times. In 1960 it also became very successful in moto-cross competitions, being ridden to victory in the World Championship in three consecutive years, 1966, 1967 and 1968. Both cross-country and moto-cross bikes were available based on the same recipe, sharing the same first-class frame fitted with 125, 175, 250, 350 or 380-cc engines. With the latter the Czechs even went on to win the 500-cc title in spite of having a smaller cylinder capacity.

Model:	MC 250
Year:	1974
Power:	34 bhp
Capacity:	246 cc
Type:	Single-cylinder, 2-stroke

DKW – 'The little miracle' ('Das kleine Wunder')

The origins of DKW go back to the Dane Jörgen Skafte Rasmussen. In 1906 this engineer bought an empty cloth mill in Zschopau. In 1920 the company launched its first moped, and the first DKW motorbike, the 'Reichsfahrt' model, was launched in 1922. This snappy little bike was given its name after winning the 'ADAC-Reichsfahrt' (the German Automobile Club Tour of Germany). Purchase on the instalment plan was a brilliant business idea and after-sales training ensured good servicing. For the first time assembly-line production was introduced into motorbike manufacturing to increase output. DKW was also successful in the world of competition with victories in the German road championship and wins in the German Grand Prix. In 1928 DKW took over the Audi factory at Zwickau. In the same year DKW became the world's largest motorbike manufacturer with about 2,400 workers and over 45,000 motorbikes produced per year. In 1929 production rose to 60,000 but then the world economic crisis struck. DKW survived the crisis with only 850 workers producing 2-stroke bikes. In 1932 Audi, Horch, Wanderer and DKW joined forces, all the motorbikes they made being sold under the name DKW. In 1936 the company's market share was 35% and in 1939 the 500,000th DKW motorbike came off the assembly line. Afer the war the production of motorbikes was resumed as part of the 'peace production' emerging in the newly-born German Democratic Republic. In 1952 the former DKW-Werk became VEB Motorradwerk Zschopau or MZ for short. In the Federal Republic the long-standing East German tradition of 2-stroke engine continued in 1949 in Ingolstadt with the launch of the RT 125. DKW remained loyal to the concept of the 2-stroke engine until it ceased production of motorbikes in 1958. After the RT 125, the company launched single-cylinder bikes with 175, 200 and 250-cc engines and in 1955 they went to build the RT 350 S. But even then the end of the motorbike business was already in sight.

DKW Fahrrad-Hilfsmotor (motor-assisted bicycle)

Cycling improves fitness and is good for your health. Only when you start struggling does the fun stop; this is when you need an engine. This was the idea that Jörgen Skafte Rasmussen turned into a reality in 1920. He fitted the little 1-bhp 118-cc engine behind the carrier; the power was transferred to the rear wheel by a belt. The DKW ('Das kleine Wunder' – 'the little miracle') was ready. This auxiliary-engined bicycle led in 1921 to DKW starting the manufacture of bicycle engines for other manufacturers and also for private buyers to fit to the rear wheels of their push-bikes. The engine was nicknamed the 'bum warmer'! Of course nobody then suspected that only six years later DKW would be the world's largest motorcycle manufacturer.

Model:	Fahrrad-Hilfsmotor (motor-assisted bicycle)
Year:	1922
Power:	1 bhp
Capacity:	118 cc
Type:	Single-cylinder, 2-stroke

DKW Reichsfahrtmodell

The first motorbike launched on the market by DKW came out in 1922. Admittedly, this very light motorcycle with a power of 2.25 bhp was very similar to a bicycle, but with its streamlined fairing it could reach 60 km/h (37 mph), and thus it became successful in racing. DKW won the prestigious Reichsfahrt.national race with it in 1922.

Model:	Reichsfahrtmodell
Year:	1922
Power:	2.25 bhp
Capacity:	148 cc
Type:	Single-cylinder, 2-stroke

DKW Rennmotorrad (racing motorcycle)

Following its motto 'Wins promote sales', DKW concentratd seriously on motorbike racing competitons. As early as 1925 it built a racing bike with a single-cylinder water-cooled 2-stroke engine. From the 142-cc engine the DKW engineers managed to squeeze an impressive 7 bhp, enough for it to reach a top speed of nearly 100 km/h (62 mph).

Model:	Rennmotorrad (racing motorcycle)
Year:	1925
Power:	7 bhp
Capacity:	172 cc
Type:	Single-cylinder, 2-stroke

DKW Z 500

DKW's boss Rasmussen was incredibly successful in his manufacture of motorbikes. In 1927 this clever businessman was already employing 15,000 workers. The top model in 1927 was the Z 500 with a 2-cylinder 2-stroke engine and three-speed gearbox. This elegant bike could develop 12 bhp and reach a top speed of 100 km/h (62 bhp).

Model:	Z 500
Year:	1927
Power:	12 bhp
Capacity:	494 cc
Type:	2-cylinder, 2-stroke

DKW E 200

Indian was the largest motorbike manufacturer in the 1920s but by 1929 DKW had overtaken the leading American brand and became market leader. The variety of its range included the E 200, a mature mid-range motorbike. The E 200 became the 'people's motorbike', which could be ridden without a driving licence and without being liable to tax. As the least expensive DKW it was the most popular bike in its class.

Model:	E 200
Year:	1929
Power:	4 bhp
Capacity:	199 cc
Type:	Single-cylinder, 2-stroke

DKW Luxus 200 ZS200

The world economic crisis also affected DKW. The ZS200 may have been called the 'Luxus 200' but in fact it was a simple everyday motorbike with fan-cooled 2-stroke engine, two-speed gearbox, chain drive and inexpensive pressed steel frame. It was popularly known as the 'blood blister'.

Model:	Luxus 200 ZS200
Year:	1931
Power:	4 bhp
Capacity:	199 cc
Type:	Single-cylinder, 2-stroke

Ducati 450 R/T

Following the modular construction principle, the vertical shaft single-cylinder gave rise to tourer, sport and scrambler models. While the latter appealed more to the enthusiast, this 450 R/T was designed for serious competition. Unlike the scrambler it was fitted with the desmo engine of the road-racing model and had a completely different frame. It was with this bike that the Italian national team took part in the international Six Days cross-country race on the Isle of Man.

Model:	450 R/T
Year:	1971
Power:	36 bhp
Capacity:	436 cc
Type:	Single-cylinder, 4-stroke

Ducati 125 Six Days

In order to keep up in the increasingly popular cross-country sport during the 2-stroke era, and in view of the sales success of the Spanish manufacturer and the indigenous manufacturers Beta and SWM, Ducati launched the enduro 125 Six Days in 1975. Originally a moto-cross version was also planned. Not least because of technical problems, its success as a competition and enduro version remained fairly modest among ordinary customers, which is why it is increasingly rare today.

Model:	125 Six Days
Year:	1976
Power:	22 bhp
Capacity:	124 cc
Type:	Single-cylinder, 2-stroke

Ducati 900 SS

The prototype of the vertical shaft 2-cylinder bike was launched in the form of the 750 GT in August 1970. After the double victory in Imola, there was first a small edition of the 750-cc Super-Sport with desmodromic valvegear, followed later by the mass-produced version. This was followed in 1975 by this 900 Supersport which was based on the Tourer 860 GT presented the year before. Because of its reduced frontal area and corresponding higher gear ratio, it even beat the 900-cc Kawasaki as far as top speed was concerned, and with its speed capability of 225 km/h (140 mph) it was for a short time the fastest mass-produced motorbike in the world.

Model:	900 Super Sport
Year:	1976
Power:	75 bhp
Capacity:	864 cc
Type:	V-twin, 4-stroke

Ducati 860 GTS

In 1973 a bike using the pistons of the 450-cc single-cylinder with a capacity of 864 cc was created for the 24-hour Barcelona race. Immediately after its victory in this race, Ducati presented the tourer bike, the 860 GT, at the Milan show. There it failed to delight many people with its squared-off features which were typical of the designer Giugiaro. Two years later this design was slightly modified in this version with twin disc brakes. Nevertheless the 860 GTS remained rather unpopular and many of them were rebuilt to look like the 900 SS.

Model:	860 GTS
Year:	1977
Power:	65 bhp
Capacity:	864 cc
Type:	V-twin, 4-stroke

Ducati 500 D

The history of the Ducati parallel twins dates back to the 175-cc 2-cylinder racing bike of 1957 which led to subsequent variations with 250, 350, 500 and even 700-cc engines. Because of the success of the single-cylinder engine, Taglioni was not interested and rejected any further development. It was only in 1975, when trying to produce less-expensive vertical-shaft models, that this 2-cylinder engine with a chain-driven but still horizontal camshaft attracted the attention of Taglioni.

Model:	500 Sport Desmo
Year:	1977
Power:	40 bhp
Capacity:	497 cc
Type:	2-cylinder, 4-stroke

Ducati 350 GTL

Strongly resembling the design of the 860 GTS the 350-cc variation of the parallel twin was hardly likely to please the customers any more. In addition, the fact that the performance was quite modest, as had been the case with the old singles, and therefore even considerably less than the 500-cc variant, meant that the sporty desmo version was unlikely appeal to Ducati's fans. In its search for new market niches, the management had forgotten its old customer base and the bikes of this series were not a commercial success.

Model:	350 GTL
Year:	1977
Power:	29 bhp
Capacity:	349 cc
Type:	2-cylinder, 4-stroke

Ducati 500 Desmo

The largest model produced under licence by Mototrans in Spain was the 500 Desmo. Its parallel-twin engine was the same as the Italian 500 Sport Desmo. The Spanish twins could be distinguished from their siblings from the parent company by details such as a different petrol tank, aluminium wheels consisting of several parts and an oil cooler. Similarly, as with the single-cylinder models, only a few spare parts were the same as those for the Italian models.

Model:	500 Desmo
Year:	1978
Power:	42 bhp
Capacity:	498 cc
Type:	2-cylinder, 4-stroke

Ducati Darmah

With the Darmah the desmo engine was used for the first time in a Ducati tourer bike. A smaller carburettor and less extreme camshafts limited the performance of the engine to 68 bhp but it was still able to reach a top speed of 195 km/h (121 mph). Leopoldo Tartarini was responsible for the styling. Under the name SSD, Ducati also produced a sports half-faired version of the Darmah.

Model:	Darmah SD 900
Year:	1978
Power:	68 bhp
Capacity:	864 cc
Type:	V-twin, 4-stroke

Ducati 350 F3

In 1985 at the Milan show Ducati presented several models including the 350 F3. The snappy sports bike soon became extremely popular and because of this a range of special models such as the Montjuich, Santamonica and Laguna Seca became one of the mainstays in the Italian company's catalogue.

Model:	350 F3
Year:	1987
Power:	39 bhp
Capacity:	349 cc
Type:	2-cylinder, 4-stroke

Ducati Indiana

Besides the 750-cc Paso and the 350-cc F3 another new model was presented at the Milan Fair in 1985 which made the hair of Ducati enthusiasts stand on end. The Indiana was Ducati's unfortunate attempt to break into the chopper sector of the market. Fitted with a Pantah engine, it was available in 350, 650 and 750-cc capacities, but after only three yearrs Ducati gave up its attempt to enter the chopper market.

Model:	Indiana Custom 650
Year:	1987
Power:	53 bhp
Capacity:	649 cc
Type:	2-cylinder, 4-stroke

Ducati 851

In 1988 Ducati for the first time presented a water-cooled 4-valve superbike, the Ducati 851. Both sport and road versions of the 851 sold very well, a fact which was due to the dramatic supersport design of the bike a well as its performance capability; the stronger SP version was capable of developing 100 bhp.

Model:	851 SP
Year:	1989
Power:	100 bhp
Capacity:	851 cc
Type:	V-twin, 4-stroke

Ducati ST 2

In 1997 Ducati was exploring new ground. As a sports tourer bikes it offered the ST 2 as an alternative to Honda's VFR and the tourer models by BMW. Comparatively light with its dry weight of 207 kg (456 lb), the strong 85-bhp 2-valve V-twin engine of the ST 2 ensured a considerable but by no means breathtaking performance. It was only in 1999 with the ST 4, which was fitted with a slightly modified version of the engine from the 916, that it was able to achieve 105 bhp and a top speed of 240 km/h (149 mph), thus meeting the requirements of the performance-hungry Ducati tourer enthusiasts.

Model:	ST 2
Year:	2000
Power:	85 bhp
Capacity:	940 cc
Type:	V-twin, 4-stroke

91

Ducati 916 / 996

In 1994 the already-legendary Ducati 916 became available in Strada and SP versions. The fantastic design, the impressive and very distinctive desmo V-twin engine and numerous details such as the patented steering shock absorber, the magnificent single-arm fork and the aggressive forged twin-tube exhaust system under the rear cowling made this motorbike one of the milestones of motorbike history. In addition, the sturdy frame is still setting the standard today. Its performance was demonstrated when Carl Fogarty won the Superbike World Championship in the first year in which the 916 was raced. Numerous other models followed. In 1999 the 916 underwent an overall technical re-working. This included a new name which corresponded to its cubic capacity, the Ducati 996.

Model:	996
Year:	2000
Power:	112 bhp
Capacity:	996 cc
Type:	V-twin, 4-stroke

Ducati MH 900e

Already presented as a design study at Inter-mot 1998, Ducati produced a limited edition of 2,000 examples of the MH 900e in the year 2000. The wonderfully beautiful retro sports bike was – as the name of the model hinted – a tribute to the racing legend Mike Hailwood. To whet the appetite it was only necessary to look on the Internet at the animation of the air-cooled 79-bhp Desmo V2 engine of the 900 cc Supersport.

Model:	MH 900e
Year:	2000
Power:	79 bhp
Capacity:	904 cc
Type:	V-twin, 4-stroke

Ducati 748

As a cheaper version of the 916/996 model range with slighly lower performance, Ducati launched the 748 in 1995. The R version was used as the basis for competing in the Supersport World Championship, in which twin-cylinder models with a maximum of 750 cc were allowed, while 4-cylinder models were only permitted to have a capacity of up to 600 cc.

Model:	748
Year:	2001
Power:	97 bhp
Capacity:	748 cc
Type:	V-twin, 4-stroke

Ducati Multistrada

With the Multistrada in 2002, Ducati presented a highly unusual funbike, which because
of its very droll design and swinging front fairing was not universally popular. In addition, the
easy-to-handle chassis was blessed with
supermoto characteristics. On winding roads
the Multistrada is very hard to beat. Since 2005
it has also been available in a 620-cc version

Model:	Multistrada 1000 DS
Year:	2003
Power:	84 bhp
Capacity:	992 cc
Type:	V-twin, 4-stroke

Ducati Monster

In 1992 the Ducati Monster 900 heralded the comeback of 'naked' bikes.
The chassis was based on that of the Ducati 888, the timeless design by
Signore Galluzzi, who worked in the design studio of Massimo Tamburini
in San Marino. Ducati produced many monster versions as the years went
by. The list began with the 620-cc variant with 63 bhp, while at the top
end of the model range the Monster S4R with 117 bhp and the V-twin
engine of the Ducati 996 provided great excitement for its riders. Since
2005 there has also been an S2R, the air-cooled 800-cc V-twin engine of
which 'only' developed 77 bhp, but which was graced with the delight-
ful aluminium single arm and high-mounted twin-tube exhaust of the S4R.

Model:	Monster S4R
Year:	2004
Power:	117 bhp
Capacity:	996 cc
Type:	V-twin, 4-stroke

Ducati Supersport 1000

In 1998 the new Supersport range was
launched which continued the SS series
which had been almost unchanged since
1991. At first as a 900-cc bike but later also
with 620, 800 and 1000-cc versions, it
remained exteremly successful, not least
because of its comparatively straightforward
appearance. In addition, the technical qualities of its frame were completely typical of
Ducati, not super-easy to handle but ultra-
sturdy. Thus the Supersport models were
clearly worthy of their name...

Model:	Supersport 1000 DS
Year:	2004
Power:	86 bhp
Capacity:	992 cc
Type:	V-twin, 4-stroke

Ducati ST3

The next generation of tourer sports bikes, the ST2/ST4, was launched in 2004. Admittedly the ST3 was inspired by the previous models, but it was given a new chassis, a clearly updated fairing, and a water-cooled three-valve engine. The ST4S model had the optimised torque of the previous 996 which in this case developed 121 bhp. Like its predecessors, the ST3/ST4S as complete tourer bikes and had an ABS brake system.

Model: ST3
Year: 2004
Power: 107 bhp
Capacity: 992 cc
Type: V-twin, 4-stroke

Ducati 999

It is not easy to be the successor to a legend. This was the situation of the Ducati 999 on its debut in 2002. Since then it has had to live with the fact that it is not such a remarkable success as its forerunner the 916. But this is not because of any shortcomings in its technical qualities. The chassis is a model of precision and in the top version, the 999 RS, the Testastretta engine now developed an unbelievable 150 bhp. Not bad for a V-twin unit! However, the controversial appearance gave rise to heated debate, and not only among Ducati enthusasts. With a slight facelift for the 2005 season, Ducati tried to smooth out the design to achieve wider acceptance.

Model: 999
Year: 2005
Power: 140 bhp
Capacity: 998 cc
Type: V-twin, 4-stroke

Ducati 749

With the 748 already available as a more affordable supersport sibling for the 916/996-cc generation, in the 2005 season an affordable 750-cc alternative to the 999 appeared. Perhaps one should say four models, because, in addition to the standard 749, Ducati entered S, R, and Dark versions into races. While the race versions were developed for ambitious race track performance, the matt black 'Dark' with103 bhp was a relatively modest entry level model.

Model: 749 Dark
Year: 2005
Power: 103 bhp
Capacity: 748 cc
Type: V-twin, 4-stroke

Ducati Sport 1000   Ducati Paul Smart   Ducati GT 1000

Not a bad idea: Ducati created these three remarkable concept bikes and displayed this so-called 'Sport Classic family' at all the most important motorbike salons in the world, gathering praise and recognition from all sides.

It was therefore no surprise that the Italians decided to put all three Sport Classic models into production. The 'Paul Smart' was the first of the three neo-traditional models to appear in November 2005. Initially, the machine is being produced in a limited edition of 1,000 examples. This has the same appearance as the 750-cc racing bike with which Paul Smart won at Imola in 1972. Later, the purist 'Sport 1000' café racer goes into production, and six months after that (in September 2006) customers will have the opportunity of acquiring the purist 'GT 1000'.

Ducati Sport 1000

Model:	Sport 1000
Year:	from March 2006
Power:	86 bhp
Capacity:	992 cc
Type:	V-twin, 4-stroke

Ducati Paul Smart

Model:	Paul Smart
Year:	from November 2005
Power:	86 bhp
Capacity:	992 cc
Type:	V-twin, 4-stroke

Ducati GT 1000

Model:	GT 1000
Year:	from September 2006
Power:	86 bhp
Capacity:	992 cc
Type:	V-twin, 4-stroke

FN – Belgium's greatest

The famous Belgian motorbike manufacturer Fabrique Nationale d'Armes de Guerre – FN for short – was founded in 1889 as an arms factory. In 1901 the company expanded its range of activities and produced motorised two-wheelers. The first motorbike to leave the factory in Herstal had a simple bicycle frame. The Belgian company became famous in 1904 when it launched the first mass-produced 4-cylinder motorbikes. Like these heavy 4-cylinder bikes, FN's single-cylinder machines also had the reputation of being very reliable vehicles. Although the maker's manufacturing faciles were destroyed during the war, the company resumed production in 1946. In the mid-1950s the reasonably-priced 2-stroke bikes replaced the no longer up-to-date M 13 4-stroke range. FN eventually stopped producing motorbikes in 1962.

FN 133 cc

Motorcycle production began in Herstal in Belgium with this 133-cc model. The power of these little single-cylinder bikes was transferred directly to a friction disc on the rear wheel by a belt. There was still an unmistakable resemblance to a push-bike, with an unsprung front fork and a frame without any stabilizing reinforcing struts. However the succeeding model which came out in 1903 with an engine of 188 cc had different dimensions.

Model:	133 cc
Year:	1901
Capacity:	133 cc
Power:	2 bhp
Type:	Single-cylinder, 4-stroke

FN 4-cylinder

In 1904 the Belgian motorcycle manufacturer added a luxurious 4-cylinder model to its single-cylinder production. The engine of this first 4-cylinder motorbike in the history of technology had such tractive power that it could do without a gearbox. The first 362-cc engine was succeeded by one of 410 cc. Then in 1909 an improved model with 492 cc and a two-speed gearbox was launched in response to popular demand. All the 4-cylinder bikes had a low-maintenance shaft drive to the rear wheel.

Model:	4-cylinder
Year:	1909
Power:	4 bhp
Capacity:	492 cc
Type:	4-cylinder, 4-stroke

FN 285 T

From 1914 to 1923 the FN range included a good everyday motorbike in the form of the 285 T. During this period FN made 3,305 examples of this little touring bike. The power of the large 4-cylinder engine was transferred to the rear wheel by a shaft drive.

Model:	285 T
Year:	1914
Power:	3 bhp
Capacity:	285 cc
Type:	Single-cylinder, 4-stroke

FN M 70

The reliable side-valve-engined M 70 went down into history as the 'Sahara'. This machine proved that it was possible to cross the Sahara on a motorcycle. The legendary reliability of this touring motorbike rubbed off on the whole model range of the Belgian maker from Herstal. These motorbikes were also made on an assembly-line in Aachen under the name 'BAM'.

Model: M 70	Year: 1935	Power: 10 bhp
Capacity: 348 cc	Type: Single cylinder 4-stroke	

FN M 13

In 1946 FN came out with a completely newly-developed motorbike, the M 13. This reliable bike was available in different versions ranging from 250 to 450 cc, and as well as the side-valve engine an overhead-valve model was offered. A special version for the authorities also existed in Belgium. The impressive details of this modern machine included very large swinging forks extending forwards with broad long-travel suspension for the forks using springs on rubber mountings or, later on, coil springs. Production ended in 1958.

Model:	M 13
Year:	1948
Power:	11 bhp
Capacity:	449 cc
Type:	Single-cylinder, 4-stroke

FN 500 OHC

When it became apparent that the old 500-cc single-cylinder motorbikes could only be sold in small quantities, the Belgian maker developed an ultra-modern 500-cc 2-cylinder machine with overhead camshaft. But the manufacturing costs of the extravagant parallel twin were too high and at the end of the 1950s the demand for motorbikes was in decline. Consequently this interesting motorcycle remained in the prototype stage.

Model:	500 OHC
Year:	1955
Power:	28 bhp
Capacity:	498 cc
Type:	2-cylinder, 4-stroke

Gilera – World champion from Italy

The Gilera make was founded by Giuseppe Gilera in 1909 and distinguished itself in competition with its very first model. It attracted international attention when it won the Six Day Trial. The name Gilera is inseparably linked to its legendary 4-cylinder racing bikes. Starting with the super-charged Rondine in the 1930s, its successors with normal induction engines won six victories in World Championship road events and countless other wins in various competitions. Another successful model was the single-cylinder Saturno 500, developed before the Second World War, which with its racing, moto-cross, cross-country and trial versions was comparable to the English BSA Gold Star. It was the model produced in far the largest numbers until the 1950s. In 1959 the company launched the Giubileo to celebrate its 50th anniversary. The successful Regolaritas of the 1960s, based on the Giubileo, were in turn the basis for the 150 Arcore. When the company was taken over by the Piaggio group in 1969, Gilera's light motorcycles were sold through selected Vespa dealers. This brought in money for racing and the modern 2-stroke gave the company, many victories in enduro championships and in moto-cross World Championships. The high points of its off-road successes were three victories in the Paris-Dakar Rally (1990, 1991 and 1992). When the company became involved in the expensive road World Championship, the important 125-cc market collapsed in Italy and Piaggio closed down the old-established factory in Arcore.

Gilera 500

After the first Gilera 17 which was produced from 1909 until the First World War, a machine which bore more than a passing resemblance to a bicycle, this Gilera 500 made in 1919 was the first postwar model. Later, Turismo, Gran Sport and Super Sport models were added to the range. The model was very modern for the time, with trapezoid forks and a three-speed gearbox. The founder of the firm, Giuseppe Gilera himself, competed in races on this bike, for instance in the Tour of Lombardy.

Model	500
Year:	1921
Power:	3.5 bhp
Capacity:	499 cc
Type:	Single-cylinder, 4-stroke

Gilera Rondine

After being bought by Gilera, the OPRA 500 developed by Pietro Remor was the basis for the Gilera Rondine 500. The water-cooled turbo-charged engine was not only European champion, but in fully-streamlined form it was involved in duels for the World Speed Record with the supercharged BMW of Ernst Henne. Without streamlining it could exceed 230 km/h (143 mph), while it reached 274 km/h (170 mph) in its speed record attempts before they were ended by the outbreak of the Second World War.

Model:	500 Rondine
Year:	1936
Power:	75 bhp
Capacity:	493 cc
Type:	4-cylinder, 4-stroke

Gilera Sei Giorni

Based on the successful side-valve model of 1931, the first model for cross-country competitions such as the Six Day Endurance Trial can be seen in the background of the photograph. From 1938 more modern bikes such as the 'Otto Bullini' in the foreground began to appear. The model name 'Sei Giorni' ('Six Days') was retained for the various capacities until the 1980s because of the many well-known international cross-country wins achieved by Gileras in these events.

Model:	500 Sei Giorni
Year:	1938
Power:	22 bhp
Capacity:	499 cc
Type:	Single-cylinder, 4-stroke

Gilera 125

With the support of the USA's Marshall Plan, in 1948 Gilera created a light motorbike for everyone as a means of helping to bring powered transport to post-war Italy. In order to emphasise its simple handling and impeccable performance, Gilera ran several advertising campaigns with women in the saddle, some even driving blindfold. Later there was also a successful sports version.

Model :	125 Turismo
Year:	1950
Power :	6 bhp
Capacity:	124 cc
Type:	Single-cylinder, 4-stroke

Gilera Saturno

A direct development of the 'Otto Bulloni' single-cylinder overhead-valve machine, the Saturn appeared immediately after the Second World War. It was probably the best-known of Gilera's road bikes throughout the world. It went through various stages of development from the first version of 1946 with trapezoid forks and articulated rear-wheel shock absorbers to this model equipped with modern telescopic forks and swing-arms. Manufacture continued until 1958. There were also various models for official authorities.

Model:	Saturno 500
Year:	1951
Power:	22 bhp
Capacity :	499 cc
Type:	Single-cylinder, 4-stroke

Gilera Saturno Cross

Like the English BSA Gold Star, the Gilera Saturno was suitable for virtually all purposes. By 1948 Ettore Villa had developed a moto-cross bike from the normal Saturno, and between 1952 and 1960 the company entered it as a works bike in moto-cross competitions. During this period drivers such as Domenico Fenocchio and Charles Molinari became French and Italian moto-cross champions several times thanks to the low weight and modern suspension of this bike.

Model:	Saturno 500 Cross
Year:	1952
Power:	35 bhp
Capacity:	499 cc
Type:	Single-cylinder, 4-stroke

Gilera 125 GP

In the course of 1955 Giuseppe Gilera, after the departure of the engineer Remor with his young colleague Franco Passoni, continued with the development of a Grand Prix bike for the 125-cc category. So was created the first dohc-twin, which not only took a number of world speed records but also won several Grand Prix events. However it never won the 125-cc world title. It reached a speed of over 190 km/h (118 mph) and continued to race for well over ten years until 1967.

Model:	125 GP
Year:	1956
Power:	20 bhp
Capacity:	124 cc
Type:	2-cylinder, 4-stroke

Gilera Piuma

This version of the Saturno with increased power was very successful as a road-racing machine and even challenged the fast 4-cylinder works bikes in Grand Prix races. Gilera won famous events such as the San Remo and the Milan-Taranto Tour on several occasions, and as a result versions for talented private entrants were sold. In photograph is the last works racing bike which won the Grand Prix des Nations with a speed of over 210 km/h (130 mph).

Model:	Piuma 500
Year:	1957
Power:	42 bhp
Capacity:	499 cc
Type:	Single-cylinder, 4-stroke

Gilera Quattro

As a development of the Rondine, Remor created this works racer with an air-cooled dohc 4-cylinder engine. Between 1949 and 1957, Gilera won six World Championship titles with it until the company had to withdraw from competition because of the economic situation. Under the management of former works driver Geoff Duke, its power enabled in it to be the runner-up in the World Championship in 1963.

Model:	500 Quattro
Year:	1957
Power:	77 bhp
Capacity:	499 cc
Type:	4-cylinder, 4-stroke

Gilera Giubileo

For the company's 50th anniversary in 1959, the Gilera Giubileo appeared. This bike was built in many variations until 1970 as a road or off-road motorbike with capacities ranging from 98 to 202 cc. On the basis of its economy and reliability, it became the best-selling Gilera model. Riding it in moto-cross competitions, the Italian team was successful on many occasions; the picture shows the moto-cross version prepared by the engine tuner Mario Bessone.

Model:	Giubileo 124 Cross
Year:	1966
Power:	18 bhp
Capacity:	124 cc
Type:	Single-cylinder, 4-stroke

Gilera 150 Strada

As a completely new development of the Piaggio era, this road bike for everyday use in the best tradition of the house appeared in 1972. It was compact, easy to maintain and reliable. While other makers almost only offered 2-strokes, the Gilera was one of the few motorbikes for 4-stroke enthusiasts. To meet Italian regulations, there was a 125-cc version which could be ridden by 16-year-olds and a model of over 150 cc which could be ridden on the autostradas.

Model:	Strada 150 Arcore
Year:	1972
Power:	14 bhp
Capacity:	153 cc
Type:	Single-cylinder, 4-stroke

Gilera 50 RS

Even before the takeover by Piaggio, Gilera had started developing modern 2-stroke bikes for off-road sport. However, as well as competition motorbikes, light motorcycles for teenagers were also offered, such as the 50 RS, which existed both as a tourer and as a trials (enduro) bike. Unlike the German 50-cc bikes of the time, the Gileras had a double-cradle type of frame which unmistakably used the technology of the large motorbikes, based on the company's experience in off-road competition.

Model:	50 RS Touring
Year:	1973
Power:	6 bhp
Capacity:	49 cc
Type:	Single-cylinder, 2-stroke

Gilera SP 01

As the Italian 125-cc market expanded strongly at the end of the 1980s, and above all because the youth market expected ever more powerful machines, Gilera brought out the SP01 with the technology of a large superbike; with, for example, an ultra-modern aluminium Deltabox frame and 300-mm disc brakes with twin piston callipers. Given the enormous performance of these high-revving bikes with a weight of only 115 kg (254 lb), a 16-year-old could fly past many an old war-horse and leave it standing.

Model:	SP 01
Year:	1988
Power:	35 bhp
Capacity:	49 cc
Type:	Single-cylinder, 2-stroke

Gilera RC 600 R

After the 1985 launch of the enduro 350 Dakota with a modern dohc 4-stroke engine which won the Tunis Rally and took the Hungary Trophy, the production RC 600 appeared in 1989. The Rally version ridden by the Gilera works team won the Pharaoh and Tunis Rallies and entered the Paris Dakar. A year later the RC was followed by the 750 RS, which won the production class of the Dakar Rally in 1990, 1991 and 1992, and in 1995 it also won the Pharoah and Baja Qatar events.

Model:	RC 600 R
Year:	1989
Power:	62 bhp
Capacity:	569 cc
Type:	Single-cylinder, 4-stroke

Gilera Piuma

The Nuovo Saturno Bialbero production machine caused a sensation in 1988 and was frequently entered into the Supermono formula which was popular at the time. A year later the factory offered racing riders another modern Piuma which was equipped with the engine of the RC 600 in its aluminium frame. The Piuma was built purely as a racing bike; with a full tank it weighed 130 kg (287 lb) and had a top speed of over 215 km/h (134 mph), winning with riders such as Tardozzi and Cathcart.

Model:	Piuma 560
Year:	1990
Power:	62 bhp
Capacity:	569 cc
Type:	Single-cylinder, 4-stroke

Gilera Supersport 600 Prototype

At the Milan Motorcycle Salon Gilera presented the Supersport 600 model with which it hoped to make its comeback in the motorbike world. However this did not take place, because the plans of the parent company Piaggio had changed in the meantime, and it had decided to position Gilera as (only) a sporty scooter manufacturer. In addition Piaggio had already developed a new generation of V-twin power units.

Model:	Supersport 600
Year:	2001
Power:	98 bhp
Capacity:	600 cc
Type:	4-cylinder in-line, 4-stroke (Suzuki)

105

Harley-Davidson – An American legend

It was in a courtyard in Milwaukee, Wisconsin, that the Davidson brothers Walter and Arthur built their first motorbike with William 'Bill' Harley in 1903. By 1909 the company had grown so much that the 'Harley-Davidson Motor Company Incorporated' was founded. The '61' model was the first motorbike with the characteristic 45° V-2 engine. By 1920 Harley-Davidson had become the leading motorbike manufacturer in America and subsequently also the largest motorbike manufacturer in the world. The company weathered the economic crisis and during the two World Wars it turned to producing military motorbikes. The post-war years also proved to be hard because of reduced supplies of raw materials and the dwindling of export markets. Harley-Davidson survived these difficult times but was the only American motorbike manufacturer to do so. In the 1960s Harley-Davidson acquired 50% of the shares in the Italian company Aermacchi. Because of the high levels of capital required, the company looked for a strong partner and as a result became integrated in the conglomerate American Machine and Foundry Company (AMF). But there were too many poor decisions on the part of AMF which annoyed customers and dealers alike. As a result Harley-Davidson became a family-owned company again at a cost of US$80 million. The introduction of the 'Evolution' engine and the Softail range heralded happier times. In 1999 the company introduced the new Big Twin 'Twin Cam 88' engine with two camshafts. In 2002 the company presented the spectacular Power-Cruiser V-Rod. The first water-cooled Harley soon became a bestseller. In 2005, the company launched the V-Rod off-shoot which paved the way for the next 100 years of Harley history.

Harley-Davidson 'The First'

The first motorbike to carry the Harley-Davidson name was assembled in a shed with an area of only 12 m² (129 sq ft) in Milwaukee by two school friends, William Harley and Arthur Davidson. The 400 cc single-cylinder engine was a copy of a French De Dion engine and generated about 3 bhp. The bike's rear wheel was driven by a loosely-fixed leather belt. Three of the so-called 'Zero Series' were made in the first year.

Model:	Model 0
Year:	1903
Power:	3 bhp
Capacity:	400 cc
Type:	Single-cylinder, 4-stroke

Harley-Davidson Model 4

'Silent Gray Fellow': the picture shows a Model 4 with a 440-cc single cylinder engine. This 4-bhp bike, which was distinguished by its standard Renault-grey paint job, had a sprung fork but was still powered by a leather belt final drive. Its simplicity and mature reliability won it the name 'Silent Gray Fellow'. H-D built 450 of these bikes in 1908.

Model:	Model 4
Year:	1908
Power:	4 bhp
Capacity:	440 cc
Type:	Single-cylinder, 4-stroke

Harley-Davidson Model 5D

The 1909 Model 5D was Harley-Davidson's first bike with twin cylinders arranged in a V at a 45° cylinder angle. But the lowly leather belt drive caused serious problems now that it was married to a racy 7-bhp engine. Also the developers only had experience with single cylinders and they were unable get the carburettor setting right. The result was a stuttering engine that even started involuntarily. But the V-2 was still very promising. Sensibly, H-D opted to stop production after 25 examples so that the V-2 engine could be perfected.

Model:	Model 5D
Year:	1909
Power:	7 bhp
Capacity:	810 cc (49.48 cu in)
Type:	V-twin, 4-stroke

Harley-Davidson Model IOE

The 1914 model IOE looked familiar – Harley used the same IOE (Inlet Over Exhaust) V-2 engine from the 5D – but the problematic leather belt was replaced at last with a chain to form the final drive to the rear wheel. The illustration shows the contemporary acetylene headlight with its own external fuel storage.

Model:	Model IOE
Year:	1914
Power:	6.5 bhp
Capacity:	810 cc (49,48 cu in)
Type:	V-twin, 4-stroke

Harley-Davidson Racer

'Wrecking Crew' member Fred Ludlow is seen here on an 8-valve prototype racer in 1915. The racer weighed only 120 kg (265 lb) but developed about 50 bhp at 4,000 rpm thanks to innovations in the cylinders. Each had four overhead valves and a hemispherical combustion chamber. This gave a top speed of 180 km/h (112 mph), incredible for the time.

Model:	8-valve Racer
Year:	1915
Power:	about 50 bhp
Capacity:	989 cc
Type:	V-twin, 4-stroke

Harley-Davidson Model 28 JD

It was on this 1928 JD model that Peter Rudolf Schmidt from Dresden rode across the USA. He spent almost 10 years planning his adventure. The motorbike consumed 7 litres every 100 km (40 mpg) regardless of the terrain. During his journey he came to know the bike in all its strengths and weaknesses, 'an utterly tough vehicle' as he reported. Despite travelling a momentous 90,000 km (56,000 miles), he never had to open up the engine once. 'If you give the push rods a can of oil a day that machine will go on for ever' Schmidt predicted. And what could possibly go wrong? The solid steel chassis was designed for tough conditions, the cast iron pistons were built for eternity and roller bearings that size would not be out of place on a tractor.

The bike never let him down, right from his first stretch which took him the 7,000 km (4,350 miles) from Chicago to New Orleans. He drove via Daytona Beach, naturally, where he put a few wannabe hardcore bikers in their place.

Model:	Model 28 JD
Year:	1928
Power:	12 bhp
Capacity:	1200 cc
Type:	V-twin, 4-stroke

Harley-Davidson Servi-Car

In 1932 Harley began producing the Servi-Car. The post office, small businesses, milkmen and even the police took to the agile three-wheeler with its spacious boot. The Servi-Cars were equipped with the 750-cc Flathead engine and rolled off the production lines practically unaltered until 1973.

Model:	Servi-Car
Year:	1932
Power:	18 bhp
Capacity:	750 cc
Type:	V-twin, 4-stroke

Harley-Davidson EL

The 1936 EL model heralded a new era at Harley-Davidson. It was the first model powered by an engine with overhead valves (OHV) and was nicknamed simply 'Knucklehead' by its owners. The Knucklehead engine initially had a capacity of 1000 cc. An improved Springer fork and giant mudguards marked it out from the rest. The 1000-cc version developed about 40 bhp, making the Knucklehead a true 'Superbike'.

Model:	Model EL
Year:	1936
Power:	40 bhp
Capacity:	989 cc
Type:	V-twin, 4-stroke

Harley-Davidson Knucklehead Racer

Harley-Davidson rider Joe Petrali is here shown on the world record-breaking covered-frame racer. With its 65-bhp Knucklehead engine the bike clocked 136.18 miles per hour, or 219 km/h, the world record for a motorbike in 1937.

Model:	8-valve Knucklehead Racer
Year:	1937
Power:	65 bhp
Capacity:	1000 cc
Type:	V-twin, 4-stroke

Harley-Davidson FL

In 1941 the company continued the Knucklehead success story with a 1200-cc version named the FL. Many enthusiasts still consider this bike to be the ideal Harley-Davidson. The FL had four-gear transmission and could hit about 150 km/h (93 mph). The Springer fork provided a comfortable front suspension.

Model:	Model FL
Year:	1941
Power:	48 bhp
Capacity:	1208 cc
Type:	V-twin, 4-stroke

Harley-Davidson WLA

With the USA's entry into the Second World War, production for the civilian market ceased almost entirely. Harley won lucrative military contracts and concentrated on producing bikes for the army, delivering a total of 88,000 WLAs, a military version of the 750 cc Flathead V-2, by the end of the war.

Model:	Model WLA (Army)
Year:	1941
Power:	23 bhp
Capacity:	743 cc
Type:	V-twin, 4-stroke

Harley-Davidson XA

The US military also commissioned Harley to develop a boxer during the Second World War. The XA model was a copy of a BMW type already in service with the German army. Harley finished development of the bike and built about 1,000 examples, but they never saw active service.   (Pictured is a sidecar variant.)

Model:	Model XA
Year:	1943
Power:	23 bhp
Capacity:	738 cc
Type:	2-cylinder boxer, 4-stroke

Harley-Davidson Panhead Springer

In 1948 Harley overhauled its old models; the Knuckleheads dated back to before the war and it was time for something new. The design was essentially the same: Springer fork at the front, fixed frame at the back. But by simply putting new cylinder heads on the basic Knucklehead engine the engineers gave birth to the legendary 'Panhead'. The model delivered 50 bhp and could achieve a top speed of 160 km/h (100 mph).

Model:	FL 74
Year:	1948
Power:	60 bhp
Capacity:	1206 cc
Type:	V-twin, 4-stroke

Harley-Davidson Hydra Glide

1949 brought with it a revolution. The venerable Springer fork still found on the top-of-the-range FL Panhead was replaced by a telescopic fork with hydraulic suspension. The factory named the bike 'Hydra Glide'. But it was only a minor revolution; everything else was old technology, including the rear wheel without suspension.

Model:	FL 74 Hydra Glide
Year:	1948
Power:	60 bhp
Capacity:	1206 cc
Type:	V-twin, 4-stroke

Harley-Davidson Duo Glide

In 1958 Harley finally equipped its leading model with rear-wheel suspension, and made it worth the wait. This new Panhead, named the Duo Glide, had modern hydraulic suspension on both wheels. The Duo Glide was also fitted with hydraulically-assisted rear brakes. Equipped with all available extras, the Duo Glide was the most comfortable, most imposing motorbike in the world.

Model:	FL 74 Duo Glide
Year:	1958
Power:	60 bhp
Capacity:	1206 cc
Type:	V-twin, 4-stroke

Harley-Davidson Model K

To appeal to a younger generation the company launched the K range in 1952. It was fitted with a Flathead engine and weighed 180 kg (397 lb), making it a well-powered machine. The K was the first Harley with telescopic forks, rear swing arm and rear shock absorbers.

Model:	Model K
Year:	1952
Power:	30 bhp
Capacity:	741 cc
Type:	V-twin, 4-stroke

Harley-Davidson KH Sportster

The KH hit the market in 1954, a K variant with 883 cc and a good 38 bhp. This was the very first model to be labelled 'Sportster'. But even the souped-up KH was held back by the ageing side-valve technology of its engine and it could not match the power of competing bikes made by the likes of Triumph, Norton and BSA. In 1957 the K model was replaced by the XL Sportster.

Model:	Model KH
Year:	1954
Power:	38 bhp
Capacity:	741 cc
Type:	V-twin, 4-stroke

Harley-Davidson Electra Glide

In 1965 the flagship of the Big Twin generation was a bike whose name is still a legend: the Electra Glide. This 1965 Panhead FL owed its name to its new electric starter. A larger battery was required and the new starter weighed that little bit extra too, so the frame had to be beefed up. This heavier bike needed more horsepower if it was not to be slower, but there was no opportunity for that with the existing engine. One problem led to another and eventually led to a new engine design: the Shovelhead.

Model:	FL Electra Glide
Year:	1965
Power:	68 bhp
Capacity:	1206 cc
Type:	V-twin, 4-stroke

Harley-Davidson Boat-Tail

The 'Boat Tail' Super Glide was Harley's first ever factory-custom bike. It was styled in 1971 by the young designer Willie G. Davidson, grandson of one of the company's founders. The name 'Boat Tail' suggested itself to anyone looking at the bike: its rear was stretched out like a boat and, again like a boat, was made out of fibreglass.

Model:	FX Boat-Tail
Year:	1971
Power:	about 62 bhp
Capacity:	1206 cc
Type:	V-twin, 4-stroke

Harley-Davidson Super Glide

In 1966 the revered Panhead motor was replaced by the Shovelhead. But the early Shovelheads shared the same engine block as the final generation of Panheads. It was not until 1970 that the Shovelhead was given its own engine block. The 1972 Super Glide pictured here developed 65 bhp and could reach almost 180 km/h (112 mph).

Model:	FX Super Glide
Year:	1972
Power:	about 65 bhp
Capacity:	1206 cc
Type:	V-twin, 4-stroke

Harley-Davidson XL 55

In 1957 Harley replaced the K model with the Sportster model of the XL series. The XL Sportsters were inspired technically by the big Shovelhead models; they had overhead valves in the cylinder heads, which were connected to push rods and tappets through a total of four camshafts. The 883-cc engine delivered 40 bhp, allowing the machine, which weighed 'only' 225 kg (496 lb), to reach a speed of 155 km/h (96 mph).

Model:	XL 55
Year:	1965
Power:	about 40 bhp
Capacity:	883 cc
Type:	V-twin, 4-stroke

Harley-Davidson XR 750

The XR 750 racing bike became a legend on America's highly popular dirt tracks. The engine was based on a sport version of the XL while the frame was taken from KR model stocks which were still in the ware-house. New cylinder heads enabled the XR 750 to develop a power of 90 bhp, giving speeds of up to 210 km/h (130 bhp).

Model:	XR 750
Year:	1970 to 1980
Power:	90 bhp
Capacity:	750 cc
Type:	V-twin, 4-stroke

Harley-Davidson Café Racer

The Café Racer from 1977 was the young Willie G. Davidson's most uncompromising design. The long stretched line of the seat and fuel tank, the twin disc brakes at the front and slim, concealed exhausts gave the Café Racer the most dynamic lines of any Harley series yet pro-duced. But it was not embraced by a conservative American public. Only 3,133 examples were built between 1977 and 1979. Today they are highly-prized collectors' pieces.

Model:	XLCR Café Racer
Year:	1977
Power:	61 bhp
Capacity:	996 cc
Type:	V-twin, 4-stroke

Harley-Davidson Sportster 1000

Like the Café Racer, the 1979 Sportster XLH possessed a 1000-cc engine but the high, curved handlebars and chunky split-level seat distanced this model from the original concept of a 'light, sporty machine'. It was a design phenomenon with lasting resonance.

Model:	Sportster XLH 1000
Year:	1979
Power:	61 bhp
Capacity:	996 cc
Type:	V-twin, 4-stroke

Harley-Davidson Electra Glide

The Electra Glide was and still is the dinosaur of the Harley range. This fully-equipped pleasure cruiser was the model for all the heavy cruiser bikes which followed. The wide mudguards, substantial handlebar coverings and hard side and top cases dominated the appearance of this enduring icon.

Model:	FLH Electra Glide
Year:	1979
Power:	66 bhp
Capacity:	1206 cc
Type:	V-twin, 4-stroke

Harley-Davidson Wide Glide

The 1980 'Wide Glide' was the most dramatic factory-custom series Harley had so far produced. The slim forks, narrow 21-inch wheels and tiny headlight made the front look as if it had been customised. The low seat, the sissy bar typical of the series and the flame motif on the fuel tank added to the bike's individual feel. It became one of the company's most successful models.

Model:	FXWG Wide Glide
Year:	1980
Power:	68 bhp
Capacity:	1338 cc
Type:	V-twin, 4-stroke

Harley-Davidson Softail

The FXST Softail marked a turning point in the Harley-Davidson success story. Equipped with what was then the brand new Evolution engine, which took over from the Shovelhead in 1984, its rear end appeared to be part of a fixed frame. But this was a mere optical illusion, a trick given away by the name 'Softail'. The Softail models were the start of a triumphant chapter in the company's history and one that is still being written.

Model:	FXST Softail
Year:	1984
Power:	65 bhp
Capacity:	1338 cc
Type:	V-twin, 4-stroke

Harley-Davidson Sportster 1200

From 1985 onwards the Sportster series benefited from new engines. The small XL Shovelheads were replaced by the XL Evolution generation. The Evo Sportsters were available in capacities of 883, 1000 and 1100 cc, while the 1200 later completed the range. Pictured is an 883 Standard from 1985.

Model:	XLH 883 Standard
Year:	1985
Power:	46 bhp
Capacity:	883 cc
Type:	V-twin, 4-stroke

Harley-Davidson Heritage Softail

The Evolution engine, developed by Porsche in Weissach, Germany, was well-established by 1988 when Harley paid tribute to its own history and brought out the 'Heritage Softail'. Visually, the Softail conjured up the era of the Panhead and was warmly welcomed by the conservative Harley fan base.

Model:	FLST Heritage Softail
Year:	1988
Power:	65 bhp
Capacity:	1338 cc
Type:	V-twin, 4-stroke

Harley-Davidson Electra Glide Classic

Even in this new Harley generation, the Electra Glide remained the king due to its enormous weight of almost 400 kg (882 lb). It received a huge boost in 1984 when it became the first model to be fitted with the new 60-bhp Evolution engine, meaning that it was now at least satisfactorily powered.

Model:	FLHTC Electra Glide Classic
Year:	1988
Power:	60 bhp
Capacity:	1338 cc
Type:	V-twin, 4-stroke

Harley-Davidson Fat Boy

The FLSTF, or 'Fat Boy' as it was christened by Willie G. Davidson, appeared in 1990. Cloaked in cool silver and with very striking single-disc aluminium wheels, the design took the market by storm and remains to this day the best-selling Harley model of all time.

Model:	FLSTF Fat Boy
Year:	1990
Power:	56 bhp
Capacity:	1338 cc
Type:	V-twin, 4-stroke

Harley-Davidson Low Rider

The 1990 Low Rider was a successor to the Low Glide and was first produced in 1984. All models of the then FXR series had the rubber-mounted V engine in common. The Low Rider spawned a whole series of custom models.

Model:	FXRS Low Rider
Year:	1990
Power:	60 bhp
Capacity:	1338 cc
Type:	V-twin, 4-stroke

Harley-Davidson Bad Boy

The Bad Boy was a factory-custom model. With a black Springer fork, whole-disc rear wheel and generously kitted out in chrome, the Bad Boy could also be fitted with a tinted front windshield. This last fixture, however, tended to detract from the bike's 'mean' quality.

Model:	FXSTB Bad Boy
Year:	1995
Power:	65 bhp
Capacity:	1338 cc
Type:	V-twin, 4-stroke

Harley-Davidson Dyna Wide Glide

The FXRs were replaced by the FXD Dyna Glide series in 1991 as the company's 90th birthday approached. They were distinguished by a fork which was angled at 35°, high 'Ape Hanger' handlebars, a 'Boat Tail' rear end and foot-rests positioned towards the front. Exactly 1,993 Wide Glides were produced.

Model:	FXDWG Dyna Wide Glide
Year:	1993
Power:	56 bhp
Capacity:	1338 cc
Type:	V-twin, 4-stroke

Harley-Davidson Road Glide

From 1998 the Harley range added a second heavyweight touring bike alongside the Electra Glide – the Road Glide. With its twin headlamps and ornate half-fairing the design was an acquired taste and was not exported to Europe as a result. Pictured is the 2000 version with a twin-cam engine and fuel injection.

Model:	FLTRI Road Glide
Year:	2000
Power:	67 bhp
Capacity:	1449 cc
Type:	V-twin, 4-stroke

Harley-Davidson Jordan F1 Promotion Bike

The Jordan F1 Promotion was planned and designed by computer in the space of two months. The idea was to leave the relaxed air of the tourers far behind and go with an aggressive dragster look, so a drag-style frame was built with a headset angle of 40°. The tank was taken from the small Evo Sportster and the bike was powered by the reliable 1340 Evo. Edelbock cylinder heads, Wiseco forged pistons, an Andrews Camshaft and an S&S carburettor pushed the engine up to 80 bhp. A fat 240 tyre helped to propel it along the road.

Model:	Jordan F1 Promotion Bike
Year:	2000
Power:	80 bhp
Capacity:	1340 cc
Type:	V-twin, 4-stroke

Harley-Davidson VR 1000

In the 1990s Harley-Davidson allowed itself the luxury of developing a special engine to enable it to participate in American Superbikes events. Breaking with the firm's V-2 tradition, the engine was water-cooled, had a 60° cylinder angle, overhead camshafts and four valves. It is clear today that in building the VR 1000 Harley's aim was to gather experience for a future generation of engines. The result was the V-Rod.

Model:	VR 1000 Racing
Year:	2000
Power:	140 bhp
Capacity:	998 cc
Type:	V-twin, 4-stroke

Harley-Davidson Deuce

With the Softail Deuce, Harley-Davidson presented a highlight of the factory-custom genre, a bike that blurred the line between the chopper and the cruiser. While the front was slim and light, the rear looked chunky and compressed. This opposition was also reflected in the wheels: at the front was a narrow 21-inch wire-spoked wheel, while at the rear was a solid 17-inch whole disc.

Model:	FXSTD Softail Deuce
Year:	2000
Power:	64 bhp
Capacity:	1449 cc
Type:	V-twin, 4-stroke

Harley-Davidson Sportster 1200 Custom

With its slim dragster handlebars, forward foot-rests and Fat Boy-style fuel tank, the 1200 Custom became the best-loved of the 1200 Sportster series. The 2000 version had a larger fuel tank and a new seat, giving driver and passenger a much more comfortable ride.

Model:	XL 1200 C
Year:	2000
Power:	58 bhp
Capacity:	1199 cc
Type:	V-twin, 4-stroke

Harley-Davidson T-Sport

Every Harley-Davidson offers a comfortable ride over long distances, but only a few are designed to take twisting country roads at speed. The 2001 Dyna Super Glide T-Sport was one of them. It boasted fully-adjustable suspension, killer brakes and handlebar protection at the front together with an adjustable windshield giving protection from wind and bad weather.

Model:	FXDXT Dyna Super Glide T-Sport
Year:	2001
Power:	68 bhp
Capacity:	1449 cc
Type:	V-twin, 4-stroke

Harley-Davidson Sportster Custom 53

The 'little' Sportster version with a capacity of 883 cc could also be obtained as a Custom variant. It had the traditional sport tank rather than the Fat Boy tank of the 1200 Custom. In line with the Custom philosophy, Harley-Davidson specified a massive 16-inch light metal disc rear wheel.

Model:	XL 53 C
Year:	2002
Power:	53 bhp
Capacity:	883 cc
Type:	V-twin, 4-stroke

Harley-Davidson Sportster 883 R

The styling of the Sportster 883 R was based on Harley's dirt track racing machines and it was only obtainable in racing orange. The Evolution power unit was coated with black powder as were the dirt track handlebar, rear mirror, oil tank and air filter. It was the only Sportster to have a sports two-into-one exhaust system.

Model:	XL 883 R
Year:	2002
Power:	53 bhp
Capacity:	883 cc
Type:	V-twin, 4-stroke

Harley-Davidson Night Train

In the Night Train everything was dark in colour. The twin-cam power unit was coated with black powder. The tank console, mudguard holder, oil tank, air filter and many other attachments were also coloured solid black. Likewise the stretched front forks with 21-inch wire spoke wheel and the massive 16-inch full disc rear wheel contributed to the powerful impression that the Night Train gives to anyone who sees this laid-back machine.

Model:	FXSTB Night Train
Year:	2002
Power:	63 bhp
Capacity:	1449 cc
Type:	V-twin, 4-stroke

Harley-Davidson Electra Glide Classic

In 2003 Harley-Davidson celebrated the 100th anniversary of the company's foundation and labelled the complete production range as the '100th Anniversary Edition'. This included the Electra Glide, which had been powered since 1999 by Harley's new twin-cam V-2. Apart from the CD player for the radio equipment which had been fitted as standard since the 2003 model year, the Electra Glide was distinguished by the unsurpassed comfort it provided for the driver and passenger.

Model:	FLHTCI Electra Glide Classic
Year:	2003
Power:	67 bhp
Capacity:	1449 cc
Type:	V-twin, 4-stroke

Harley-Davidson Fat Boy

After the Touring and Dyna ranges were fitted with the new twin-cam power unit in 1999, the Softail model was first fitted with the new engine in the year 2000. For it, Harley fitted the power unit with balancing shafts, because since the frame tube ran close to an engine mounting point it was not possible to mount the engine on rubber Silentblocks.

Model:	FLSTFI Fat Boy
Year:	2003
Power:	64 bhp
Capacity:	1449 cc
Type:	V-twin, 4-stroke

Harley-Davidson Road King Classic

The Road King Classic radiated pure nostalgia. Custom features such as the wide whitewall tyres and the extravagant hard shell case covered with leather gave it the Harley-Davidson look. Impressive too was the large headlight with chromium-plated casing which enclosed two additional headlights. The twin-cam engine on the Road King was mounted on Silentblocks, which effectively damped out vibration.

Model:	FLHRCI Road King Classic
Year:	2003
Power:	68 bhp
Capacity:	1449 cc
Type:	V-twin, 4-stroke

Harley-Davidson V-Rod

When the V-Rod was launched in 2002 the Harley world looked in disbelief. A water-cooled V-2 with a 60° cylinder angle in a Harley-Davidson? After the qualities of the machine had been discussed, scepticism gave way to enthusiasm. Then it was apparent that this sporty, elegant 'power cruiser' provided a lot of enjoyable riding thanks to the Revolution power unit developed by Porsche.

Model:	VRSCA V-Rod
Year:	2003
Power:	117 bhp
Capacity:	1130 cc
Type:	V-twin, 4-stroke

Harley-Davidson Road King Custom

The Road King Custom was characterised by soft curved lines that were inspired by the California beach look. Its rear end was low in order to give the machine a long, stretched, flat appearance. To emphasise the clean 'no frills' look, it was decided not to fit trim to the mudguards. Instead of a windshield, a new fork bridge covering and a chrome-plated wind deflector were installed. The last refinement were the wide beach handlebars cranked towards the back.

Model:	FLHRSI Road King Custom
Year:	2004
Power:	71 bhp
Capacity:	1449 cc
Type:	V-twin, 4-stroke

Harley-Davidson Sportster 1200R

The 1200 Roadster interpreted the Sportster theme more dynamically than ever. Its Evolution engine now developed a maximum of 66 bhp and a maximum torque of 93 Nm. The wide polished handlebars gave a semi-sports seating position and a twin disc brake on the front wheel provided sufficient deceleration. Finally, thanks to the return to chromium plated spoked wheels, the 2005 generation was perhaps the most beautiful machine that had so far been produced.

Model:	XL 1200R Sportster 1200 Roadster
Year:	2005
Power:	66 bhp
Capacity:	1202 cc
Type:	V-twin, 4-stroke

Harley-Davidson Softail Springer Classic

For 2005 Harley-Davidson looked back at its long history and produced the Softail Springer Classic. This motorbike paid tribute to the legendary Panhead of 1948. Its outstanding feature being the Springer fork with black powder coating. A traditional bumper light adorned the front mudguard, which was otherwise free from any decoration. The Springer Softail Classic was fitted with a crossover exhaust system: one chromium-plated silencer was located on the left and the other one on the right next to the rear wheel. The new tombstone rear light completed the classic look.

Model:	FLSTSCI Softail Springer Classic
Year:	2005
Power:	67 bhp
Capacity:	1449 cc
Type:	V-twin, 4-stroke

Harley-Davidson Dyna

The new Super Glide Custom supplemented the factory custom bikes of the Dyna Glide series from the 2005 model year. This continued a Harley-Davidson tradition, started with the introduction of the first FX Custom models in the 1970s. Polished chrome was a feature of the new Custom, with its silver and chrome twin-cam 88 engine, and even the headlamp fairing and tachometer housing were chrome plated. Finally, the new, flat seat rounded off the original appearance of the Super Glide Custom.

Model:	FXDCI Dyna Super Glide Custom
Year:	2005
Power:	67 bhp
Capacity:	1449 cc
Type:	V-twin, 4-stroke

Harley-Davidson Softail Deluxe

The Softail Deluxe was a synthesis of many of the nostalgic and graceful elements of various epochs of Harley-Davidson styling. Thus Harley fitted a beautiful tombstone rear light to the rear mudguard. The chrome-plated shotgun exhaust pipes harmonised well with the chrome covers of the black engine and the whitewall tyres completed the 'de luxe' look, which from the very first glance shouted 'pure classic'. The low-slung chassis gives a very low sitting height of just 62 cm (24½ in).

Model:	FLSTN Softail Deluxe
Year:	2005
Power:	64 bhp
Capacity:	1449 cc
Type:	V-twin, 4-stroke

Harley-Davidson Street Rod

With the Street Rod, Harley-Davidson had put a real hot rod on wheels. The 'Straight Shot Dual' exhaust system contributed to the increase in power of about 3 bhp compared with the V-Rod. The improved vehicle dynamics were due to the higher positioning of the chassis, which was combined with a steering head angle of 30° for more agility. In order to provide a rate of deceleration to match the aggressiveness of the engine Harley-Davidson installed a new Brembo brake system with two 300-mm disc brakes and four-piston callipers on the front wheel.

Model:	VRSCR Street Rod
Year:	2005
Power:	120 bhp
Capacity:	1131 cc
Type:	V-twin, 4-stroke

Henderson – Powerful 4-cylinders from the United States

William Henderson was a determined advocate of the 4-cylinder in-line engine. In his factory set up in Detroit/Michigan in 1911, he built a single model of motorbike with an unusually long wheelbase. Both inlet and outlet valves were on the same side and the bike was started by a crank. In 1917 the company merged with Excelsior in Chicago, the maker for the future motorbike giants Schwinn. But for William Henderson this union only lasted two years. The obstinate engineer left the company and founded his own maker ACE. From then on it was Arthur O. Lemon who was responsible for the further development of the Henderson-Excelsior motorbikes for Schwinn. He created the completely newly developed Model K with an underhead-valve engine. The range also included a de luxe version with reverse gear. Because of their impressive top speed of about 160 km/h (100 mph), the bikes were also very popular with police forces. In 1929 Henderson motorbikes had a streamlined profile, fashionable at the time, with large mudguards and a tear-drop-shaped tank. Schwinn sensed the impending economic crisis and stopped the production of the large 4-cylinder bikes in spite of good sales figures.

Henderson 4

The first motorcycle from Henderson had the 4-cylinder engine installed longitudinally which was typical of the make. The heavy machine with its long, deep frame looked different from any other motorcycle. The footrest for the rider's feet was a long way in front of the engine. The maximum speed was about 75 km/h (47 mph). In spite of this Henderson did not fit a front brake but instead chose two rear brakes for his vehicle.

Model:	4
Year:	1912
Power:	13 bhp
Capacity:	1068 cc
Type:	4-cylinder in-line, 4-stroke

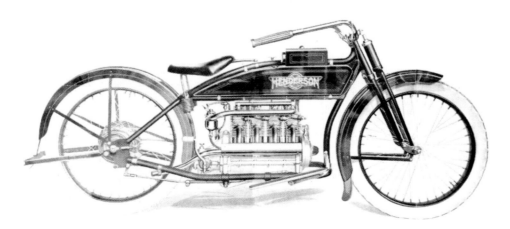

Henderson 4

In 1917 the Henderson 4-cylinder bike was fitted with a three-speed gearbox and a more reliable clutch. In addition the frame was shortened, which gave the machine a more agreeable appearance. 1917 was the last year before the takeover by the Excelsior factory. The motorbikes built after this had a large 'X' logo on the tank. In the next model in 1918, a sidecar connection was included as standard, the forks were strengthened and the engine was modified.

Model:	4
Year:	1917
Power:	15 bhp
Capacity:	1068 cc
Type:	4-cylinder in-line, 4-stroke

Henderson K Model

In 1925 the motorcycle with 4-cylinder in-line engine was given a new frame. As a result the seat could be placed lower. The toolbox mounted on the fuel tank also served as a lock for the oil and petrol tank. A significantly improved lubrication system and new materials for pistons, valves and crankshaft led to even greater reliability for the engine of 80 cubic inches (1300 cc) which was fitted.

Model: K
Year: 1925
Power: 25 bhp
Capacity: 1301 cc
Type: 4-cylinder in-line, 4-stroke

Henderson K Special

In the 1950s many motorcycle riders were looking for a heavy machine which could take a sidecar and which also had the reliability of a car. Since such a vehicle could not be had for love or money, a gifted fitter built this 'buffalo' himself, by transplanting a car engine into a motorcycle frame. The installation of an Austin 4-cylinder engine in a lengthened Henderson chassis was certainly very different from the normal designs of the maker.

Model: K Special
Year: 1955
Power: 40 bhp
Capacity: 998 cc
Type: 4-cylinder, 4-stroke

Henderson Super-X

In 1990 the rights to the names owned by the Hanlon Manufacturing Group were purchased, and thus there was a comeback for Excelsior-Henderson a couple of years later. At the ostentatious headquarters of the firm in Belle Plaine, Minnesota, only one model was produced, the Super X, illustrated here. The 1400-cc V-2 came from the aftermarket, as did many other parts of the machine. The design had too little originality to make it a serious competitor to Harley-Davidson. At the end of 1999 the firm had to go into bankruptcy – after several million dollars of funding had been spent.

Model: Super-X
Year: 1998
Power: 70 bhp
Capacity: 1386 cc
Type: V-twin, 4-stroke

Hercules 315

An ILO engine propelled this 250-cc machine and consequently the 315 was considered very sporty. A few manufacturers such as Hercules dared to build bikes falling into the larger-capacity classes, but many others did not because the vast majority of motorbike riders were still riding with pre-war driving licences which only allowed machines up to 250 cc to be ridden.

Model:	315
Year:	1952
Power:	11.4 bhp, later 12.8 bhp
Capacity:	247 cc
Type:	Single-cylinder, 2-stroke

Hercules 316

In the early 1950s the production programme was broadened to include a small 98-cc 2-stroke engine from Fichtel & Sachs. The two-speed gearbox was operated by means of a tank-mounted gear change. If required telescopic forks could be fitted instead of the trapezoid forks.

Model:	316
Year:	1952
Power:	3 bhp
Capacity:	98 cc
Type:	Single-cylinder, 2-stroke

Hercules 317

Price-wise, the Hercules 200 cc came between the 200-cc Derby and the Zündapp Norma, but in terms of equipment and power output it was superior to the two Nuremberg competitors. The ILO engine developed 11 bhp and with this power it could take on competitive models such as the Triumph Cornet (10.1 bhp) and the Adler M 200 (9.6 bhp). The chrome tank gave the bike a glamorous appearance. Apart from the chain case, the 317 did not differ from the other models of the 3 series..

Model:	317
Year:	1953
Power:	11 bhp
Capacity:	197 cc
Type:	Single-cylinder, 2-stroke

Hercules 318

The frame and equipment were already known from the other models in the series; but only the legendary ILO 'M 2 x 125' engine was used and the result was the first post-war 2-cylinder machine offered by Hercules. The old 25-cc 315 bike was removed from the range when the 318 was introduced.

Model:	318
Year:	1953
Power:	15 bhp
Capacity:	246 cc
Type:	2-cylinder, 2-stroke

Hercules 319

The replacement for the 314 in the favourable 175-cc insurance category was the 319. Instead of the ILO engine, a Fichtel & Sachs unit was fitted. The mass-produced machine offered as a single-seater could be supplemented by a seat for a passenger including foot-rests. It also had a friction disk steering damper.

Model:	319
Year:	1953
Power:	9.5 bhp
Capacity:	173 cc
Type:	Single-cylinder, 2-stroke

Hercules 320

The same Fichtel & Sachs engine as the 319 was used in this newly-developed machine with swing-arm rear suspension. Visually it was given a face-lift with its rounded sheet metal forms blending with the bulging cover of the baroque timing case. The chromed parts were evidence of a prosperous business.

Model:	320
Year:	1953
Power:	9.5 bhp
Capacity:	173 cc
Type:	Single-cylinder, 2-stroke

Hercules 321

Structurally identical to the 320, this model had a 200-cc ILO engine developing 11.2 bhp. But even with this comparatively powerful unit the swing-arm rear suspension came nowhere near its limits.

Model:	321
Year:	1953
Power:	11 bhp
Capacity:	197 cc
Type:	Single-cylinder, 2-stroke

Hercules 322

This was the top model of the 3 series. An ILO twin-cylinder engine, affectionately known as the 'Pinneberg Singer', was fitted within the swinging frame. The brightest item in the equipment list was the Prä-nafa drum brake supplied by Jurisch, which had a performance that was more than sufficient even when running with a sidecar.

Model:	322
Year:	1953
Power:	15.1 bhp
Capacity:	246 cc
Type:	2-cylinder, 2-stroke

Hercules A 175

The Nuremberg firm kept the A 175 in its range for ten years. Like the preceding 320 model, it was fitted with a Fichtel & Sachs engine. A new feature was the use of 16-inch wheels, which emphasised the bike's compact appearance. At the same time it boasted a Siba dynastarter, which during the 1950s was otherwise only offered on the Triumph Cornet.

Model:	A 175
Year:	1956
Power:	9.3 bhp
Capacity:	173 cc
Type:	Single-cylinder, 2-stroke

Hercules K 100

At the start of the 1960s the K 100 was the company's best-seller and together with its other models, Hercules was extremely successful at the time. The purchase price was its most attractive feature. In addition it could do 75 km/h (47 mph). This led many purchasers to ignore the bike's problems, such as the rotary gear change which was difficult to adjust and the inadequate dimensions of the single-tube frame.

Model:	K 100
Year:	1956
Power:	5.2 bhp
Capacity:	98 cc
Type:	Single-cylinder, 2-stroke

Hercules K 101

With foot gear change, chrome-plated tank and double seat, the improved K 100 was set to win the customers in 1959. The publicity literature was aimed primarily at young married couples, who could now enjoy the low-cost pleasure of motorcycle riding in the 100-cc class. The frame and fully floating axles had been strengthened and new brakes provided the necessary deceleration. In addition the K 101 was also available in a GS version and this was offered in competition with Maico which was the only producer of off-road machines for scrambling.

Model:	K 101
Year:	1959
Power:	5.2 bhp
Capacity:	98 cc
Type:	Single-cylinder, 2-stroke

Hercules 220 S

The 220-cc model was the first low-powered bike from Hercules, with a pressed-steel frame and hydraulically-damped telescopic struts. But the chassis was really too weak to carry two people. In 1962 the fast 220 K-4 appeared, which could reach 75 km/h (47 mph). It had a four-speed foot gear change instead of the three-speed rotary hand system and this was responsible for the beautiful feel of the motorcycle.

Model:	220 S
Year:	1960
Power:	3.4 bhp
Capacity:	220 cc
Type:	Single-cylinder, 2-stroke

Hercules K 102

Two years after the introduction of the K 101 came the sports version, the K 102. It was rather more expensive than the rival product, the Florett from Kreidler, but, particularly after the introduction of the four-speed foot gear change system in 1962, its riders found them not only smart and convenient but also quick off the mark.

Model:	K 102
Year:	1961
Power:	7 bhp
Capacity:	98 cc
Type:	Single-cylinder, 2-stroke

Hercules K 103 S

This model had to be more comfortable than the K 102 but without losing its sports character. With a new appearance and with the Sachs 100/4 engine it reached a maximum speed of 90 km/h (56 mph) and was more competitively priced than the arch-rival Zündapp. The K 103 could also be converted to an off-road bike.

Model:	K 103 S
Year:	1964
Power:	8.2 bhp
Capacity:	97 cc
Type:	Single-cylinder, 2-stroke

Hercules K 105

'For experts and connoisseurs who ride: the Hercules K 105'. With this slogan Hercules wooed the customer and offered a 'real motorbike' with the 10-bhp Sachs engine, the five-speed gearbox and the frame that had proved reliable for scrambling. Characteristic of the K 105 was the half-length suspension at the front, while at the rear there was a rear-wheel swing-arm with two telescopic struts.

Model:	K 105
Year:	1970
Power:	10 bhp
Capacity:	97 cc
Type:	Single-cylinder, 2-stroke

Hercules K 125 X

The relatively light K 125 fought for market share against the big competitors in the 125 range. Maico, Honda, Yamaha, Zündapp and BMW also offered similar-powered machines and were very popular with customers with their lightweight cradle frames and 17-inch wheels. However the 2-stroke bikes from Nuremberg had the advantage of the high-torque Hercules engine.

Model:	K 125 X
Year:	1970
Power:	15 bhp
Capacity:	123 cc
Type:	Single-cylinder, 2-stroke

Hercules K 125 MC

The K 125 MC five-speed moto-cross bike, whose frame was indeed good, but whose engine only unleashed its power at high revs was not successful. After two years Hercules removed it from its range.

Model: K 125 MC
Year: 1974
Power: 22 bhp
Capacity: 123 cc
Type: Single-cylinder, 2-stroke

Hercules W 2000

From the middle of the 1960s Sachs experimented with the development of a rotary piston engine. Eventually Hercules presented the first prototype of the W 2000 in 1970 which was intended to go into production in 1973. The power output at 25 bhp was certainly modest. In addition it had several technical problems, such as an overloaded cooling fan and vibrations, The Wankel-Hercules was also difficult to produce. Against the more powerful and significantly more reasonably priced machines from Japan the W 2000 did not have much to offer. For this reason production was terminated in 1979.

Model: W 2000
Year: 1975
Power: 27 bhp
Chamber volume: 294 cc
Type: Single rotor rotary engine

Hercules GS 250

For a wide spectrum of machines for off-road sport, Sachs developed a sports engine with a seven-speed gearbox. As much magnesium as possible was used in the extremely light engine which was fitted with a new type of forged piston. The crankshaft was supported by three deep-groove ball bearings and the big-end bearing of the connecting rod was designed for extreme loads. To match the competition, there was a kick-starter which worked directly on the crankshaft, so that in each gear when the clutch was released the engine could be started again. The GS was offered in versions with 125, 175, 250 and 350-cc engines. The short frame designed by Hercules was very manoeuvrable and easy to control even by amateurs.

Model: GS 250
Year: 1976
Power: 26 bhp
Capacity: 245 cc
Type: Single-cylinder, 2-stroke

Hercules K 125 BW

Hercules landed a lucrative contract in 1970 when the German army withdrew its Maico M 250 BW bikes and signed up for the K 125 BW. It was at first criticised as being too loud and heavy, weighing 130 kg (287 lb), and because the engine speed range was too narrow. These problems were at least partly resolved in 1988 with the K 125 BW Variant 2. The double-underslung frame was extremely stable as was the very effective swing-arm suspension

Model: K 125 BW
Year: 1988
Power: 12.5 bhp
Capacity: 123 cc
Type: Single-cylinder, 2-stroke

Honda – World market leader in record time

Soichiro Honda has revolutionised the world of motorcycle technology with his smart ideas. But everything started quite modestly. He founded the Honda Motor Company in September 1948 with his partner Takeo Fujisawa and in 1950 almost half the motorbikes built in Japan displayed the Honda logo. At the end of 1951 Honda launched the first 4-stroke OHV (overhead valve) engine on the market. The 250-cc Dream C70 of 1957, developed by Honda itself, was to be the forerunner of many other Honda models. The next milestone was the 250 cc Dream CB72 launched in 1960 and in 1965 Honda launched the Dream CB450. At the end of 1968 Soichiro Honda presented the CB750 Four. It was the first mass-produced 4-cylinder motorbike in the world and Honda hoped to conquer the world market with this bike. Honda had plenty of experience of mass-production, having built over ten million bikes by 1968. But it also had the technical design know-how. After all, at that time the founding head of the company could look back on 16 World Championship titles. His racing bikes were technical masterpieces. The CB750 Four became a best-seller and by 1978 over one million examples had come off the assembly line. Today life without Japanese motorbikes is hardly conceivable. It is impossible to imagine how the motorbike market would have developed without Soichiro Honda.

Honda Model A

The first Honda was designed to be very simple: The air-cooled 2-stroke machine was based on the frame of a man's bicycle and drove the rear wheel by means of a belt. The design of the tank was equally bizarre, based on a bed warmer. Since petrol was in short supply, it was eked out with turpentine and distilled pine resin extract, which naturally resulted in a dark exhaust plume.

Model:	A
Year:	1947
Power:	1 bhp
Capacity:	50 cc
Type:	Single-cylinder, 2-stroke

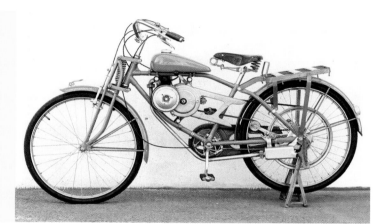

Honda Dream

In many ways Honda broke fresh ground in 1950 with the D Type. It was not only the first genuine Honda motorcycle, but also the first Japanese machine which was completely produced by a single manufacturer. The belt drive had in the meantime been replaced by a chain and a two-speed gearbox was also included. The solid steel frame was combined with modern telescopic forks.

Model:	Dream (Typ D)
Year:	1950
Power:	3 bhp
Capacity:	98 cc
Type:	Single-cylinder, 2-stroke

Honda C100 Super Cub

Today everybody knows that the Honda Super Cub was the most important model in the history of the motorcycle. It is still the bestest selling means of motor driven transport of all time. Beneath the weather-protection casing, an air-cooled engine delivered sufficient power to transport the driver and his load at a wind-creating pace.

Model:	C100 Super Cub
Year:	1958
Power:	4.3 bhp
Capacity:	49 cc
Type:	Single-cylinder, 4-stroke

Honda Benly C92

The next step after the D type was the C92 Benly, a comparatively lively 125 of the completely new generation. It was very unusual at that time for a motorcycle of this capacity to have two cylinders. Its chirpy engine had an overhead camshaft, a technical feature which most manufacturers of the day only fitted on their racing machines, if at all, and with its electric starter it set quite a new standard of rider-friendliness.

Model:	Benly C92
Year:	1959
Power:	11.5 bhp
Capacity:	124 cc
Type:	2-cylinder in-line, 4-stroke

Honda CB72

The CB72 set new standards. Such high power could previously only be obtained from large machines, which in general were unwieldy, unreliable and always covered in oil. The high-revving CB72 was completely oil-tight and its compact tubular frame, high performance brakes and 12-volt electrical system were very advanced features.

Model:	CB72
Year:	1960
Power:	24 bhp
Capacity:	247 cc
Type:	2-cylinder in-line, 4-stroke

Honda CB450 1965

When the CB450 was launched on the market in 1966, it was the largest capacity Honda of all time. At the same time it had a series of technical features which had never been seen before in the 500-cc class. The power unit was a 2-cylinder engine with double overhead camshafts. A minor sensation was caused by the valve springs, which were designed in the form of torsion bars. Because of its high engine power and maximum speed the machine, many parts of which were painted black, was quickly nicknamed the 'Black Bomber'.

Model:	CB450
Year:	1965
Power:	43 bhp
Capacity:	444 cc
Type:	2-cylinder in-line, 4-stroke

Honda RC166

Honda's Grand Prix Racer RC166 was really the technical highlight of all time. The amazing 6-cylinder engine ran at an unbelievable 17,000 rpm, had 24 valves and double overhead camshafts. The legendary Mike Hailwood rode to victory ten times in 12 races on the outstanding RC166 in the 250-cc GP class. An improved version, the RC174, proved very successful in the 350-cc class, since Hailwood won every GP.

Model:	RC166
Year:	1966
Power:	over 60 bhp
Capacity:	249 cc
Type:	6-cylinder, 4-stroke

Honda RC181

In 1966 there was only one category in the World Championships in which Honda had yet to produce the champion: the 500-cc class. This was for many years dominated by MV Agusta. When the Honda rider Jim Redman became the many-times World Champion at the German Grand Prix in 1966 and beat the MV Star Giacomo Agostini with the brand new RC181, the dominance of the Italians in the senior category was broken. Honda won the manufacturers' title, but had to wait until 1983 before the riders' title was won on it.

Model:	RC181
Year:	1967
Power:	over 85 bhp
Capacity:	499 cc
Type:	4-cylinder, 4-stroke

Honda CB750 Four

The technical journalists and fans raved about the CB750 when it was shown at the Tokyo Motor Show in 1968. This 4-cylinder machine marked a new epoch in the story of motorcycle construction. It set new standards for riding and equipment: overhead camshaft, disc brakes at the front, five-speed gearbox, electric starter and first-class workmanship. The result was that Honda had put the first superbike on the road. In 1969 the CB750 Four won the Bol d'Or and, in the following year, the 200 miles at Daytona.

Model:	CB750 Four
Year:	1969
Power:	67 bhp
Capacity:	736 cc
Type:	4-cylinder, 4-stroke

Honda CB500 Four

After the brilliant introduction of the CB750, Honda decided to apply the 4-cylinder concept to smaller-capacity machines. The compact CB500 impressed with its good riding properties, comfort and reliability, and it also had sufficient power to carry a pillion passenger. Its maximum speed was only 15 km/h (9 mph) below that of its larger sibling. Because of this and its favourable price many riders interested in sports performance bought this model in the 1970s.

Model:	CB500 Four
Year:	1971
Power:	48 bhp
Capacity:	498 cc
Type:	4-cylinder in-line, 4-stroke

Honda SL250S

The design of the trail bike, a motorbike permitted on the roads with genuine off-road qualities, was first produced in this form in the 1970s. Honda had presented a forerunner in the 1960s with its little 'Scrambler', which had a high-placed exhaust and plenty of ground clearance, and this enabled off-road excursions to be made.

Model:	SL250S
Year:	1972
Power:	22 bhp
Capacity:	248 cc
Type:	Single-cylinder, 4-stroke

Honda CR250M Elsinore

To European ears the name 'Elsinore' may be reminiscent of Hamlet's castle in Denmark, but in reality the machine was named after a Grand Prix course in California. With the 250-cc machine built to emulate the CR works machine, Honda had a hot contender in the amateur moto-cross field right from the start. The CR250M was delivered more or less ready to race, and could, without any significant modifications, be driven straight 'out of the box' down to the start and from there to the winning post.

Model:	CR250M Elsinore
Year:	1972
Power:	33 bhp
Capacity:	247 cc
Type:	Single-cylinder, 2-stroke

Honda TL125 Bials

With the construction of the first thoroughbred trials bike in Japan Honda again challenged an iron rule – namely that only 2-stroke engines were light and powerful enough to compete in trials. In spite of its weight the TL125 Bials (the name is a combination of 'Bike' and 'Trials') saw off the competition. With this deliberately narrow and correspondingly manoeuvrable machine, Honda could reach the top places in this sport as well.

Model:	TL125 Bials
Year:	1973
Power:	8 bhp
Capacity:	122 cc
Type:	Single-cylinder, 4-stroke

Honda CB 400 Four

Honda introduced a true classic in 1975 with the CB 400 Four, which was immediately a sales success. The sports character was a prime feature of this model. Its clear lines and brightly coloured paintwork were the visual characteristics of this machine, which was the first to be fitted with a prominent 4-into-1 exhaust system. People who were looking for thoroughbred riding excitement in the finest café racer style were well served by the 400-cc Four.

Model:	CB 400 Four
Year:	1974
Power:	37 bhp
Capacity:	408 cc
Type:	4-cylinder in-line, 4-stroke

Honda GL1000 Gold Wing

The trail-blazing Gold Wing, which received the name of Honda's traditional emblem, set new standards for power and comfort in motorbike design. The whole motorbike world was fascinated by the enormous size and the luxurious equipment of this new super-tourer and its water-cooled 4-cylinder boxer engine. The Gold Wing originated out of the 'King of Motor Cycles', a prototype from 1972 with a 6-cylinder flat engine. In 1980 the GL was fitted with a more powerful 1100-cc engine.

Model:	GL1000 Gold Wing
Year:	1974
Power:	80 bhp
Capacity:	996 cc
Type:	4-cylinder boxer, 4-stroke

Honda RCB1000

The Le Mans 24-hour race for motorbikes first took place in 1978 and Honda was the first to win it. With further wins in the following two years, the RCB 1000 with its in-line 4-cylinder engine became an almost unbeatable machine in the European long distance championship. Specifically, the pair of riders Jean-Claude Chemarin and Christian Leon, who were responsible for this success, were able to win four titles in succession on the machines provided by Honda France.

Model:	RCB1000
Year:	1976
Power:	over 120 bhp
Capacity:	997 cc
Type:	4-cylinder in-line, 4-stroke

Honda CB900F Bol d'Or

The most demanding 24-hour long-distance race in the world is the 'Bol d'Or'. In the middle of the 1970s Honda won this gruelling marathon three times in a row. After these successes Honda launched the CB900F Bol d'Or on the market in 1978. Technical people talked about milestones while the racing fans knew that the big thing about this bike was that it would go over 220 km/h (137 mph).

Model:	CB900F Bol d' Or
Year:	1978
Power:	95 bhp
Capacity:	901 cc
Type:	4-cylinder in-line, 4-stroke

Honda RC500M

Success for Honda in the 500-cc Moto-Cross World Championship took longer to come than was expected by the demanding market, which had been accustomed to seeing the company win. In 1979 the British rider Graham Noyce won the first victory on a Honda and the Belgian, André Malherbe, carried off the World Championship title in 1980 and 1981 on his RC500M. In the development of moto-cross racing machines Honda tried out a few novel ideas. One of these was an articulated rear spring to increase freedom of movement, without raising the motorbike too high. However, this system did not function satisfactorily due to too little power being transmitted to the back wheel.

Model:	RC500M
Year:	1979
Power:	55 bhp
Capacity:	493 cc
Type:	Single-cylinder, 2-stroke

Honda CBX1000

In the 1960s Honda had shown the astonished technical world how it was possible to put six cylinders on a racetrack machine. In 1978 Honda dropped another bombshell by announcing a 6-cylinder machine suitable for the road. The project was managed by the brilliant engineer Soichiro Irimajiri, who later rose to become managing director of the Honda Motor Company. The air-cooled 6-cylinder engine with its six exhaust manifolds not only looked magnificent but delivered breathtaking power in conjunction with a ride that was as soft as silk.

Model:	CBX1000
Year:	1979
Power:	105 bhp
Capacity:	1047 cc
Type:	6-cylinder in-line, 4-stroke

Honda CBX1000FII Pro-Link

In 1981 the CBX 1000F II with fairing, panniers and – as a first – Pro-Link rear-wheel suspension with single spring damper was introduced as a touring bike. It was based on the CBX 1000F which was originally designed as a sports bike.

Model:	CBX1000FII Pro-Link
Year:	1981
Power:	105 bhp
Capacity:	1047 cc
Type:	6-cylinder in-line, 4-stroke

Honda CX500E

At the end of 1977 the Honda CX500 was introduced to the market, which caused a major problem. Honda was totally convinced about its new machine, but for the bikers the CX500 was too unexciting and too simple. The future of the model was therefore in doubt. However what happened next was unexpected. The CX tourer series went to the hearts of touring riders. The CX500E, the 'E' standing for 'Euro', was put on the market and Honda found that this model went down well with the European motorcycle fraternity. The transverse 80° V-2 engine was the most reliable motorbike power unit ever built and engine lives of 500,000 km (300,000 miles) and more were not unusual.

Model:	CX500E
Year:	1982
Power:	50 bhp
Capacity:	498 cc
Type:	V-twin, 4-stroke

Honda VF750S

In 1982 Honda chose a new way to break into the high-power range with the V-4 configuration of the VF750S. For this it abandoned the power and smooth running of an in-line four in favour of the enormous torque of a large V engine. The V-4 configuration was also considerably narrower than an in-line four. Already in its first version the liquid-cooled 90° V-4 engine with 16 valves delivered a powerful 85 bhp. Although the crankshaft was at right angles to the direction of travel, the final drive was through a cardan shaft. The front wheel had an anti-dive system and the rear wheel suspension consisted of a Pro-Link system with central spring damper.

Model:	VF750S
Year:	1982
Power:	82 bhp
Capacity:	748 cc
Type:	V-4, 4-stroke

Honda VT250F

Until the early 1980s people thought that high performance in the 250-cc class was the domain of the 2-stroke engine. Then came the VT250F which proved the opposite. The lively liquid-cooled V-2 engine with conventional 90° cylinder angle ran fast and visually it had a lot to offer. Many features appealed to the younger sports riders of the time; for example, ideal weight distribution, a solid frame with Pro-Link rear wheel suspension and a disc brake at the front.

Model: VT250F
Year: 1982
Power: 35 bhp
Capacity: 248 cc
Type: V-twin, 4-stroke

Honda CB650C Chopper

At the beginning of the 1980s the soft chopper was very fashionable. The Honda CB650C, the 'C' standing for Chopper, was, of course, no exception. But it could hardly be considered a genuine dyed-in-the-wool long-fork chopper. Honda fitted the standard CB650 high handlebars, drop tank, stepped seat and chubby exhaust pipes in order to create the 'Easy Rider' effect.

Model: CB650C Chopper
Year: 1982
Power: 63 bhp
Capacity: 648 cc
Type: 4-cylinder, 4-stroke

Honda CX650 Turbo

With the CX500, Honda ventured into the world of turbocharger technology. The irregular exhaust rhythm of a V-twin compared to an in-line engine did not make this easier, but the finished design, the CX650, was the first production machine with a turbocharger and delivered at least 100 bhp. It was also Honda's first machine with fuel injection. A large fairing was then supposed to give the CX650 tourer qualities, however neither this nor the turbocharger turned out to be big breakthroughs for motorcycles.

Model: CX650 Turbo
Year: 1983
Power: 100 bhp
Capacity: 673 cc
Type: V-twin, 4-stroke

Honda VF1100C Magna

The large volume V-4 engine was developed by Honda in the early 1980s and was intended for use in bikes with a relaxed seating position ridden on long highways. This model marked the entry into the area of choppers and cruisers which was traditionally dominated by the American V-twins in particular, but with a more modern, more powerful design. As far as period designs were concerned, the Japanese at that time still had a long way to go.

Model: VF1100C Magna
Year: 1983
Power: 120 bhp
Capacity: 1098 cc
Type: V-4, 4-stroke

Honda XL600V Transalp

Honda presented a new facet of the enduro concept in 1986 with the consciously 'civilised' Transalp. The power was supplied by a six-valve V-2 engine bored out to 600 cc, which had already proved successful in the VT500. The European Honda Design Department was allowed to have its say in the styling of the machine. So far as the name was concerned, anyone who thought of the bike only in terms of alpine passes soon learned otherwise. The Transalp was from the start designed to run on country roads, motorways and in the city, but it was just as much at home on the long hairpin bends in the Alps.

Model:	XL600V Transalp
Year:	1987
Power:	50 bhp
Capacity:	583 cc
Type:	V-twin, 4-stroke

Honda NX650 Dominator

The Dominator was presented as the perfect street machine with a very visible enduro character. It was a further development of the XL600R. In the European roadster market the Dominator has been a fixture for 15 years. Its main market ran through the lower and middle ranges, and the chassis with its Pro-Link central telescopic strut was in no way unsuitable for this. As a multi-functional bike for everyday use it has proved itself as a reliable companion both on the tarmac in cities and on the dusty tracks of many rallies.

Model:	NX650 Dominator
Year:	1988
Power:	45 bhp
Capacity:	644 cc
Type:	Single-cylinder, 4-stroke

Honda VFR750R/RC30

The V-4 design reached a new dimension with the VFR750F of 1985. This machine also proved how simple and uncomplicated the compact and sophisticated V-4 design could be as far as maintenance was concerned. A real surprise followed in 1988 in the form of the now legendary VFR750R RC30, with which Honda produced a bike that was practically a racing machine that could run on ordinary roads. The hand-made engine offered breathtaking performance.

Honda GL1500 Gold Wing

As a further development of the Gold Wing concept, Honda presented a very impressive flagship with what was, for that time, the very futuristically styled GL 1500 SE. The integral brake system and reverse gear of the GL 1500 set new operating standards. The soft-as-silk engine, the smooth springing and the well-balanced handling made the rider feel he was riding on a flying carpet.

Honda PC800 Pacific Coast

Designers from the Honda car department were responsible for the styling of the PC800 Pacific Coast. This machine was aimed at customers who felt left out by the normal motorcycle attributes arising from competitive two-wheel technology and sport. So, based on knowledge from the car business, a completely 'clean' line with noise-swallowing fairing was created without any hint of aggression or sportiness.

Model:	VFR750R/RC30
Year:	1988
Power:	112 bhp
Capacity:	748 cc
Type:	V-4, 4-stroke

Model:	GL1500 Gold Wing
Year:	1988
Power:	98 bhp
Capacity:	1520 cc
Type:	6-cyl. boxer, 4-stroke

Model:	PC800 Pacific Coast
Year:	1989
Power:	56 bhp
Capacity:	800 cc
Type:	V-twin, 4-stroke

Honda ST1100 Pan European

The ST1100 Pan European was a comparatively slim alternative to the Gold Wing. Like the latter, it offered optimum conditions for extended touring with a passenger and luggage. Both machines had the engine arranged so that the crankshaft and cardan shaft were in the direction of travel, while the ST was 'only' fitted with a 90° V-4 power unit. The European designers of HRE (Honda Research Europe) and the European Honda retailers were very much involved in the design right from the beginning of the project.

Model:	ST1100 Pan European
Year:	1990
Power:	101 bhp
Capacity:	1085 cc
Type:	V-4, 4-stroke

Honda NR750

In 1979 the NR500 racing machine radically did away with one of the oldest dogmas in motorcycle history: that pistons must be round. The four pistons in the V-engine of the NR500 were actually oval and thus permitted a larger valve area and consequently a better gas flow. The result was, among other things, a green area for the rev range which only ended at an unbelievable 19,500 rpm. The first NR500 had overcome many technical problems. The NR750 road bike introduced in 1992 was an interesting piece of engineering for well-heeled motorcycling enthusiasts.

Model:	NR750
Year:	1992
Power:	130 bhp
Capacity:	747 cc
Type:	V-4, 4-stroke

Honda CBR900RR FireBlade

The ultimate supersports experience of the 1990s was defined by Honda with its CBR900RR. It was amazingly light to handle and the performance package justified the high expectations suggested by the name. The machine, which was originally only designed for a small niche market, combined for the first time the performance of a 900 with the handling of a 600. But in this case the technology used was not exactly revolutionary. What made the difference was the detailed and consistent implementation of knowledge gained from motor sport.

Model:	CBR900RR FireBlade
Year:	1993
Power:	124 bhp
Capacity:	893 cc
Type:	4 cyl. in-line, 4-stroke

Honda XRV750 Africa Twin

Its engine capacity alone proved that the Africa Twin was the absolute king of the Honda enduros for a long time. The XRV750 was to a large extent based on the NXR750, which in the 1980s ruled the tracks between Paris and Dakar. The identification features of the Africa Twin were surely its enormous front fairing with the double headlights and the 52° V-2 engine with six-valve technology. The Africa Twin is still being built and has conquered the hearts of a loyal fan community who regard it as an extremely reliable adventure tourer.

Model:	XRV750 Africa Twin
Year:	1990
Power:	59 bhp
Capacity:	742 cc
Type:	V-twin, 4-stroke

Honda NTV650 Revere

Pricewise, the Honda NTV650 Revere was a real bargain in 1993. But thiss certainly did not mean that it was a 'cheap' motorcycle; quite the reverse. The three-valve V-2 engine was fully developed and in principle could not be faulted, while the bridge frame with single swing arm and cardan shaft drive was torsionally stiff and stable. The Revere was an ideal entry-level bike which could be fitted with engines which developed either 27 bhp, 50 bhp or, in the open version, 57 bhp.

Model:	NTV650 Revere
Year:	1993
Power:	57 bhp
Capacity:	647 cc
Type:	V-twin, 4-stroke

Honda VF750C

The fame of the 750 Honda Custom models was based on the fact that these perfectly represented the American style of riding. In addition they had very good acceleration, which made every outing an experience. The outstanding engine performance, noticeable in particular in the first three gears, was delivered in a controlled way by a carburettor system based on the Fireblade. It was easy to drive in town traffic and at high speeds on roads with no speed restrictions.

Model:	VF750C
Year:	1993
Power:	88 bhp
Capacity:	748 cc
Type:	V-4, 4-stroke

Honda F6C

Up to that time Honda's most powerful contribution to the cruiser/chopper segment exceeded the normal standards of this class. The F6C had the enormous 1500-cc 6-cylinder engine of the Gold Wing. However, what distinguished the F6C from other mega-cruisers was its sensational acceleration, the powerful brakes and, in view of the weight, its amazingly precise handling. This heavyweight cruiser had a big following particularly in the United States.

Model:	F6C
Year:	1996
Power:	101 bhp
Capacity:	1520 cc
Type:	6-cylinder boxer, 4-stroke

Honda VF750/RC45

John Kocinski's win in the 1997 World Superbike Series confirmed the exceptional qualities of the RC45. The phenomenal V-4 engine with electronic fuel injection and the chassis which had been continually optimised on the most demanding race tracks of the world harmonised perfectly. The unmistakable signature of the Honda Racing Corporation was written on the fairing which, without compromise, gave the RC45 excellent stability at maximum speed.

Model:	VF750/RC45
Year:	1994
Power:	120 bhp
Capacity:	749 cc
Type:	V-4, 4-stroke

Honda CBR600F

In 1987 when Honda first showed the CBR600F, people had never seen anything like it in the 600 Super Sport class. This machine offered the power of a significantly higher capacity at a more favourable price – but with the lighter handling of a 600. The sales figures were a great success. In October 1996 the 200,000th CBR 600 F was licensed, which was a tremendous result for a sports bike. Introduced in 1995, the model had developed into a machine that was primarily suitable for everyday use but was increasingly a serious sports machine.

Model:	CBR600F
Year:	1995
Power:	100 bhp
Capacity:	599 cc
Type:	4-cylinder in-line, 4-stroke

Honda CB Sevenfifty

With the no-frills Sevenfifty, Honda resurrected its former successful model from the 1960s. The ingredients were the same: an air-cooled 4-cylinder in-line engine in a conventional lightweight cradle frame of timeless design. Honda also produced a 1000-cc version for the power hungry 'naked biker'.

Model:	CB Sevenfifty
Year:	1996
Power:	73 bhp
Capacity:	747 cc
Type:	4-cylinder in-line, 4-stroke

Honda CB1000

Honda offered a 1000-cc version of the CB designed on the same purist philosophy as the CB Sevenfifty. Even more powerful than the 750 power unit, the big CB with the irrepressible in-line 4-cylinder engine, which was mounted in a conventional chassis with duo telescopic struts, was an absolutely classic road motorcycle.

Model:	CB1000
Year:	1996
Power:	98 bhp
Capacity:	998 cc
Type:	4-cylinder in-line, 4-stroke

Honda VT600C Shadow

At the end of the 1980s, with the 600 Shadow Honda offered an uncomplicated mid-range cruiser of straightforward design. The period of embarrassing Harley copies came to an end with the appearance of the little Shadow.

Model:	VT600C Shadow
Year:	1996
Power:	39 bhp
Capacity:	583 cc
Type:	V-twin, 4-stroke

Honda CB500

The Honda CB500 was the classic entry-level motorcycle. It was extremely robust, good value for money and, thanks to a moderate seat height it was also easy for smaller people to ride. Produced in the Italian Honda factory, the machine was also offered as an S version with tourer-friendly half-shell fairing.

Model:	CB500
Year:	1997
Power:	57 bhp
Capacity:	499 cc
Type:	2-cylinder in-line, 4-stroke

Honda CR250R

The CR250R was an off-road racing machine of the finest calibre with modern features such as Power Jet Control and digital ignition. The only surprise, however, was the frame. The CR250R was the first moto-cross machine to have a frame made of aluminium. Together with the Delta-Pro-Link rear wheel suspension, the whole chassis was designed for the high loadings of the moto-cross world. How well this succeeded at the first attempt was seen in 1997 when the Moto-Cross World Championship in the 250-cc class was won by Stefan Everts.

Model:	CR250R
Year:	1997
Power:	58 bhp
Capacity:	249 cc
Type:	Single-cylinder, 2-stroke

Honda SLR650

As a straightforward low-cost scrambler, the SLR has still not really caught on in Europe. Yet the SLR, powered by the proven 4-stroke unit of the Dominator, could be thoroughly convincing thanks to its light-footed handling and pleasant appearance. Also the model revision for the 1999 season added, among other things, a discreet headlight fairing and a new name, Vigor.

Model:	SLR650
Year:	1997
Power:	39 bhp
Capacity:	644 cc
Type:	Single-cylinder, 4-stroke

Honda VT1100 Shadow

Honda's Shadow series was available in three capacities: 600, 750 and 1100 cc. The big Shadow known as 'C2' came with a comparatively plain appearance, while the 'C3' model with projecting mudguards and enormous use of chrome swam on the waves of earlier nostalgia. The power output of 50 bhp from a large 1100-cc engine was really modest, since the V-2 in the 'C3' delivered at least 57 bhp.

Model:	VT1100 C2 Shadow
Year:	1997
Power:	50 bhp
Capacity:	1099 cc
Type:	V-twin, 4-stroke

Honda CBR1000F

The CBR1000F has been part of Honda's model range since the mid-1980s. The tasteful sports tourer with somewhat limited sports qualities based its appeal, in particular, on the extremely powerful 4-cylinder engine which in some countries was only offered in the insurance-friendly 98-bhp version.

Model:	CBR1000F
Year:	1997
Power:	98 bhp
Capacity:	998 cc
Type:	4-cylinder in-line, 4-stroke

Honda CBR1100XX

What the Hayabusa was for Suzuki, the CBR1100XX was for Honda – a powerful speed bike with good wind protection and imposing appearance. The motorcycle could travel at up to 280 km/h (174 mph) and in order to brake effectively, the 'Double XX' was fitted with Honda's advanced CBS Combibrake system which was first used in 1993 in the CBR1000F. With the use of fuel injection equipment and two computer-controlled catalytic converters, the original power of 164 bhp was reduced to a still-luxurious 150 bhp.

Model:	CBR1100XX
Year:	1997
Power:	150 bhp
Capacity:	1137 cc
Type:	4-cylinder in-line, 4-stroke

Honda VFR

With this machine Honda again produced a technological marvel on wheels. Fitted with fuel injection, computer-controlled catalytic converters and a gear-driven valve unit, the VFR set a new standard so far as environmental friendliness was concerned. The VFR was also full of advanced technical features in other areas. Thus, the single swing-arm was attached not to the frame but directly to the engine. When the handbrake lever was operated, the Dual-CBS (Dual Combined Braking System) activated the two external brake pistons of the front brake calliper and the central piston of the rear brake calliper. The foot-brake pedal operated the external pistons of the rear brake calliper and on the central piston of the front brake calliper.

Model:	VFR
Year:	1998
Power:	106 bhp
Capacity:	781 cc
Type:	V-4, 4-stroke

Honda Deauville

In 1998 Honda launched the Deauville with full fairing, based on the tried and tested NTV650 Revere. This was an unpretentious tourer for everyday use with standard case system and combination brake system. Developing a comparatively low performance of 56 bhp, the V-2 power unit was more geared to durability than to the highest possible performance.

Model:	Deauville
Year:	1999
Power:	56 bhp
Capacity:	647 cc
Type:	V-twin, 4-stroke

Honda CB600 Hornet

Launched in 1998, the Hornet became the absolute best-seller in the Honda catalogue in a record short time. This snappy all-rounder had a 94-bhp 600-cc 4-cylinder in-line engine which in the past had also been used in the Super-Sport CBR600F. After many years the little Hornet was still the best-selling motorbike in Europe.

Model:	CB600 Hornet
Year:	1999
Power:	94 bhp
Capacity:	599 cc
Type:	4-cylinder in-line, 4-stroke

Honda CB600 Hornet S

Its little sibling with half-fairing also contributed much to the Hornet's success. It allowed the rider to speed down the motorway without the air-flow spoiling his pleasure at higher speeds. In the year 2000 the 'S' version was fitted with an easier-to-handle 17-inch front wheel and the power was increased to 95 bhp.

Model:	CB600 Hornet S
Year:	2000
Power:	95 bhp
Capacity:	599 cc
Type:	4-cylinder in-line, 4-stroke

Honda CBR900RR Fireblade

After Yamaha started a new chapter in the history of supersport motorbikes with the R1, Honda came under pressure with the Fireblade. In 2000 it presented a completely new 'Fireblade' for which the market leader had left no stone unturned. The 4-cylinder in-line powerplant was a short-stroke engine, more efficient and with its manifold injection and computer-controlled catalytic converter more environmentally friendly. The frame with inverted forks and 17-inch front wheel was extremely rider-friendly and precise without the CBR suffering from an everyday appearance.

Model: CBR900RR Fireblade
Year: 2000
Power: 147 bhp
Capacity: 929 cc
Type: 4-cylinder in-line,
            4-stroke

Honda XR650R

With the 650-cc XR, Honda again had a sporty, high capacity single-cylinder enduro bike in its catalogue. Its 61 bhp made it powerful enough for ambitious enduro riders, but the homologated version developed only 50 bhp. Because Honda brought out the 61-bhp model without homologation, type approval had to be undertaken individually, which proved possible without too many problems.

Model:	XR650R
Year:	2000
Power:	61 bhp
Capacity:	649 cc
Type:	Single-cylinder, 4-stroke

Honda X11

The X-11 was almost the naked bike variation of the 1100-cc 'Double-X'. It had a powerful 4-cylinder engine which for this purpose was tuned for even greater high-end torque and a higher top speed. The X-11 was also fitted with the powerful Honda Dual-brake system.

Model:	X11
Year:	2000
Power:	136 bhp
Capacity:	1137 cc
Type:	4-cylinder in-line, 4-stroke

Honda VTR1000SP-1

To keep up with the enormously powerful Ducatis in the Superbike World Championship, Honda also launched a 2-cylinder racer at the beginning of the 2000 season: the VTR1000SP-1. In the homologated version the V-2 power unit with manifold injection and Ram-Air system developed a strapping 136 bhp.

Model:	VTR1000SP-1
Year:	2000
Power:	136 bhp
Capacity:	999 cc
Type:	2-cylinder in-line, 4-stroke

Honda VT750 Shadow

The medium-sized model in the Shadow range was also designed with great love and care. Massive mudguards, the indispensable V-twin engine and the extravagant two-colour paint scheme which differentiated the C2 from the C1, gave the bike a true cruiser look. Its substantial torque of over 60 Nm made controlled skids possible in spite of its maximum power of only 45 bhp.

Model:	VT750C2 Shadow
Year:	2001
Power:	45 bhp
Capacity:	745 cc
Type:	V-twin, 4-stroke

Honda CBR600F

The new CBR600 generation launched in 2001 was available in two versions: the 'normal' F-version and the 'sport' version. Both versions had a 600-cc 4-cylinder in-line engine with computer-controlled catalytic converter and exhaust emission, capable of developing 109 bhp. The 'sport' aspect was reflected by the absence of a centre stand and the narrow seat. Both had completely adjustable suspension elements and an excellent braking system, and for its class it was unusually well-suited to everyday use.

Model:	CBR600F Sport
Year:	2001
Power:	109 bhp
Capacity:	599 cc
Type:	4-cylinder in-line, 4-stroke

Honda Black Widow

In 2000 Honda presented the Black Widow as a sporty alternative to the 750-cc Shadow. Admittedly it was still powered by the relatively tame 45-bhp power unit of the Shadow but it no longer had its cruiser appearance. Instead it had a low chopper look reminiscent of the Harley-Davidson sports models.

Model:	VT750DC Black Shadow
Year:	2001
Power:	45 bhp
Capacity:	745 cc
Type:	V-twin, 4-stroke

Honda VTX1800

At least at the beginning the VTX was the absolute engine capacity champion of the ever-more powerful cruisers. An impressive 1800 cc and a power of over 100 bhp – this is what many cruiser fans had been waiting for. With its elegant appearance, maintenance-free cardan shaft drive, inverted forks and combination brake system, this monster cruiser became extremely popular and well-loved.

Model:	VTX1800
Year:	2001
Power:	105 bhp
Capacity:	1795 cc
Type:	V-twin, 4-stroke

Honda Gold Wing

In 2001 Honda launched a completely new generation of the Gold Wing, equipped for maximum comfort. Powered by a 1.8-litre 6-cylinder boxer engine, capable of developing 119 bhp, and fitted with ABS, combination brakes, audio system, cruise control and reverse gear, it satisfied every wish of the most spoilt tourer biker. In fact, the gap between it and a car was not at all wide any more.

Model:	GL1800 Gold Wing
Year:	2001
Power:	119 bhp
Capacity:	1832 cc
Type:	6-cylinder boxer, 4-stroke

Honda VTR1000 Firestorm

Already on the market in the mid-1990s, Honda's Firestorm was unable to find its niche in the market. Possibly its appearance was too unsophisticated compared to its Italian V-twin rivals, because all the other features of the 2-cylinder sports bike were first class. First and foremost was the powerful engine, the output of which was reduced from 110 to 98 bhp in some countries. Its comparatively thirsty fuel consumption might have played a part in the lack of interest.

Model:	VTR1000 Firestorm
Year:	2002
Power:	98 bhp
Capacity:	996 cc
Type:	V-twin, 4-stroke

Honda VFR

Honda called its variable valve operating mechanism V-4-Tec and it was fitted to the new VFR, launched in 2002. At first one inlet or exhaust valve always remained open, which meant that more power was available at the lower end of the speed range. When the rev counter reached the magical figure of 7,000 rpm, the valves closed and this was reflected in a sudden thrust of power. Apart from this the VFR remained a straightforward motorbike: safe, sporty, environmentally friendly and very suitable for touring.

Model:	VFR
Year:	2002
Power:	106 bhp
Capacity:	782 cc
Type:	V-4, 4-stroke

Honda CB900F Hornet

Just as the power unit of the sporty CBR600F had been fitted to the 600-cc Hornet, in 2002 the 900-cc Hornet engine was mounted in the same frame as the Fireblade. The power, and therefore the maximum speed, of the 4-cylinder in-line engine was slightly reduced in order to achieve more torque. But with 110 bhp the Hornet still had no need to fear any opponents – at least on country roads.

Model:	CB900F Hornet
Year:	2002
Power:	109 bhp
Capacity:	919 cc
Type:	4-cylinder in-line, 4-stroke

Honda Fireblade

Only two years after the launch of the last Fireblade generation, in 2002 Honda launched an even lighter, more powerful and more sporty CBR on the market. The styling of the new bike was clearly more aggressive in appearance. With over 150 bhp and a dry weight of less than 170 kg (375 lb), this Super-Sport bike combined the performance of a 1000-cc bike with the handling of a 600-cc one.

Model:	CBR900RR Fireblade
Year:	2002
Power:	151 bhp
Capacity:	954 cc
Type:	4-cylinder in-line, 4-stroke

Honda Pan European

In 2002 Honda after 12 years put the original 1100-cc Pan European into retirement so as to create a new model to challenge the new generation of BMW bikes in the heavy-travelling tourer-bike market. From the newly-developed V-4 engine and the newly-designed bridge-type frame – now always in aluminium – to the strikingly more stylish overall design, nothing remained of the older generation of bikes. Apart, that is, from the fact that the 'Panni' was still a nimble, agile first-class Supertourer as it had been before.

Model:	ST1100 Pan European
Year:	2002
Power:	118 bhp
Capacity:	1261 cc
Type:	V-4, 4-stroke

Honda Varadero

To keep up with BMW on the market of the powerful travel-enduro bikes, Honda launched the Varadero in 1999. The V-2 engine was derived from the Firestorm but with modified torque to suit its new role. Initially still with carburettor fuel supply and high fuel consumption, it was fitted with a fuel injection system which significantly reduced the latter.

Model:	XRV1000 Varadero	Year:	2003	Power:	94 bhp
Capacity:	996 cc	Type:	V-4, 4-stroke		

Honda CBR600RR

In 2003 Honda presented a completely new 600-cc CBR. Admittedly the F-version remained unchanged in the catalogue but it appeared rather old-fashioned compared to the new 'RR'. It was designed in the style of Valentino Rossi's World Championship bikes so that, for instance, the exhaust naturally had to be moved under the seat. To develop 117 bhp from 599 cc was quite incredible in itself and the amazingly lively 4-cylinder in-line engine turning at up to 15,000 rpm was enough to make the heart of any experienced supersport rider beat even faster.

Model:	CBR600RR
Year:	2003
Power:	117 bhp
Capacity:	599 cc
Type:	4-cylinder in-line, 4-stroke

Honda CB1300

In 2003 Honda launched an extremely powerful muscle-bike on the market.The traditionally designed CB was powered by an impressive 1300-cc 4-cylinder in-line engine which enabled the CB1300 to reach a top speed of 230 km/h (143 mph). In contrast to Yamaha's XJR 1300 or Suzuki's 1400-cc-GSX, the Honda engine was water-cooled.

Model:	CB1300
Year:	2003
Power:	116 bhp
Capacity:	1284 cc
Type:	4-cylinder in-line, 4-stroke

Honda VTX1300

The VTX1800 was unable to get a successful foothold in some markets, which was partly due to its price. To boost sales, Honda brought out a 1300-cc version which was cheaper because it did not have some of the fittings.

Model:	VTX1300S
Year:	2003
Power:	75 bhp
Capacity:	1312 cc
Type:	V-twin, 4-stroke

Honda CBF600

In 2004 Honda launched a new generation of the CBF which was available in three versions: as a 500-cc 2-cylinder and a 600-cc 4-cylinder bike, with or without half-shell fairing. All the models were extremely well designed with a stylish, crisp frame and optional ABS. Customers were immediately won over so that the CBF soon became the best-selling motorbike of 2004.

Model:	CBF600S
Year:	2004
Power:	76 bhp
Capacity:	599 cc
Type:	4-cylinder in-line, 4-stroke

Honda Fireblade

Naturally Fireblades could not continue to be unaffected by the increasingly shorter model cycles. The version launched in 2004 was admittedly slightly less powerful and a little heavier than its rivals but it was therefore pleasanter to ride in everyday life than the R1, ZX-10 and GSX-R. They were the first to be fitted with an electronic steering shock-absorber.

Model:	CBR1000RR Fireblade
Year:	2004
Power:	171 bhp
Capacity:	998 cc
Type:	4-cylinder in-line, 4-stroke

Honda CB600F Hornet

Even in 2003 the Hornets had been carefully reworked to improve their appearance and in addition, their performance had been increased as the design of the frame improved. As result the bhp was increased to 97. In 2005 the Hornets were further improved and now boasted new inverted forks with gold-anodised 41-mm sliding tubes.

Model:	CB600F Hornet
Year:	2005
Power:	97 bhp
Capacity:	599 cc
Type:	4-cylinder in-line, 4-stroke

Honda FMX650

In 2005, to appeal to a younger clientele, Honda developed the FMX650, a superbike which was comparatively cheap. As well as a very elegant appearance it also had the robustness of the blessed Dominator. Because of the new exhaust emissions limits the FMX now only developed 38 bhp.

Model:	FMX650	Year:	2005	Power:	38 bhp
Capacity:	644 cc	Type:	Single-cylinder, 4-stroke

HOREX – The queen of singles

To speak of Horex is to speak of its most celebrated bike, the Regina. At the end of 1948 Horex was the first company in West Germany which could offer a 350-cc machine at a reasonable price. There was work again and people were earning a little money. Generally people needed a motorbike to go to work since very few people could afford a car. In the following two years Horex sold well over 1,000 SB35 bikes. At the beginning of 1949 Horex began work on the development of a new motorbike and by the end of the year it was ready: Horex launched the 350-cc Regina and it immediately became a best-seller. In the autumn of 1951 Horex presented the Imperator at the IFMA motorbike show. The 350 cc Regina Sport stood on the podium right next to the 500-cc prototype. But then the market began to look less good for two-wheelers. In October 1960 Horex was sold to Daimler-Benz AG.

Horex 350 Regina

Representing a 'dream of escape' for a relatively modest sum, this Regina was a wonderfully beautiful 18-bhp single-cylinder 4-stroke bike with modern telescopic fork, direct rear wheel suspension, effective hub brakes, chrome tank and silencer. The totally enclosed drive chain was also standard. This Horex had eye-catching wheels with chrome-plated steel rims, set off by white edging with a red central stripe. It immediately became a best-seller and sold the largest number of motorbikes in its category.

Model:	350 Regina	Year: 1950	Power: 18 bhp
Capacity: 350 cc		Type: Single-cylinder, 4-stroke	

Horex 350 Regina Sport

As the first Regina, the Sport also had a newly developed aluminium cylinder head with a single port exhaust system. This gave it a top speed of 125 km/h (78 mph). But this racer was also visually very pleasing. With its silver-grey paintwork, the Sport had a kick-starter, brake pedal, foot-operated gear change, clutch lever engaging the gearbox and chrome-plated seat springs. The aluminium handlebars were also standard, as was the racing saddle on the sprung seat.

Model:	350 Regina Sport	Year: 1952	Power: 20 bhp
Capacity: 350 cc		Type: Single-cylinder, 4-stroke	

Horex 350 Regina

In 1953 Horex brought the third Regina generation on to the market. The iron-grey cylinder head was replaced by a newly developed aluminium cylinder head with twin-port system. The compression ratio was close to 6.8:1 and new silencers increased the power to 19 bhp. The standard fittings included mudguards which enclosed the tyres much more, and light metal tapered wheel rims.

Model:	350 Regina	Year: 1953	Power: 19 bhp
Capacity: 350 cc		Type: Single-cylinder, 4-stroke	

Horex 400 Regina

In 1953 Horex presented the Horex 400 Regina, available to choice with aluminium tapered rims for solo riding or as a combination with steel rims and a S-500 Steib sidecar attached.

Model:	400 Regina 4
Year:	1953
Power:	22 bhp
Capacity:	400 cc
Type:	Single-cylinder, 4-stroke

Husaberg – Swedish competition bikes from Austria

Building motorbikes which would win moto-cross, supermoto and enduro championships was Husaberg's dream. After the Swedish Elektrolux group sold the Husqvarna motorbike division to the Cagiva group in 1986, five former Husqvarna employees joined forces in 1988 and founded the Hudabergs Udde company on the peninsula of the same name. The launch of the niche products on the market was successful. In 1995 Husaberg was taken over by KTM Sportmotorcycle AG. Both makes concentrated on different niches in the market, but in the year 2000 KTM intended to sell Husaberg so that the Austrian side could concentrate entirely on their own plans for expansion. Since the middle of 2004 all Husaberg bikes have been assembled at KTM under the latter's strict conditions of quality control.

Husaberg FS 400 E

An ambitious manufacturer of enduro and moto-cross bikes, Husaberg launched a supermoto on the market at the beginning of the new millennium. The main difference between it and the cross-country versions lay in the fact that it had 17-inch wheels with road tyres. The 400-cc version was already fitted with the new engine with balancing shaft and the bike was started by an electric starter.

Model:	FS 400 E	Year:	2001	Power:	17 bhp
Capacity:	399 cc	Type:	Single-cylinder, 4-stroke		

Husaberg FC 470 E

The Husaberg moto-cross range was identified by the initials FC. The weight of these slender bikes whose dry weight was only 110 kg (242 lb) was reduced by a further 6 kg (13 lb) to a mere 104 kg (229 lb) – not bad for a 500 cc 4-stroke moto-cross machine. In 2002 Husaberg improved the engine in several ways. The model illustrated here was also available in a 550-cc version but even this was not permissible for road use.

Model:	FC 470 E	Year:	2002	Power:	n.a.*
Capacity:	472 cc	Type:	Single-cylinder, 4-stroke		

* The maker does not publish the power of its competition bikes

Husaberg FS 650 E

Supermoto racing is extremely spectacular. Mostly held on go-kart circuits, riders skid around the track with thrilling power slides. The leading Husaberg supermoto had a magnificent 650-cc single-cylinder engine which propelled it like a rocket with its weight of a mere 112 kg (247 lb). The components of the frame were also distinctive: suspension elements by White Power, brakes by Beringer (at the front) and Brembo (at the back), wheels by Behr and aluminium handlebars by Magura.

Model:	FS 650 E	Year:	2004	Power:	15 bhp
Capacity:	501 cc	Type:	Single-cylinder, 4-stroke		

Husaberg FE 550 E

The FE 550 E was the successor to the 501-cc model. But after the implementation of measures to meet the exhaust emission and noise regulations, only 15 bhp remained of the original 60.

Model:	FE 550 E
Year:	2004
Power:	15 bhp
Capacity:	549 cc
Type:	Single-cylinder, 4-stroke

Husqvarna – Swedish off-roader

The Swedish company Husqvarna Vapenfabrik Aktiebolag was founded in 1867 as an armaments factory. The company had already started producing bicycles in the late 19th century and in 1903 it also built its first motorbike. In 1928 Folke Mannerstadt, one of the best engineers around, joined the company and developed a 500-cc V-engine. However it was the little 98-cc 2-stroke bikes which brought the company financial success and they continued to be sold even during and after the Second World War. After a tough apprenticeship in road racing in the pre-war years, the company moved away from that kind of competition and, in 1953, decided to take part in Six Day trial events with 2-stroke bikes. After Rolf Tobblin became European moto-cross champion, Husqvarna increased its range of models and versions. Bill Nelson won the World Championship titles in 1962 and 1963 in the 250 and 500 cc categories and thus put an end once and for all to the era of the chunky 4-stroke bike represented by the BSA Gold Star. The Swedish bikes not only had a simpler drive assembly but also a lighter frame. In the 1970s the Swedes were still world leaders. In 1986 Husqvarna motorbikes were no longer made in Sweden but in Italy. However this did not affect their success.

Husqvarna MC 250 CR

After Sweden won the moto-cross World Championship in 1969 with Bengt Aberg on a 400-cc bike in the up-to-500 cc category, sales figures rocketed. Technical development was therefore intensified and cross-country bikes, derived from the moto-cross ones, also benefited from this success, doing very well in for instance the 1973 Six Day Endurance Trial in the United States where the American Husqvarna riders won the Silver Cup. Between 1962 and 1975 bikes such as the 250 CR, illustrated here, won 11 Italian moto-cross titles.

Model:	MC 250 CR	Year:	1975	Power:	35 bhp
Capacity:	245 cc	Type:	Single cylinder	2-stroke	

Husqvarna 420 AE

In 1982 Husqvarna developed a completely unique automatic bike for the Swedish army. The expensive construction proved very functional and robust for military purposes but it did not prove so attractive as a sports bike.

Model:	420 AE
Year:	1982
Power:	25 bhp
Capacity:	420 cc
Type:	Single-cylinder, 2-stroke

Husqvarna 430 WR

While a new engine replaced the 430 CR, used in another frame until 1983, the smaller engine of the GS version was kept but also with a new frame. Later the suspension was replaced by a central suspension system.

Model:	430 WR
Year:	1983
Power:	26 bhp
Capacity:	430 cc
Type:	Single-cylinder, 2-stroke

Husqvarna WR 360

It is always bad for a competition bike if its existence depends on being suitable for homologation. It means that often its power is only half what it could be. This was the case with the Husqvarna WR range, available with 125, 250 and 350-cc engines.

Model:	WR 360
Year:	2000
Power:	17 bhp
Capacity:	349 cc
Type:	Single-cylinder, 2-stroke

Husqvarna SM 610

Besides two hard-core supermoto bikes, Husqvarna had a relatively 'softer' SM version, with the 570-cc engine also used in other models. Nevertheless it chose the model designation '610', probably to emphasise the main difference, which lay in the fact that it was an everyday bike. So much was this the case that Husqvarna even offered a top case for it. This was perfect for bike enthusiasts who also wanted to use it to go shopping on their supermoto, but real husky fans turned up their nose at it.

Model:	SM 610 S
Year:	2000
Power:	46 bhp
Capacity:	576 cc
Type:	Single-cylinder, 4-stroke

Husqvarna CR 125

Having won several moto-cross World Championship titles, Husqvarna justified its reputation as a brilliant manufacturer of racing bikes. In 2000 the comprehensively revamped 125-cc hard-core moto-cross machine conquered the circuits with its 39-bhp 2-stroke engine, combined with an impressively light weight of 88 kg (194 lb).

Model:	CR 125
Year:	2000
Power:	39 bhp
Capacity:	125 cc
Type:	Single-cylinder, 2-stroke

Husqvarna TE 510

This special model, produced as a limited edition of 500 examples, was in fact designed to celebrate Husqvarna's hundredth anniversary. However, because of stringent economic circumstances, this 'centenary' bike, made even more desirable by the use of exotic materials such as carbon fibre, titanium and aluminium, would only be produced a year later. The costly execution and limited number made the Jubilee Husky one of the most exclusive enduros ever built.

Model:	TE 510 Centennial
Year:	2004
Power:	55 bhp
Capacity:	501 cc
Type:	Single-cylinder, 4-stroke

Husqvarna SM 610

In 2005, Husqvarna launched the SM 610, an ultra-sophisticated supermoto bike in the distinctive style of the house. As a pioneer of off-road sport, it now wanted to build a bike that would meet urban requirements. In other words, the vibrations of the four-valve engine were toned down by means of a balancing shaft and it also included an electric starter which had hitherto been unthinkable for a Husqvarna. There were further significant additions such as multi-adjustable suspension elements and the best Brembo brakes able to meet the requirements of the most demanding rider. In addition, the appearance was perfect.

Model:	SM 610
Year:	2005
Power:	60 bhp
Capacity:	576 cc
Type:	Single-cylinder, 4-stroke

Hyosung – Newcomer from Korea

Hyosung was founded as a business concern in 1957 and in the course of the following 15 years it grew to be a very large group. In 1978 Hyosung Motors & Machinery was founded as a second arm of the empire. The main works of the company are situated in Changwon and its output is 200,000 units a year. One of the company's characteristics, and at the same time one of its strengths, is its capacity to manufacture most components itself. Many parts of the chassis and even the brakes are developed and produced by Hyosung for its own use. Internationally the Koreans currently play a only secondary role. It is true that its scooters and motorbikes are sold all over the world, but the maker still does not have a clear image in the world of motorbikes, so sales are mainly boosted by the unbeatable price-performance ratio. But as in the Korean car industry, it is likely that the problem of image will soon be resolved.

Hyosung Aquila GV 250

The 250 cc Aquila was the first bike with a capacity of over 125 cc exported by Hyosung. Admittedly, the small cruiser bike was fairly ordinary from a technical point of view. There was also a 125 cc version for the price-conscious 'Easy-Rider'.

Hyosung Comet GT 250

The Comet 250 had the same air-cooled V-twin engine as the Aquila. It was extremely convincing as a classic road bike with sturdy box frame and a very pleasing appearance for its price. Well established in the 250-cc category, the manufacturer could not really have offered more.

Hyosung Karion RT 125

In Asian climes the Karion was immediately popular with the young. Because of the thick, low-pressure tyres and the relaxed seating position, it was easy and great fun to ride through the traffic, and it could even make some small forays on rough terrain without any problem. It was powerd by a robust single-cylinder engine of 12 bhp which enabled the Karion to reach a top speed of 101 km/h (68 mph).

Model:	Aquila GV 250
Year:	2001
Power:	28 bhp
Capacity:	249 cc
Type:	V-twin, 4-stroke

Model:	Comet GT 250
Year:	2002
Power:	28 bhp
Capacity:	249 cc
Type:	V-twin, 4-stroke

Model:	Karion RT 125
Year:	2002
Power:	12 bhp
Capacity:	125 cc
Type:	Single-cylinder, 4-stroke

Hyosung Comet GT 600

After the air-cooled 125 and 250-cc Comet versions, Hyosung presented the Comet 600 with water-cooled V-2 engine at the Milan Motorcycle Fair in the autumn of 2001. The modern 8-valve engine with 90° cylinder angle had two overhead camshafts. Unusual for this category was the fitting of ABS as standard in an ordinary 'naked bike'. Wheelbase and steering head corresponded to the smaller variants. But it was not until 2003 that the Comet 600 cc was delivered to the European Hyosung dealers.

Model:	Comet GT 600
Year:	2003
Power:	65 bhp
Capacity:	600 cc
Type:	V-twin, 4-stroke

Hyosung Comet GT 650

As a successor to the 600-cc Comet, the 650 cc version was undeniably very similar to the Suzuki SV 650. Developed and built by Hyosung, the engine was almost identical in all basic details to the Suzuki power unit. This was hardly surprising since both companies are closely linked by a comprehensive collaboration agreement. In contrast to its predecessor, the 650-cc Comet had a beautiful aluminium frame with two parallel bars. But tipping the scales at 190 kg (419 lb) dry weight, it was by no means light, and this is in spite of the fact that it did not have the standard ABS which the 600 cc could still boast.

Model:	Comet GT 650	Year:	2004	Power:	79 bhp
Capacity:	647 cc	Type:	V-twin, 4-stroke		

Hyosung Comet GT 650 R

As a sporty offshoot of the GT 650, the fully-faired R-version was designed to appeal to passionate hobby-racers. By shortening the wheelbase, the Hyosung engineers gave the bikes more agility in tight corners. The power of the 650-cc engine remained unchanged at 79 bhp. All in all it was a perfect mid-range motorbike.

Model:	Comet GT 650 R
Year:	2004
Power:	79 bhp
Capacity:	647 cc
Type:	V-twin, 4-stroke

Hyosung Comet GT 650 S

For reasonably weather-tolerant riders, Hyosung also developed a partly-faired version of the Comet 650 which included the letter S in its designation. This version also had the shorter wheelbase and stylish fairing of the R version. The S version provided a clear view of the V-2 power unit which remained unchanged at 79 bhp. Both S and R versions were fitted with a digital speedometer.

Model:	Comet GT 650 S
Year:	2004
Power:	79 bhp
Capacity:	647 cc
Type:	V-twin, 4-stroke

Hyosung Aquila GV 650

Hyosung called its cruiser range 'Aquila', inspired by astronomy, after the constellation of the Eagle. After the rather toothless Aquila models with 125 and 250-cc engines, Hyosung presented this very impressive cruiser bike at the Intermot motorbike fair in Munich. It was fitted with the 650-cc V-2 power unit used in the Comet models. This magnificent motorbike had a wheelbase of 1.7 m (5 ft 7 in).

Model:	Aquila GV 650
Year:	2005
Power:	79 bhp
Capacity:	647 cc
Type:	V-twin, 4-stroke

INDIAN – Winnetou and Old Shatterhand

The 'Hendee Manufacturing Company' was founded in 1900 by bicycle manufacturer George M. Hendee and engine designer Carl Oscar Hedström. A year later they launched the first 4-stroke-single on the market. The company's 'Indian' logo was registered as a trademark without the founders realising that the name would soon become famous in the history of the motorbike. Hendee and Hedström were extremely professional in their approach to their business and in 1906, six years after the company was founded, Hedström built a V-2 engine. By 1913 the company had developed into a major motorbike manufacturer employing over 3,000 workers. The quality, reliability and resistance to wear of Indian bikes were unequalled. The next milestones in the history of the company came in 1921 with the launch of the 600-cc Scout and the 1000-cc Chief. A year later Indian launched the Big Chief with a powerful 1200-cc engine. Whenever a big Indian made an appearance, people always believed it was a 'Big Chief'. In 1929 Indian only built one large V-model and this was the 1200-cc which had now been 'demoted' to Chief. This remained unchanged until the company closed and production ceased in August 1953.

Hedstrom motorcycle

The first 'motor bicycle' was built by the Hendee Manufacturing Company in 1901 and it was originally described as the Hedstrom motorcycle. But soon after, the company's bosses changed the name of their firm to 'Indian'. The name 'Indian' was intended to emphasise and symbolise the true American nature of the product. This motorbike capable of reaching 50km/h (31 mph) was faster than any mail coach.

Model:	Hedstrom motorcycle
Year:	1901
Power:	1.75 bhp
Capacity:	213 cc
Type:	Single-cylinder, 4-stroke

Indian Twin

As early as 1908, Indian had three single-cylinder bikes in its range with capacities of 311, 443 and 492 cc respectively. But the real sensation was the big V-2 motorbike. In spite of the relatively vast proportions of the power unit, the resemblance to a bicycle was still unmistakable. The advantage was that anyone who ran out of petrol or suffered a breakdown on the vast prairie could always pedal home.

Model:	Twin
Year:	1908
Power:	4 bhp
Capacity:	633 cc
Type:	V-twin, 4-stroke

Indian Hendee-Special 1000 Big Twin

Indian made the big leap from 'motor bicycle' to a true 'motorcycle' in 1914 when it launched the Hendee Special. This motorbike was miles ahead of those built by its competitors and in particular Harley-Davidson. In the Big Twin both front and rear wheels were sprung, there was a lighting system to ensure safety and comfort and an electric starter. The Hendee Special was available ex-works as a solo bike or with a sidecar.

Model:	Hendee-Special 1000 Big Twin
Year:	1914
Power:	7 bhp
Capacity:	998 cc
Type:	V-twin, 4-stroke

Indian Powerplus

The Indian Power Plus was the first model of a new generation of bikes which were not built under the supervision of the company founders but under that of the chief engineer Charles Gustafson. The performance of the then top model in the range was increased to a respectable 18 bhp and the pistons had a remarkable stroke of 100 mm. The bike had a three-speed gearbox and both it and the sidecar had a leaf-spring suspension.

Model:	Powerplus
Year:	1917
Power:	18 bhp
Capacity:	995 cc
Type:	2-cylinder, 4-stroke

Indian Prince

The smallest Indian model was the Prince, built between 1925 and 1928. This lightweight bike was conceived to appeal especially to the younger motorbike riders because the Prince retailed at the then very reasonable price of $185. For this price the customer could be the proud owner of a side-valve single-cylinder engine with modern trapezoid forks. The extremely long-stroke 350-cc engine was capable of propelling the bike at 80 km/h (50 mph) or more. The standard equipment was most impressive for the 1920s: electric headlights as well as rear lights, horn, ammeter and even a tool box and air pump

Model:	Prince
Year:	1925
Power:	8 bhp
Capacity:	350 cc
Type:	Single-cylinder, 4-stroke

Indian Scout 45

The Indian Scout made its debut in 1920. It was an extremely sturdy motorbike with a strong double-cradle frame which could also take a sidecar. The Scout had no rear-wheel suspension but at the front it had a reinforced leaf-sprung fork. The primary transmission was by means of a gear drive, the gear shift lever was on the right of the tank and the multi-disc wet clutch was operated by a pressing a giant foot pedal. Several engines were used over the years.

Model:	Scout 45
Year:	1929
Power:	16 bhp
Capacity:	746 cc
Type:	V-twin, 4-stroke

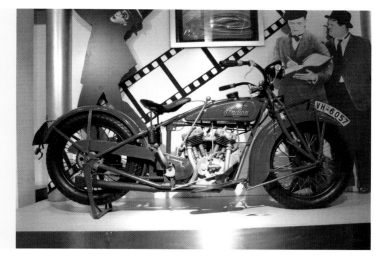

Indian 1200 Big Chief

The star in the Indian catalogue of 1935 was the 1200 Big Chief. With its new mudguards and different rear chain guard, the Big Chief had become the 'American limousine' on two wheels. Expensive paint work was a standard feature of Indian bikes, a four-speed gear-box was available on request and when used with a sidecar it was fitted with a three-speed gearbox with reverse gear. The impressive capacity of the Big Twin made it an ideal touring bike for the never-ending American highways.

Model:	1200 Big Chief
Year:	1935
Power:	40 bhp
Capacity:	1207 cc
Type:	V-twin, 4-stroke

Indian Junior Scout

With its 500-cc V-2 engine, the Junior Scout or Scout Pony was the starting bike in the Indian twin range. It was a sensational machine for its more than reasonable price of $225. At the time it was the cheapest American 2-cylinder bike around. Weighing only 150 kg (331 lb), it was extremely easy to handle and could reach a speed of well over 100 km/h (62 mph).

Indian 750 Sport Scout

Racing was also very important for Indian. The hard 'flat-track' races or the demanding sandy track of Daytona Beach where the Daytona 200 was held, provided the perfect opportunity for showing off the great qualities of the bikes. Success in competition was the best advertisement any manufacturer could wish for. Indian's greatest rival at the time was Harley-Davidson but Indian often pipped its competitor at the post.

Indian Four

The description 'car on two wheels' perfectly described the Indian Four, at least as far as the power unit was concerned. The powerful 1266-cc 4-cylinder in-line engine, capable of developing 40 bhp would have served well in a mid-range automobile. This was certainly the case with the Four which had in fact been built for this purpose. The contrast between the silky-smooth engine and its roaring power was extremely attractive. So far as handling was concerned, the Four had nothing to fear from comparison with the Big Chief. Compared to many other American 4-cylinder bikes, the Indian Four was a star, the 'king of the road'.

Model:	Junior Scout
Year:	1936
Power:	12 bhp
Capacity:	492 cc
Type:	V-twin, 4-stroke

Model:	750 Sport Scout 'Dirt Tracker'
Year:	1937
Power:	25 to 30 bhp
Capacity:	748 cc
Type:	V-twin, 4-stroke

Model:	Four
Year:	1939
Power:	40 bhp
Capacity:	1266 cc
Type:	4-cylinder, 4-stroke

Indian 1000 Sport Scout

For a long time experts believed that a rear-wheel suspension would adversely affect the roadholding qualities of a motorbike. This is why the new Sport Scout was absolutely revolutionary when it was launched in 1941. The rear wheel was fitted with direct suspension for the first time while the trapezoid forks at the front ensured a comfortable ride. Compared to the Big Chief, the Sport Scout was a good 25 kg (55 lb) lighter, which was very noticeable in its handling. The nimble 30-bhp bike could easily reach a speed of 140 km/h (87 mph).

Model:	1000 Sport Scout
Year:	1941
Power:	30 bhp
Capacity:	944 cc
Type:	V-twin, 4-stroke

Indian 1200 Civilian Chief

Even when the big V-twin Indian was officially only called the 'Chief', it was still the 'Big Chief' for motorbike fans, Indian enthusiasts and the rest of the world. And quite rightly. No other motorbike looked more impressive than the Big Chief with its extra-deep mudguards, its magnificent paintwork and its chrome decoration. In the 1940s the power of the 1200-cc V-twin engine was increased to 42 bhp. The photograph shows the 'civilian' version which, with the exception of the mighty mudguards, looked quite Spartan.

Model:	1200 Civilian Chief
Year:	1942
Power:	40 bhp
Capacity:	1207cc
Type:	V-twin, 4-stroke

Indian 1200 Chief

The Chief with its windscreen, auxiliary lights and inviting fringed seat was definitely a picture-book 'full dresser'. But it was also very heavy. Unfortunately the technical side had been obsolete for a long time and Indian had no plans to change its approach. The end of the marque which had once been so famous was already on the horizon.

Model:	1200 Chief
Year:	1946
Power:	40 bhp
Capacity:	1207 cc
Type:	V-twin, 4-stroke

Indian Chief combination

In post-war America, cars had been more popular than motorbikes for many years and Indian was fighting to survive. Bikers who wanted to see a bit of the world but to do so in comfort and with space for some luggage could order the Chief with a sidecar. The mighty 322-kg (710-lb) motorcycle combination had a hand-operated three-speed gearbox with reverse gear.

Model:	1200 Chief combination
Year:	1946
Power:	40 bhp
Capacity:	1207 cc
Type:	V-twin, 4-stroke

Indian 101 Scout

Years after the company closed its doors, attempts continued to be made to revive the Indian. This was actually achieved in 2000. The newly founded 'Indian Motorcycle Company', based in Gilroy, California, started the production of the 101 Scout and a little later it brought out the Chief. As before, the 101 Scout was the sport bike in the range. The engine was supplied by S&S while the other parts came from reputable suppliers or were made by the Indian Motorcycle Company itself.

Model:	101 Scout
Year:	2001
Power:	75 bhp
Capacity:	1442 cc
Type:	V-twin, 4-stroke

Indian Chief Deluxe

For the new Indian Motorcycle Company in Gilroy this model was an enormous technical and financial challenge. The results could be seen in the summer of 2003 when fans could once again admire the new Chief, standing proudly on its 16-inch wheels. Here again was the dream of an American motorbike, unmistakably an Indian. But this future was not to be; a few months later Indian went bankrupt again.

Model:	Chief Deluxe
Year:	2003
Power:	85 bhp
Capacity:	1638 cc
Type:	V-twin, 4-stroke

Jawa – The art of Czech engineering

This company has played a major part in the history of the motorcycle and is also the subject of numerous unlikely stories and anecdotes. One of the strangest is that of the order received from the Vatican in 1939 for two motorbikes in white with 14-carat gold fittings. The first motorbike presented by the company was a 500-cc Wanderer built under licence, a collaboration to which the company also owes its name. The first two letters of the JAnecek company and the name WAnderer soon became synonymous with innovative technology. Reflecting the then-current trend for small bikes, the company launched the 175-cc in 1932, a model which was to be the economic foundation stone of the company. Ten years after Jawa was founded, the plant came to a standstill for a time with the occupation of Czechoslovakia, which naturally also affected Jawa. The Jawa engineers continued to work in secret and under the control of the Wehrmacht so that in 1946 they were able to launch a 250-cc motorbike. This was called the 'Perak', meaning 'Jumper' in English, because of its heavy-duty suspension. In the same year Jawa won the Gold Medal with this model at the Paris Motor Salon. Its victories in competitions made Jawa famous throughout the world: it won the World Trophy 15 times, the Silver Vase in International Six Day Motorcycling races 11 times and the European Championship title 25 times, as well as numerous Grand Prix victories and many more national and international titles. In the 1950s Jawa and CZ joined forces but this was a union which only lasted until 1961. After the political changes in Eastern Europe, Jawa was unable to hold its position on the market and the buildings and stock were bought by five private individuals. The future of this great maker now lies both in speedway racing and in the new road bikes with modern Rotax power units.

Jawa Villiers

'A better bike for less money' was the Jawa slogan for the 175 cc Villiers. The bike had an English Villiers engine and sold for 30% less than comparable bikes made by the competition.

Model:	Villiers
Year:	1932 to 1946
Power:	5.5 bhp
Capacity:	172,6 cc
Type:	Single-cylinder, 2-stroke

Jawa Duplex BLOC

Shortly before the start of the Second World War Jawa developed a new type of bike. With a 2-stroke engine, it was the first to have gearbox, primary transmission and twin chain drive integrated into the engine block.

Model:	Duplex BLOC
Year:	1939
Power:	9 bhp
Capacity:	250 cc
Type:	Single-cylinder, 2-stroke

Jawa Perak

The history of the Perak is legendary. Its name, meaning 'Jumper', referred to the hard rear wheel suspension. It satisfied the requirements of discriminating customers.

Model:	250 „Perak'
Year:	1946 to 1953
Power:	9 bhp
Capacity:	249 cc
Type:	Single-cylinder, 2-stroke

Jawa 500 OHC

First presented in Paris, the Jawa 500 OHC went into production two years later and was one of the legendary bikes to come from Czechoslovakia. It had an air-cooled 2-cylinder 4-stroke engine with parallel pistons. The overhead camshaft, driven by a vertical drive shaft, was capable of developing 26 bhp. Until 1953 this was achieved by means of a worm-gear drive but the next model (from 1953) was revised because of thermal problems with the whole cylinder head. The model was never exported, although it was the only mass-produced 2-cylinder OHC in the 500-cc category.

Model:	500 OHC	Year:	1954 to 1958	Power:	26–28 bhp
Capacity:	488 cc	Type:	2-cylinder, 4-stroke		

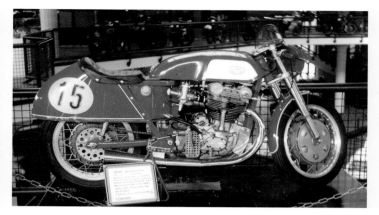

Jawa racing bike

With its brilliant racing bikes Jawa was very successful on international race tracks, winning many important victories. This works racing-bike with 2-cylinder dohc engine was able to display its great qualities with riders such Havel, Stasny and Steiner.

Model:	500 dohc
Year:	1954
Power:	55 bhp
Capacity:	499 cc
Type:	2-cylinder, 4-stroke

Jawa Californian 350

Jawa built other models for export, based on the 250 and 350-cc engines with front and rear telescopic forks. The 350, derived from the 360 model, had 19-inch wheels and a rapid twist grip. Besides supplying this model to police forces in Mexico, Finland and Yugoslavia, Jawa produced a model with protected frame, direction indicators and the words 'Road King' for the Canadian and US markets. These models were produced in two versions for the American market: a standard version and a lighter version without side cases, with Bosch headlights and a new fuel tank.

Model:	Californian 350
Year:	1967 to 2000
Power:	23 bhp
Capacity:	343 cc
Type:	2-cylinder, 2-stroke

Jawa 640 Classic

75 years after the founding of the company and 57 years after the launch of the legendary ohc twins, Jawa launched two new models to capture the market. With a traditional steel frame with two shock-absorbers at the back and telescopic forks at the front, chrome spoked wheels and black paint covering all metal parts, it had all the features of a classic bike. Yet its appearance was rather reminiscent of the Japanese soft choppers. It was powered by single-cylinder Rotax engine.

Model:	640 Classic
Year:	2001
Power:	24 bhp
Capacity:	343 cc
Type:	Single-cylinder, 4-stroke

Jawa 650 Bizon

Pictures of the Bizon prototype revealed a conventional steel frame and water-cooled Rotax 4-stroke engine. The front wheel was controlled by sprung forks while the rear wheel sat in a steel swing-arm supported by two suspension struts. The design was unusual, somewhere between a soft chopper and a dragster.

Model:	650 Bizon
Year:	2005
Power:	46 bhp
Capacity:	652 cc
Type:	Single-cylinder, 4-stroke

Kawasaki – The 'power-factory'

Kawasaki is the youngest of the four Japanese motorcycle makers. But 'Kawasaki Heavy Industries Ltd' is undoubtedly a gigantic manufacturing company of world-wide reputation. The products it manufactures range from tracked vehicles, ocean-going freighters, oil-drilling platforms, aeroplanes, helicopters, satellites, construction machinery, power stations and industrial robots, and of course motorbikes. It was in 1878 in a shipyard in Tsukiji near Tokyo that Shozo Kawasaki laid the foundation of his future industrial empire. The company expanded with breathtaking speed and soon Kawasaki was successfully involved in all three spheres: land, sea and air. In the Second World War the industrial giant was the largest supplier of armaments in Japan. Many of Kawasaki's factories were destroyed during the war and afterwards with the surrender of Japan the company was forbidden to build any kind of aircraft. To ensure that its plants worked at full capacity, the factories which had escaped destruction were converted by highly-qualified aeronautical engineers to the manufacture of ranges of gearboxes for mopeds and motorcycles. Kawasaki, always interested in big things, also wanted to set standards in the field of motorbike manufacture. It wanted to build something superlative, unique and extravagant. This meant a bike which was faster and more powerful than those of the competition, and it is this concept which still guides Kawasaki today. The Kawasaki bosses proudly presented their top model the W1 in October 1965. But Western experts could hardly suppress an amused smile. The similarity to the long-outdated BSA A7 was only too obvious. The bike was a flop. In the same year Kawasaki launched the A1 Samurai. The Samurai, and later the 350-cc A7 Avenger and then the 500-cc H1 'Mach III' were fantastic sports bikes which enabled anyone to have a really good time riding them. This time Kawasaki had succeeded. Neither Honda, Suzuki nor Yamaha could aspire to project such a sporty and aggressive image. At the beginning of the 1970s the development of a 4-cylinder 4-stroke high-speed motorbike took place and in 1972 it became famous under the name of 'Z1'. In 2005 the 175 bhp ZX-10R showed what it was capable of and those who were confident enough could ride this amazing speed-machine at 300 km/h (186 mph). Today there is still no end in sight for this 'gigantomania'. It is still a matter of 'faster, larger, better'.

Kawasaki 650 W1

The first big Kawasaki was not really a Kawasaki at all. In the late 1950s the company had acquired shares in Meguro whose top model was the 500-cc K1. But Meguro had not developed the K1 itself. The bike was in fact a reproduction of the English BSA A7. This 'thunderbolt' had been somewhat dolled up visually but technically it had not been updated. The company bosses hoped this 'character-bike' would give the firm its big break, but in this they were disappointed.

Model:	650 W1
Year:	1966
Power:	47 bhp
Capacity:	624 cc
Type:	2-cylinder, 4-stroke

Kawasaki 650 W2

At first glance the Kawasaki W1 and W2 appear absolutely identical. But those who have a technical eye will immediately recognise that the W1 has one carburettor and the W2 two. At first the more powerful 650-cc W2 could develop 50 bhp but later the engine was modified so that the power output was increased to 53 bhp. The W-range remained more or less unknown in Europe.

Model:	650 W2
Year:	1966
Power:	53 bhp
Capacity:	624 cc
Type:	2-cylinder, 4-stroke

Kawasaki 250 A1 Samurai

In the middle of the 1966 season the maker presented the 2-stroke A1 Samurai rocket. It was a sports bike which was originally intended for export. The Samurai scored a bull's eye. The nimble bike with rotary valves was exactly the opposite of the ponderous W1 and W2 series.

Model:	250 A1 Samurai
Year:	1966
Power:	31 bhp
Capacity:	247 cc
Type:	2-cylinder, 2-stroke

Kawasaki 500 H1 'Mach III'

In 1968, at a time when hardly an expert was left who believed in 2-stroke bikes, Kawasaki launched an incredible machine on the market. This was the 500 H1 'Mach III' with a 3-cylinder 2-stroke engine able to develop 60 bhp and a maximum speed of 200 km/h (124 mph). Anyone riding a 'Mach III' was definitely the fastest on the block, and this was exactly what the rider experienced: the 500-cc Kawa went like greased lightning, although the chassis could be a little worrying at times. Malicious gossip had it that the 'Mach III' wobbled even when standing. But that was exactly what the bike's fans enjoyed. The general consensus was that the Mach III was not for 'weaklings' or 'cowards'.

Model:	500 H1 'Mach III'
Year:	1968
Power:	60 bhp
Capacity:	498 cc
Type:	3-cylinder, 2-stroke

Kawasaki 750 H2 'Mach IV'

The Kawasaki 'Mach III' was acclaimed as the 'rodeo bike'. Only a Mach IV could possibly be an improvement and at the same time the culmination of the 3-cylinder 2-stroke range. In 1971 Kawasaki launched the 750 H2 with a power of 71 bhp and a speed of over 210 km/h (130 mph) on the market. Anyone riding a Mach IV was the undisputed 'king of the road' because there was simply nothing faster around.

Model:	750 H2
	'Mach IV'
Year:	1973
Power:	71 bhp
Capacity:	748 cc
Type:	3-cylinder, 2-stroke

Kawasaki 900 Z1 'Super Four'

There was a 'gentlemen's agreement' among Japanese motorbike manufacturers not to build any bikes with a capacity of more than 750 cc. In spite of this agreement, in autumn 1972 Kawasaki presented the 900 Z1 'Super Four' at the IFMA motorbike show in Cologne. The industry was flabbergasted, motorbike fans rubbed their eyes and the competition was lost for words. But it was no illusion. With the 900-cc 4-cylinder big bike, Kawasaki opened a new chapter in motorbike history. When the first Z1s were eventually delivered at the start of 1973, great stories about the Big Bike spread like wild fire. In conversations among enthusiasts and also in various test reports, it was said that it was a motorbike with 'pure power', or that 'it is only good on a straight road, but when it comes to cornering…'. The Z1 legend was born.

Model:	900 Z1
Year:	1973
Power:	79 bhp
Capacity:	903 cc
Type:	4-cylinder, 4-stroke

Kawasaki KZ 900 LTD

In 1976 Kawasaki developed the Z 900 LTD especially for the US market (LTD indicates 'limited edition') and indeed only 2,000 were produced. It was recognised worldwide as the first mass-produced 'soft chopper' made in Japan. Among its distinctive features were the high handlebars, teardrop-shaped fuel tank, stepped seat, 16-inch rear wheel and short silencer. Only a few of these bikes were imported into Europe.

Model:	KZ 900 LTD
Year:	1976
Power:	81 bhp
Capacity:	903 cc
Type:	4-cylinder, 4-stroke

Kawasaki Z 1000

In 1977 Kawasaki went even further. The engine capacity of 900 cc was increased to 1 litre. This 'big bike' was now called the Z 1000. At a first glance only the new 4-into-2 exhaust system and disc brakes on the rear wheel of the new big bike seemed to differ from the previous model. But other changes had been made. It now developed 85 bhp and the quality of the frame was visibly better. Overall it was a very impressive bike.

Model:	Z 1000
Year:	1977
Power:	85 bhp
Capacity:	1016 cc
Type:	4-cylinder, 4-stroke

Kawasaki Z1-R

Kawasaki clearly defined the concept of supersport bike when it launched the Z 900 'Z1' in 1972. No one at the time thought of a fairing. But five years later the world saw things very differently. The new Kawasaki Z1-R was available from dealers, and the readers of at least one specialist motorbike magazine chose it as the 'Motorcycle of the Year'. The new, angular design was enormously popular. With half-fairing, 4-into-1 exhaust system, modern cast wheels and a top speed of 200 km/h (124 mph), it was the quintessential sports bike.

Model:	Z1-R
Year:	1977
Power:	90 bhp
Capacity:	1016 cc
Type:	4-cylinder, 4-stroke

Kawasaki Z 650 LTD

The Kawasaki Z 650 LTD was conceived as a special sports series. The LTD did not stand as it often did for a soft chopper model but for 'limited edition'. With upper fairing, sporty handlebars and sports seat, the LTD was the basic model for the Kawasaki Makers Cup which was held only in 1978.

Model:	Z 650 LTD
Year:	1978
Power:	66 bhp
Capacity:	652 cc
Type:	4-cylinder, 4-stroke

Kawasaki Z 550 LTD

In the 1980s, Japanese soft choppers were all the rage and there was a wide range of engine capacities. Kawasaki presented the Z 550 LTD at IFMA in 1980. A low seat and fun handling made this medium-sized soft chopper the ideal beginner's bike. The stepped seat and high handlebars also conveyed an Easy Rider feeling.

Model:	Z 550 LTD
Year:	1980
Power:	50 bhp
Capacity:	554 cc
Type:	4-cylinder, 4-stroke

Kawasaki Z 750

The Z 900 'Z1' launched in 1972 was not only a milestone in the history of the company but the 4-cylinder concept was used for many years in a wide range of models, ranging from 400 cc to 1100 cc. In 1980 Kawasaki brought out the Z 750 for the popular 750 class. This nimble 4-cylinder bike could develop 77 bhp and had a top speed of 200 km/h (124 mph).

Model:	Z 750
Year:	1981
Power:	77 bhp
Capacity:	739 cc
Type:	4-cylinder, 4-stroke

Kawasaki Z 1000 LTD

While the Z 1000 had been considered the quintessential big bike since 1977, Kawasaki had no problem in transforming the 1000-cc machine into a soft chopper with only a few modifications. The recipe was simple: long front forks, high handlebars, teardrop-shaped 15-litre (3.3-gallon) fuel tank, stepped seat, 16-inch rear wheel, short chopper foot pegs and many chrome parts. One could never be bored with this bike, riding in the wind at 210 km/h (130 mph).

Model:	Z 1000 LTD
Year:	1981
Power:	95 bhp
Capacity:	999 cc
Type:	4-cylinder, 4-stroke

Kawasaki GT 750

Shaft-driven bikes are ideal for long-distance touring. No tiresome lubrication or tightening of the chain. As early as 1978 Kawasaki had fitted the Z 1000 ST and Z 1300 with a low-maintainenance cardan shaft drive. In 1982 it brought out the medium-sized GT 750 with shaft drive. The engine was mounted on rubber to improve the rider's comfort by eliminating irritating vibrations.

Model:	GT 750
Year:	1982
Power:	78 bhp
Capacity:	739 cc
Type:	4-cylinder, 4-stroke

Kawasaki GPZ 750

At the beginning of the 1980s there were bikes to satisfy every taste. There were enduros, tourers, sports bikes, supersport bikes and choppers in a whole range of capacities. In 1981 Kawasaki brought out the GPZ 750. Half-fairings and cast wheels were a must in sports bikes at the time. With its 2-valve engine completely painted black, it developed 80 bhp and had a top speed of at least 210 km/h (130 mph).

Model:	GPZ 750
Year:	1982
Power:	80 bhp
Capacity:	739 cc
Type:	4-cylinder, 4-stroke

Kawasaki GPZ 1100

Launched in the early 1980s, the GPZ 1100 was very much ahead of its time. Indeed, the Kawa engineers had fitted a fuel injection system to this 100-bhp bike. This modern technique was a complete innovation in the construction of motorbikes. The pitch-black engine, black exhaust system and small cockpit fairing were the epitome of sportiness at the time.

Model:	GPZ 1100
Year:	1982
Power:	100 bhp
Capacity:	1090 cc
Type:	4-cylinder, 4-stroke

Kawasaki GPZ 305

Those who thought Kawasaki only built large sports bikes soon had to change their mind after the launch of the GPZ 305. The 34-bhp 4-stroke twin spun at 10,000 rpm, and with additional tuning this small sports bike was capable of reaching a top speed of 260 km/h (162 mph). The cockpit fairing was a standard feature in Kawa sports bikes.

Model:	GPZ 305
Year:	1983
Power:	34 bhp
Capacity:	306 cc
Type:	2-cylinder, 4-stroke

Kawasaki Z 750 Turbo

The saying 'there is no subsitute for engine capacity and power' is well-known among bike experts. But what can be done when a 750-cc bike has to develop 100 bhp? The answer is to use a turbocharger. The basis of this turbo engine was the famous 4-cylinder engine which in turn was based on the Z-900-'Z1' power unit. The resulting 112 bhp caused a sensation.

Model:	Z 750 Turbo
Year:	1983
Power:	112 bhp
Capacity:	739 cc
Type:	4-cylinder, 4-stroke

Kawasaki GPZ 550

In the mid-1980s, the Kawasaki GPZ 550 was the kingpin in the medium-sized category. But this stunningly beautiful bike with elegant top fairing and amusingly-designed tank with side panels had more tricks up its sleeve. In spite of its weight of 200 kg (441 lb), it could make life very difficult on narrow winding roads for expert bikers on their powerful big bikes.

Model:	GPZ 550
Year:	1984
Power:	65 bhp
Capacity:	554 cc
Type:	4-cylinder, 4-stroke

Kawasaki Z 1300

When Kawasaki presented the Z 1300 at IFMA in 1978, the world was stunned. This was hardly surprising. The Japanese maker had once again confirmed its reputation of being 'stronger and faster than anyone'. The 320-kg (705-lb) motorbike with water-cooled 6-cylinder engine was capable of developing 120 bhp. This was much more than Honda with its 105 bhp. But the excitement roused by this powerful bike did not last long because it soon became the subject of a debate about the sense of such high-performance bikes.

Model:	Z 1300
Year:	1983
Power:	100 bhp
Capacity:	1286 cc
Type:	6-cylinder, 4-stroke

Kawasaki ZX-10R

In contrast to all other Kawasaki models the development of the Ninja ZX-10R began with chassis experiments. The Kawasaki engineers wanted to create an extremely light and compact chassis. This was achieved by reducing the wheelbase and lengthening the swing-arm which made the ZX extraordinarily nimble and easy to handle. The concave fuel tank surface and well-balanced ergonomic triangle of foot-rest, handlebars and seat contributed to the compact sitting position. Radial brake callipers at the front, wave brake discs and completely adjustable suspension elements clearly reflected Kawasaki's aim to create a bike with racing performance. With its ultra-powerful 4-cylinder in-line engine it was a bike which at the time was unbeatable on the race tracks.

Model:	ZX-10R
Year:	2004
Power:	175 bhp
Capacity:	998 cc
Type:	4-cylinder in-line 4-stroke

Kawasaki VN 1600

If the 'coolness' factor of a cruiser is based on its height and length, then the 'long and low' VN 1600 was as cool as any bike could ever be. A new frame with longer wheelbase and lower seat was combined with a long-stroke version of the VN 1500 engine. At last, Kawasaki's attempts to be seen as more than a manufacturer of supersport bikes were successful with this model.

Model:	VN 1600 Classic
Year:	2003
Power:	67 bhp
Capacity:	1552 cc
Type:	V-twin, 4-stroke

Kawasaki VN 2000

The flagship in the Kawasaki cruiser fleet moved the goal posts: the capacity was an incredible 2053 cc, which made the VN 2000 the most powerful mass-produced V-twin in the history of the motorbike. The enormous size of the 2-cylinder engine and its impressive performance matched the smart design which combined fashionable and traditional elements to form a streamlined, homogenous whole. The main and most striking feature in the design of the VN 2000 was the streamlined headlight housing with a 'projector-light'.

Model:	VN 2000
Year:	2004
Power:	103 bhp
Capacity:	2053 cc
Type:	V-twin, 4-stroke

Kawasaki KLE 500

Already present in the Kawasaki catalogue in the early 1990s, the KLE was comprehensively revamped for the 2005 season. The new half-fairing with the headlight and windshield of the Z1000 gave the KLE a more aggressive look. This more up-to-date appearance was in perfect keeping with the current Kawasaki sports models. Two catalytic converters, both incorporated in the manifold, and another one in the exhaust pipe, ensured that the exhaust emissions were within the limits imposed by the Euro-II specifications.

Model:	KLE 500
Year:	2005
Power:	48 bhp
Capacity:	498 cc
Type:	2-cylinder in-line, 4-stroke

Kawasaki VN 1600 Classic Tourer

With this model Kawasaki updated the Classic Tourer version of the VN range, albeit a year later than planned. It too now had the bigger 1600-cc V-2 engine and optimised chassis with reinforced frame. This classic tourer included a luggage compartment, windshield and seat back rest for the pillion passenger as standard equipment.

Model:	VN 1600 Classic Tourer
Year:	2005
Power:	67 bhp
Capacity:	1552 cc
Type:	V-twin, 4-stroke

Kawasaki Z 750

After the resounding success of the brilliant Z 1000 naked bike, Kawasaki launched a 750-cc version in 2004. Although the 750 retained many of the aggressive styling features of the Z 1000, it missed out on a few treats such as the wonderful 4-into-2-into-4 exhaust system of its larger sibling. In 2005 Kawasaki brought out the S-version with half-fairing, illustrated here.

Model:	Z 750 S
Year:	2005
Power:	110 bhp
Capacity:	748 cc
Type:	4-cylinder in-line, 4-stroke

Kawasaki ZX-6R

Kawasaki had made no compromises when developing the Ninja ZX-6R, which was presented in 2003: absolute racing performance was the aim of the Kawasaki engineers and the bike's performance data were sensational. But only two years later it underwent a comprehensive revamp. The engine was given new cylinder heads, new cylinders and oval throttle valves as well as two injection valves per cylinder for greater induction efficiency. A cylinder incorporated in the silencer optimised the bike's performance at lower and medium rpm. It was capable of developing 130 bhp.

Model:	Ninja ZX-6R
Year:	2005
Power:	130 bhp
Capacity:	636 cc
Type:	4-cylinder in-line, 4-stroke

Kreidler – Popular thimble-engined motorbikes

The range of models marketed by this tradition-conscious manufacturer consisted of mopeds and light motorcycles. This company, which once specialised in the manufacture of steel wire and semi-finished parts, made its successful debut in the world of motorbike manufacture in 1950 with small motorcycles. These basic but sturdy mopeds and scooters were very popular and Kreidler, based near Stuttgart, became famous with the 'Florett'. The mass-production of this small motorcycle began in the spring of 1957. A Kreidler was always a little faster than comparable bikes, it had larger brakes, a robust chassis and was considered practically indestructible. These tiny Grand Prix bikes with a top speed of 200 km/h (124 mph) were unbeatable on international racing tracks. But fashionable features such as water-cooling and partial fairing helped Kreidler's competitors in Germany to remove it from it position of advantage. In January 1981 Kreidler was finally forced to declare itself bankrupt.

Kreidler R 50

Besides the K and J moped models, Kreidler also made the R 50 motor scooter in the mid-1950s. The small 50-cc 2-speed engine was fitted with forced air cooling. It was with such a bike that in 1954–55 the Munich journalist, Günter Markert, undertook a 17-month-long trip round the world. On this small reliable bike, he covered 50,000 km (31,000 miles), crossed four continents and 33 countries. The top speed of this reliable R 50 was 50 km/h (31 mph).

Model:	R 50	Year:	1954	Power:	2.2 bhp
Capacity:	48 cc	Type:	Single-cylinder, 2-stroke		

Kreidler Florett Straßenrennmaschine (road racer)

After Kreidler had presented its modern 50-cc Florett bike in the autumn of 1956, in 1959 it launched the first official road racer with the new horizontal cylinder engine. Riders such as Rudolf Kunz and Hans Georg Anscheidt won various victories in Motocup events with this little 6 bhp road racer. The handlebars were placed well below the fuel tank so as to reduce air resistance and thus reach higher speeds.

Model:	Florett Straßenrennmaschine (road racer)
Year:	1959
Power:	6 bhp
Capacity:	49 cc
Type:	Single-cylinder, 2-stroke

Kreidler GP racing bike

In 1963 Kreidler developed a completely new chassis for the GP-racing bike. The chassis components and brakes were made of light magnesium. The powerful 2-stroke engine had an inlet port through two rotary disc valves and was fed by two carburettors. In 1963 Hans Georg Anscheid was runner-up in the World Championship.

Model:	Grand Prix
Year:	1963
Power:	14 bhp
Capacity:	49 cc
Type:	Single-cylinder, 2-stroke

Kreidler Florett Super

In the mid-1960s the Florett Super replaced the sporty luxury model in the Kreidler catalogue. With its 5.2 bhp, forced air-cooled engine, this small bike achieved a top speed of 80 km/h (50 mph).

Model:	Florett
Year:	1965
Power:	5.2 bhp
Capacity:	49 cc
Type:	Single-cylinder, 2-stroke

Kreidler MEO 1 'Zigarre'

It was on the 'Zigarre' or 'Cigar' that Rudolf Kunz set the world speed record for 50-cc vehicles on the Great Salt Lake in Utah. Kunz reached a top speed of 210 km/h (130 mph) in his record-breaking vehicle. The engine was powered by four-stage supercharger and cooled with ice cubes.

Model:	MEO 1
Year:	1965
Power:	15 bhp
Capacity:	49 cc
Type:	Single-cylinder, 2-stroke

Kreidler record-breaking bike

After its success with the 'Zigarre', Kreidler tried again to break a few records. In 1965 this bike was built to set long-distance records on the Contidrom in Hanover. Like the MEO 1, this record-breaking bike was powered by a nine-gear supercharged engine.

Model:	Record-breaking bike
Year:	1965
Power:	15 bhp
Capacity:	49 cc
Type:	Single-cylinder, 2-stroke

Kreidler Florett RM

Besides its 90-km/h (56-mph) light motorcycles, Kreidler also made small-capacity bikes which could only do 40 km/h (25 mph). Externally these two only differed in minor details such as smaller drum brakes and painted front wheel mudguard. In this way these small-capacity bikes benefited from the reputation of the Kreidler light motorbikes.

Model:	Florett RM
Year:	1973
Power:	2.9 bhp
Capacity:	49 cc
Type:	Single-cylinder, 2-stroke

Kreidler Florett RMC

The last Kreidler models had composite wheels and sports seat with small tail. But the 50-cc motorbike from Swabia was unable to survive the competition of the cheap Japanese bikes.

Model:	Florett RMC
Year:	1979
Power:	2.9 bhp
Capacity:	49 cc
Type:	Single-cylinder, 2-stroke

KTM – Austrian motorcycle history

It all started in 1934 with an ordinary locksmith's workshop, set up by Horst Trunkenpolz, which developed into the largest repair workshop for cars and motorbikes in Austria. The first road bike developed by KTM (Kraftfahrzeuge Trunkenpolz, Mattighofen), fitted with an R 100 Rotax engine, left the workshop in 1953 and a year later the company launched the 125-cc Tourist model. A mere two years later it celebrated the production of the 1,000th motorbike displaying the KTM logo on the fuel tank. The logo was followed by the new name of the company, 'Kronreif & Trunkenpolz, Mattighofen, the Salzburg businessman Ernest Kronreif having joined the company as a partner in 1955. In the mid-1950s KTM also developed its own engines. KTM became the leading manufacturer of off-road bikes in Europe thanks to the American motorbike dealer and enduro rider John Penton who commissioned light enduro bikes, designed to his requirements, from the Mattighofen factory. The countless successes in scrambling further reinforced the 'Made in Austria' quality. In 1980 Ernst Trunkenpolz bought Kronreif's shares back and KTM became a family-owned business again. But nine years later he was forced to sell the majority shareholding to GIT Trust Holding which obliged KTM Motorfahrzeug AG to go into liquidation. This led to the company being divided into four independent successor companies. One of these was KTM Sportmotorcycle GmbH which made a stylish debut at the beginning of the new millennium.

KTM R 100

A motorbike of its time: robust and straightforward, the first KTM bike was presented at the Vienna Spring Fair in 1953, after only a two-year period of development. A sprung seat replaced the rear-wheel suspension while the undamped telescopic front forks absorbed the biggest bumps. Its aluminium full hub with stub axles clearly distinguished it from its rivals.

Model:	R 100
Year:	1953 to 1955
Power:	3 bhp
Capacity:	98 cc
Type:	Rotax single-cylinder, 2-stroke

KTM 250 MX PL

The successor of the 250 MC weighed less than 200 kg (441 lb) on the scales. The centrally-mounted swing arm of the moto-cross bike for the first time consisted of the 'Pro-Lever' system; the single telescopic arm contributing to longer spring travel as well as better progression. The water-cooled 2-stroke engine had reed valves, while duplex drum brakes at the front and back looked after deceleration. The fact that this bike was used in the Moto-Cross World Championship by the Austrian Heinz Kinigadner (1984 and 1985), was the best advertising for the model.

Model:	250 MX PL
Year:	1983
Power:	n.a.
Capacity:	245 cc
Type:	Single-cylinder, 2-stroke

KTM LC 4 620 Adventure

'Adventure was the name of KTM's first 'travel bike'. In appearance it was very reminiscent of the Paris-Dakar rally bikes, but it was in fact completely suitable for everyday use. It was powered by a liquid-cooled 4-stroke engine which the Austrian make had used in enduro sport bikes since 1987 after a five-year period of development. The rear end of the chrome-molybdenum frame was reinforced so that sufficient luggage could be carried for a long journey. The exhaust system lying under the rear cowling clearly reflected the purpose of this bike.

Model: LC 4 620 Adventure
Year: 1997
Power: 50 bhp
Capacity: 609 cc
Type: Single-cylinder, 4-stroke

KTM Duke II

Having already benefited from the supermoto boom with its first Duke version, KTM brought out a completely new, radical successor in readiness for the 1999 season. With an increase of 7 bhp which raised its power to 57 bhp, the new 640-cc single-cylinder was perfectly prepared for snappy performance on winding roads. Thanks to first quality additions such as the BBS-light cast alloy wheels and aluminium swing-arm, the Duke only weighed 145 kg (320 lb) unladen. The combination of high-performance transmission, lightweight construction and first-quality chassis components made the Duke II one of the fastest bikes round corners.

Model: Duke 640
Year: 1999
Power: 57 bhp
Capacity: 625 cc
Type: Single-cylinder, 4-stroke

KTM SX 520

In 2000 KTM launched a new generation of moto-cross bikes which set the standard and are still doing so today. It was the first time that a bike combined the handling of a 250-cc with the superior performance of a large 4-stroke engine. As a result, the SX 4-stroke models proved to be unbeatable in numerous championships. But KTM continued to produce its 2-stroke moto-cross bikes, which have remained leaders in their category because of continuous further development.

Model: SX 520
Year: 2001
Power: 59 bhp
Capacity: 510 cc
Type: Single-cylinder, 4-stroke

KTM 640 Adventure

KTM naturally made use of its bike's victory in the Dakar Rally to develop a mass-produced model derived from it. Thanks to its enormous 30-litre (6.6-gallon)tank, rally fairing and optional long-distance travel accessories, the 'Adventure' version of the LC 4 was a perfect bike for travelling round the world. For hardened bikers KTM also produced a rally version with 84 bhp and a complete hard-core desert-kit.

Model: LC 4 640 Adventure
Year: 2001
Power: 50 bhp
Capacity: 625 cc
Type: Single-cylinder, 4-stroke

KTM LC4 640 Supermoto

KTM used the successful LC4 range with great skill to create a large model family. Besides enduro and rally versions, KTM also offered a 'classic' supermoto version in addition to the Duke. Although continually evolving, the LC4 range is easily recognised by its elegant mechanical features.

Model:	LC4 640 E Supermoto
Year:	2001
Power:	49 bhp
Capacity:	625 cc
Type:	Single-cylinder, 4-stroke

KTM 950 Adventure

227 kilograms (500 pounds) of adventure. 98 bhp. 210 kilometres (130 miles) of landscape in an hour. In theory. KTM's first model in the new 2-cylinder generation reached a new level of riding dynamics in the off-road motorcycle. But who races every day over hedges and ditches to record their best time? Cross-country drives are no problem with the Adventure. The rather light weight of the bike is not noticeable, whether on gravel, stones or grass. The Adventure rider need have no fear that the fork might break or the frame fall to pieces. The KTM is sturdy, very sturdy. But it is also very light, and it was this combination which was exciting. It took only 3.2 seconds for the Adventure to reach 100 km/h (62 mph)! Such figures would make many a rider break into a sweat.

Model:	950 Adventure
Year:	2003
Power:	98 bhp
Capacity:	942 cc
Type:	V-twin, 4-stroke

KTM 125 EXC

It would be impossible to list all the national and international championship titles won by the 2-stroke KTM moto-cross and enduro bikes. And KTM continues to develop its range. The 125-cc EXC version of the 2005 model range had a new frame, revised suspension elements and a new design as well as a slightly modified engine. All in all it was hotter than ever. The small 2-stroke impressed with its super-snappy transmission and excellent reworking. The 125 EXC will 'fly' over the bumpiest tracks without any part feeling as if it is not strong enough to handle it.

Model:	125 EXC
Year:	2004
Power:	35 bhp
Capacity:	125 cc
Type:	Single-cylinder, 2-stroke

KTM 950 Supermoto

As it had done with the LC4 single-cylinder bike, KTM also brought out a supermoto version of the 2-cylinder enduro. And what a bike: the ultra-streamlined 'Power-drifter' with the 98-bhp V-twin engine of the Adventure was very, very fast.

Model:	950 Supermoto
Year:	2005
Power:	98 bhp
Capacity:	942 cc
Type:	V-twin, 4-stroke

KTM 990 Superduke

KTM took its involvement in the field of road racing very seriously, and this was not only reflected in its participation in the 125-cc GP Sport category. The first serious road bike developed by KTM was the Superduke, a strikingly designed streetfighter. The V-twin power unit used in the long-legged 950-cc range had its capacity increased to 1 litre and was now capable of developing 120 bhp under any circumstances.

Model:	990 Superduke
Year:	2005
Power:	120 bhp
Capacity:	999 cc
Type:	V-twin, 4-stroke

KTM RC 8

'The ultimate weapon for the ambitious street-fighter' will be presented by KTM in 2007 at the latest. The concept of the RC 8 displays a radical concentration of masses round the compact 75° V-2 engine. This is a philosophy which Erik Buell has applied for years when developing the stunning handling qualities of his V-twin monsters. The KTM racer will also include innovative details, such as the seat doubling up as a petrol tank so that the fuel is situated at the bike's centre of gravity. Because of the dry sump lubrication, it was possible to place the entire exhaust system where it influences the bike's dynamics least: directly underneath the engine.

Model:	990 RC 8
Series production:	2007
Power:	over 120 bhp
Capacity:	999 cc
Type:	V-twin, 4-stroke

Laverda – From agricultural machinery to motorbikes

Pietro Laverda founded the company in 1870 in Breganze. After the Second World War the company was taken over by his descendants. As it happens the young engineer Francesco Laverda firmly believed that the future lay in two-wheeled vehicles and in 1949 he founded the Moto Laverda company which was to concentrate on the mass-mechanisation of post-war Italy. He also achieved remarkable results in the world of sport. But at the end of the 1950s he was forced to adapt to the new economic situation. Small, reasonably-priced bikes still sold well in 1961, but there was insufficient demand for 2-cylinder bikes. As a result the eldest son Massimo Laverda decided to turn to the USA to find new sales outlets. This led to the development of a modern 2-cylinder bike. In 1969 the first design for a 1000-cc 3-cylinder bike was presented. A new generation of sports motorbikes was developed based on this design after the 1987 bankruptcy.

Laverda 75

The first motorbike presented by Laverda in 1949, the Laverda 75, was extremely reliable. Indeed, between 1952 and 1956, these small bikes regularly won their category in the Milan-Taranto long-distance race. It also won victories in the Motogiro d'Italia. Sales of this inexpensive little motorbike rose sharply as a result and it can safely be said that it contributed in large measure to the motorisation of post-war Italy. Although the early versions had an unusual chassis with sheet-metal frame, in 1952 it was replaced by a conventional tubular frame.

Model:	75
Year:	1952
Power:	3 bhp
Capacity:	75 cc
Type:	Single-cylinder, 4-stroke

Laverda 750 SF

Laverda came to the realisation, before many other bike manufacturers did, that the future did not lie in good, everyday motorbikes but in sporty bikes, used for pleasure. Thus in 1966, after the Laverda 650, the company launched a new range including, 750 GT/S and 750 SF. The only common feature was the powerful 2-cylinder engine which was similar to a Honda CB-72 engine, scaled up in proportion. It was mounted as a load-bearing element in an original frame design without a lower frame tube.

Model:	750 SF 1
Year:	1972
Power:	52 bhp
Capacity:	744 cc
Type:	Parallel twin, 4-stroke

Laverda 750 SFC

Because the SF models provided an excellent basis for competition racing bikes, Laverda produced the SFC racer in a small series. It was fitted with a more powerful, parallel-twin engine, weight-saving elements and a complete sports package consisting of a magnificent half-fairing, tail unit seat, rear-set gear-change and brake system and 2-into-1 exhaust system. It participated in events such as Oss, Monza, Barcelona and the Isle of Man where it achieved excellent results.

Model:	750 SFC
Year:	1973
Power:	61 bhp
Capacity:	744 cc
Type:	Parallel twin, 4-stroke

Laverda Chott

In 1972, together with the Swedish manufacturer Husqvarna, Laverda built the Chott enduro bike, using a 2-stroke engine from Scandinavia. Unlike the first Japanese enduros which were conceived more for enthusiast or road use, the Laverda enduro was a real cross-country sports bike. Although it participated extremely successfully in the Valli Bergamasche event, it was not a commercial success for the company.

Model:	250 2T Chott
Year:	1975
Power:	26 bhp
Capacity:	247 cc
Type:	Single-cylinder, 2-stroke

Laverda 1000

Laverda caused a real sensation at the Milan Fair in 1969. Before even the Japanese manufacturers, the company presented a powerful motorbike with an impressive capacity of 1 litre. This had been made possible by the development of a 3-cylinder engine with twin overhead camshafts. This 250 kg (551-lb) heavyweight, capable of developing 78 hp, was one of the fastest superbikes in the world. In the late 1970s Laverda produced a sports version, the Jota, which had larger valves and carburettor and a higher compression ratio, enough to give a speed of 220 km/h (137 mph).

Model:	1000 3CL
Year:	1980
Power:	78 bhp
Capacity:	980 cc
Type:	3 cylinders parallel, 4-stroke

Laverda 1200

The Laverda 1200 was not only a slightly faster S-version of the 1000 cc, it replaced the good-natured tourer bike. Its higher torque increased the traction power, and only the clearly noticeable vibrations of the engine restricted the smoothness of the transmission. Nevertheless the 1200 was an excellent long-distance bike. Hardly any other bike in the mid-1970s was capable of achieving such a high degree of riding comfort and performance.

Model:	1200
Year:	1981
Power:	82 bhp
Capacity:	1115 cc
Type:	3 cylinders parallel, 4-stroke

Laverda 750 Formula

In 1996 Laverda launched a new generation of bikes, available in several models to meet every need. The 750 Formula, Laverda's sporty flagship, had a 2-cylinder in-line engine capable of developing 92 hp. The engine was developed and built by Laverda itself and fed by fuel injection.

Model	750 Formula
Year:	1997
Power:	92 bhp
Capacity:	747 cc
Type:	2-cylinder in-line, 4-stroke

Laverda 1000 SFC

The German Laverda importer, Witt, developed the 1000 SFC, a supersport variation of the more tourer-like Laverda RSG. Top quality add-on parts and a more powerful 3-cylinder engine transformed the SFC into an outrageously expensive but extremely fast dream bike. Because this concept only appealed to a few well-off enthusiasts, this 'Italophile' was unable to counter the strong competition from Japan.

Model	1000 SFC
Year:	1984
Power:	82 bhp
Capacity:	980 cc
Type:	3 cylinders parallel, 4-stroke

Laverda 750 S

The 750 S (sports version) was, contrary to what the name might suggest, a slightly more moderate version of the Formula, its sister model. With 82 bhp it had 10 bhp less than Formula. It had an otherwise similar power unit but without the Formula's higher compression ratio and engine management system. In addition it included a passenger seat, ordinary steel disc brakes and three-spoke wheels.

Model:	750 Sport
Year:	1998
Power:	82 bhp
Capacity:	747 cc
Type:	2-cylinder in-line, 4-stroke

Laverda Strike

The 'Strike' was the streetfighter version of the 750-cc range. It too had a water-cooled 2-cylinder engine which was comprehensively revamped in 1999. The light metal bridge-type frame which was also used in the 'Sport' and 'Formula' models remained unchanged. Laverda also produced a 'Black Strike', an all-black version of the nimble naked bikes.

Model:	Strike 750
Year:	1999
Power:	82 bhp
Capacity:	747 cc
Type:	2-cylinder in-line, 4-stroke

Laverda Super Sport

The 'Super Sport' was in principle a cross between the 'Formula' and the 'Sport'. This meant that it had a passenger seat and the slightly less high-quality chassis components of the 'Sport' while being powered by the performance-optimised 'Formula' engine from which it has also inherited the 2-into-2 exhaust system.

Model:	750 Super Sport
Year:	2000
Power:	92 bhp
Capacity:	747 cc
Type:	2-cylinder in-line, 4-stroke

Laverda Lynx

Shortly before Laverda was taken over by Aprilia, it presented the Lynx, a completely new medium-sized model which for the first time in the company's history was not powered by one of its own engines. The V-2 engine was based on Suzuki's successful 650-cc SV and was therefore an excellent choice. The Lynx might also have been successful commercially, not least because the combination of tubular space frame and cast aluminium parts gave it a very distinctive appearance. But immediately after the takeover by Aprilia, all Laverda's activites were put on ice. This is why this open-framed naked bike unfortunately disappeared again soon after it was presented.

Model:	650 Lynx
Year:	2000
Power:	72 bhp
Capacity:	645 cc
Type:	V-twin, 4-stroke

Laverda SFC 1000

In 2002 Laverda – now part of the Aprilia group – came back to life. Its prototype for a new SFC 1000 thrilled everyone, not only the hardened fans of the marque. Barely a year later at the EICMA show the production version was presented, powered by the Rotax V-twin, used in the Aprilia RSV Mille. But in fact the bike did not go into production. Its future is uncertain again after the take-over of Aprilia, Moto Guzzi and Laverda by Piaggio.

Model:	SFC 1000
Year:	2003
Power:	141 bhp
Capacity:	998 cc
Type:	V-twin, 4-stroke

Maico – Strong off-road

It was in 1926 that the Maisch brothers decided to build motorbikes. Inevitably production was interrupted by the Second World War. After the war, the Swabian motorbike company presented a new motorbike powered by the company's own single-cylinder 2-stroke engine. The elegant Taifun was a luxury top model, launched in 1953. Then a large order from the German army ensured that the company's coffers remained full. As a result, some 10,000 robust M 250 BW motorbikes, which had great cross-country mobility, went into public service. During the 1950s Maico was taking part in scrambling and moto-cross races. In the following two decades the Maico enduro motobikes were considered among the best in the world. By 1968 Maico had also produced a successful model for road racing. But in the 1980s Maico lost touch with the competition. Although financiers intervened to help the company, Maico was forced to close its doors in 1987.

Maico Maicomobil

The Maicomobil with its sturdy tubular frame and 14-inch wheels was more like a fully-faired motorbike than a motor scooter. Unlike a scooter, it had no gap in the middle, giving stable handling to this cross between a car and a motorbike, which included many aluminium parts. With a top speed of up to 85 km/h (53 mph), depending on the engine, the Maicomobile was a comfortable means of transport for long-distance journeys.

Model:	Maicomobil	Year:	1953	Power:	8.5 bhp
Capacity:	174 cc	Type:	Single-cylinder, 2-stroke		

Maico Taifun 400

With a top speed of over 130 km/h (81 mph) the Maico Taifun was one of the fastest motorbikes produced in the post-war period. Reflecting the spirit of the time, the Maico engineers had dressed their 2-cylinder top model in a sumptuous, smooth fairing. The front and rear swinging forks gave great riding comfort and the generous use of aluminium contributed to a significant reduction in weight.

Model:	Taifun 400	Year:	1955	Power:	22.5 bhp
Capacity:	395 cc	Type:	2-cylinder, 4-stroke		

Maico MC 350

The internationally very successful Maico moto-cross models could be ordered in a range of cubic capacities including 125, 250, 350 (subsequently 400) and 501 cc. These highly specialised competition bikes with double-cradle type frame were already as competitive as works bikes, and usually even superior. The company also produced cross-country models with lighting systems and otherwise approved for road use.

Model:	MC 350	Year:	1969	Power:	28 bhp
Capacity:	352 cc	Type:	Single-cylinder, 2-stroke		

Maico GS 250

The Maico models of the late 1970s and early 1980s were the last successful off-roaders. Their air-cooled 2-stroke engines and sturdy chassis with two suspension struts in the rear have made these cult Maicos very sought-after for vintage moto-cross and cross-country events.

Model:	GS 250
Year:	1978
Power:	28 bhp
Capacity:	248 cc
Type:	Single-cylinder, 2-stroke

Matchless – Sports bikes for clubmen

In the company's earliest motorbikes, the De Dion engine was mounted above the front wheel. From there it was moved via the rear wheel to the triangle of the frame. By 1904 engineers had developed a new motorbike with a JAP 2-cylinder engine. In the 1930s Matchless took over the well-established marques AJS and Sunbeam. During the Second World War Matchless developed the G3 model for the British armed forces. In 1956 AMC absorbed the Norton, Francis Barnett and James motorbike marques. In the late 1950s its range of models included both single-cylinder and 2-cylinder bikes. But the company's financial situation worsened considerably and in 1966 this firm, with its long tradition, was forced to file for bankruptcy.

Matchless Silver Hawk

Besides the Ariel Square Four there was another English 4-cylinder bike, the Matchless Silver Hawk.

.
Model:	Silver Hawk
Year	1931
Power:	18 bhp
Capacity:	598 cc
Type:	V-4, 4-stroke

Matchless G 3L

After the Second World War, many British motorbike manufacturers converted their military motorbikes into civilian vehicles so as to avoid having to develop new motorbikes immediately. Hence after the war Matchless converted the military G 3 into a successful bike for civilian use.

Model:	G 3L	Year:	1949	Power:	16 bhp
Capacity:	348 cc	Type:	Single-cylinder, 4-stroke		

Matchless G 50

The G 50 was a successful racing bike in the Matchless range. Its 496-cc single-cylinder engine with chain-driven overhead camshaft, based on an AJS design from 1948, was still winning victories in the early 1960s. This steady racer which only weighed 130 kg (287 lb) had an impressive top speed of 210 km/h (130 mph). Today the fast single-cylinder is still – like its ASJ 7R sibling — very popular at vintage bike events.

Model:	G 50	Year:	1956	Power:	50 bhp
Capacity:	496 cc	Type:	Single cylinder	4-stroke	

Matchless G 12

Besides the single-cylinder models, the Matchless range also included road and cross-country bikes with parallel twin engines. At first available in 500 cc and 650 cc variations, the 500-cc model was removed from the catalogue and replaced by a new 750-cc one. All cylinder capacities – even the single cylinder – had the same traditional British engine layout.

Model:	G 12	Year:	1963		Power:	36 bhp
Capacity:	646 cc	Type:	Parallel twin, 4-stroke			

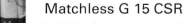

Matchless G 15 CSR

In 1966, after the merger of Norton and Matchless, a range of so-called hybrids was launched. The frame of the Matchless G-80-CS models was fitted with the engine, forks and wheels of the 750-cc Norton Atlas. These rare hybrids were sold under the Norton and Matchless labels.

Model:	G 15 CSR	Year:	1966		Power:	52 bhp
Capacity:	745 cc	Type:	Parallel twin, 4-stroke			

Mondial – A teacher for Honda

Together with his three brothers, the Italian Count Giuseppe Boselli founded the Fratelli Boselli company in 1936. Established in Croce di Casalecchio, the company at first produced three-wheeler freight vehicles under the FB name. The factory having been destroyed in 1944, the company moved to Milan and in 1948 commissioned the engineer Alfonso Drusiani from Bologna to design a fast 125-cc motorbike. Its single cylinder with two overhead camshafts driven by a vertical drive shaft developed a power output of 100 bhp per litre and could deliver over 10,000 rpm. With it Luigi Cavanna succeeded in breaking four world speed records. From then on the Count called his motorbikes 'Mondial' as a reference to their achievements. This brilliant motorbike was faster than the established 250-cc racing bikes, as Nello Pagani showed a year later when he won the World Championship title for the first time on a 125-cc machine. The Milanese company continued to dominate the Grand Prix scene for years to come. But the sale of mass-produced bikes was not sufficient to finance the company's involvement in racing and as a result the company stopped taking part in competition. Then in 1958 Boselli received a visit from the boss of an equally young Japanese motorcycle company, who was impressed by superior technology of his racing bikes. Soichiro Honda wanted to talk about competition motorbikes with the Count, who immediately gave him two racing bikes for examination. One of these bikes is still at the entrance of the Honda museum in honour of the Italian motorbike manufacturer. Meanwhile engineers in Milan were working on the development of racing bikes with a 2-stroke rotary-valve engine. The company built its first enduro motorbike in 1966. New models for younger customers followed, some of them already with disc brakes, but because of low production numbers the bikes often had to be more expensive than those of its competitors. As a result production of motorbikes ceased in 1977. When in 1999 the businessman Roberto Ziletti wanted to revive the name, the Boselli family also participated financially in the newly founded Mondial Moto SpA company in Manerbio. A year later the company presented the Mondial Piega, for which Honda produced the 1000 cc V-Twin in memory of Boselli's support in the past.

Mondial 175 TV

The Mondial 175 TV was one of the hottest motorbikes of its time. Its overhead camshaft was chain-driven and the engine developing up to 20 bhp gave this light motorbike a top speed of over 140 km/h (87 mph) which even exceeded that of many a 500-cc bike. This light motorbike with its distinctive appearance was a perfect embodiment of the technology used by the legendary long-distance racing bikes of the Motogiro d'Italia which Mondial won several times with Tarquinio Provini.

Model:	175 TV
Year:	1956
Power:	18 bhp
Capacity:	174 cc
Type:	Single-cylinder, 4-stroke

Mondial 125 dohc

This superior Mondial bike with 125-cc single cylinder engine and double overhead camshafts dominated all GP racing events for many years until the maker's retirement from racing in 1957. It also inspired no less a man than Soichiro Honda to develop his own motorbikes. The photograph shows the latest version with six-speed gearbox with which Carlo Ubbiali won the World Championship in 1957 while his team-mate Cecil Sandford won the World Championship title in the 250 cc category.

Model:	125 Sport
Year:	1957
Power:	17 bhp
Capacity:	124 cc
Type:	Single-cylinder, 4-stroke

Mondial 125 Sport

Even in its mass-produced bikes, Mondial remained highly design-conscious, as is reflected by the intake trumpet, quick-action fuel tank filler cap and steering shock absorbers. The design of the forks and the drum brakes with air scoops were not dictated by technical requirements but were merely a celebratory flourish by the designer. At the same time, the ohv engine was very straightforward and could be up-rated to perform perfectly for long-distance events such as the Milan-Taranto tour.

Model:	125 Sport
Year:	1957
Power:	6 bhp
Capacity:	123 cc
Type:	Single-cylinder, 4-stroke

Mondia Piega

In 2002 Mondial celebrated its come-back with the launch of the Piega. The stunning bike with its very elegant fairing was powered by a Honda V-2 engine as used in the VTR and which in the Evo-version shown here was capable of developing 143 bhp. Needless to say, only the very finest materials were used in constructing the Piega such as aluminium, titanium and carbon fibre. Exclusive spring elements by Öhlins and Brembo brake systems completed this outstanding chassis. But apparently there were not enough buyers for this Mondial racer whose production ceased in 2004 and plans to build a naked bike and streetfighter version were abandoned.

Model:	Piega Evo
Year:	2004
Power:	143 bhp
Capacity:	999 cc
Type:	V-twin, 4-stroke

Montesa – A people's bike for Spain

After the Second World War Spain experienced a huge increase in the demand for reasonably-priced individual motor transport. In the mid-1940s Pedro Permanyer and later Francisco Bulto developed and built the first motorbikes to satisfy this surge in demand. The simple construction, rigid-frame rear end and straightforward 2-stroke engines of these motorbikes met the requirements of the Spanish people, who wanted reasonably-priced, everyday bikes. But soon Montesa was also developing racing bikes. Because of differences in opinion between the owners of the company, Bulto left and in 1958 he founded his own company Bultaco. Montesa went through difficult times but managed to survive, thanks to the popular Impala model. The trial bikes built by Montesa proved to be particularly successful. The agile Cota, launched in 1968, won spectacular victories in trial races. In 1986 the company was taken over by the Japanese motorbike manufacturing giant Honda. The Honda models for the European market are still built in the former Montesa factory.

Montesa 125 cc D-51

Shortly after the introduction of the very first Montesa model, the company brought out a sports model, the 125 cc D-51. Instead of parallelogram forks, this top model sported modern telescopic forks and a frame with direct suspension replacing the cheap, rigid frame of the standard model. In addition, it had a large fuel tank which also distinguished it from the standard model. The D 51 was followed in 1953 by the Brio 90 which had a more powerful 125-cc 2-stroke engine.

Model:	125 cc D-51
Year:	1953
Power:	6 bhp
Capacity:	124 cc
Type:	Single-cylinder, 2-stroke

Montesa Impala

In 1960 the Impala all-round bike was the first model to be fitted with a newly developed engine of 175 cc. With long spring travel, proverbial reliability and racy performance, the Impala was known in Spain as an effective multi-purpose motorbike. Like its sibling the Comando, which had 9 bhp compared to the Impala's 10.5 bhp, it remained in Montesa's catalogue for many years and towards the end it even boasted fashionable cast aluminium wheels.

Model:	Impala
Year:	1962
Power:	10.5 bhp
Capacity:	174 cc
Type:	Single-cylinder, 2-stroke

Montesa Capra 360 V8

In 1975 Montesa launched the Capra as a successor to the Scorpion 250 moto-cross model presented in 1985. The new moto-cross range had a powerful 2-stroke engine, available in 125, 250 and 360-cc versions. Montesa also developed cross-country models approved for road use, based on the Capra. As a result of constant improvements such as longer suspension travel and in 1977 a raised exhaust system, this Iberian cross-country bike has remained very competitive.

Model:	Capra 360 V8
Year:	1973
Power:	38 bhp
Capacity:	351 cc
Type:	Single-cylinder, 2-stroke

Montesa Cota 172

For many years Spanish trial bikes were considered unbeatable. They owed this excellent reputation not only to the bikes from Bultaco but also to the Montesa Cota models. In 1967 the Trial championships were at first dominated by the 250-cc Cota. In 1976 their cylinder capacity was increased to 350 cc but without increasing their performance. Montesa continued the production of trial bikes until the 1980s with versions ranging from 50 cc to 350 cc.

Model:	Cota 172	Year:	1977	Power:	13 bhp
Capacity:	174 cc	Type:	Single-cylinder, 2-stroke		

Moto Morini – Italian family ties

In 1937 the motorbike racer Alfonso Morini founded a company which would specialise in the production of three-wheeler freight vehicles. After the Second World War Morini started developing and manufacturing motorbikes himself. The first model launched by Morini was reminiscent of the DKW RT 125. The maker was involved in racing from the very start and competed successfully against MV Agusta in road races. In 1950 Morini converted his bikes to 4-stroke engines. Nevertheless the company withdrew from the expensive GP races and launched a mass-produced 4-stroke bike, the Settebello 175, which was extremely successful in long-distance races. Then in 1958 the company returned to GP racing and at Monza competed with a 250-cc bike which inflicted a spectacular defeat on the World Champion Carlo Ubbiali. Racing enthusiasts will never forget the 1963 season when Tarquinio Provini on the fast single-cylinder bike beat Jim Redman's 4-cylinder Honda several times, thus becoming runner-up in the World Championship just two points behind the winner. Inspired by its production bikes with reliable ohv single-cylinder engines, Moto Morini was also very successful in scrambling races. Morinis were always firm favourites for a Gold Medal in the Six Days. When Gabriella took over the company after the death of her father Alfonso Morini in 1969, a new generation of bikes emerged. There were touring, sports and enduro bikes in which only the front cylinder of the twin engine was used. After the take-over by the Cagiva group the company was going downhill until Maurizio Morini bought it back and launched some new models in 2004.

Morini 125

Since the 1950s Morini had made exceedingly successful cross-country bikes with which the Italian national team often competed in the international Six Days. The ohv engine was based on the power unit of the normal road bikes and was available with 100, 125 and 164 cc. Until 1975 the small 4-stroke bikes still held their own against the up-and-coming 2-strokes before the appearance of the enduro models such as the 500 Camel, fitted with the new V-2 engine.

Model:	Regolaritá 125 Casa
Year:	1966
Power:	12 bhp
Capacity:	124 cc
Type:	Single-cylinder, 4-stroke

Morini 3 1/2

In 1971 Morini won international recognition with the so-called 3 1/2 350-cc engine. The slender bike with its unusual 72° V-engine showed itself to its best advantage in the 3 1/2 Sport model. In addition, so-called Heron-type combustion chambers ensured low fuel consumption.

Model:	3 1/2
Year:	1978
Power:	30 bhp
Capacity:	344 cc
Type:	V-twin, 4-stroke

Morini 9 1/2

Dante Lambertini had created the single-cylinder Morini engine and his son Franco later created the V-engines. The new 9 1/2 was his baby. In the space of just one year he developed the unusual dohc 87° V-twin to be ready for production.

Model:	9 1/2
Year:	2005
Power:	105 bhp
Capacity:	998 cc
Type:	V-twin, 4-stroke

Morini Corsaro 1200

The chassis of the largest bike differed from that of the smaller 9 1/2. While the tubular space frames were identical, the adjustable forks and suspension struts were different. The larger cylinder capacity was achieved by a longer stroke which increased the torque of this relatively light motorbike.

Model:	Corsaro 1200
Year:	2005
Power:	140 bhp
Capacity:	1187 cc
Type:	V-twin, 4-stroke

Moto Guzzi – The Italian legend

During the First World War, the engineer Carlo Guzzi, ship-owner's son Giorgio Parodi and pilot and racing motorbike rider Giovanni Ravelli decided to build a motorbike. Sadly Ravelli lost his life in a test flight, but the prototype for the first motorbike displayed the initials 'G.P.' for Guzzi and Parodi, together with an eagle in the logo in honour of their comrade. The first mass-produced Moto Guzzi motorbike left the factory in Mandello on Lake Como in 1921. While Carlo Guzzi remained faithful for decades to his production philosophy and continued to build simple, robust bikes, the company developed a number of unique designs for its racing bikes based on a very wide variety of engines: dohc 4-valve, 120° V-twin, 3 and 4-cylinder in-line engined and finally in 1956 a V-8 engine. But Moto Guzzi also suffered from the problems affecting the motor industry in the 1950s and the company became a partially state-controlled company. In the mid-1960s the first production model with large V-engine laid the foundation for the image of a Guzzi motorbike which exists today. The long-standing arrangments for supplying bikes to the Highway Patrol in California led to the creation of the California range of models. Aware of the company's success, the Italian-Argentine Alejandro de Tomaso bought Moto Guzzi in 1972. Meanwhile a complete range of new models was designed to challenge the supremacy of the powerful Japanese. After the failure of the De Tomaso company Moto Guzzi was taken over by Aprilia and it now belongs to the Piaggio group.

Moto Guzzi Normale

In building his first production motorcycle, Carlo Guzzi's aim was to create a robust and economical machine that did not suffer from the typical defects of the time. It was a clear success, with the concept of a horizontal single cylinder with large flywheel being used in production for over 50 years, right up to the Mandello in the 1970s.

Unlike the practice of most other manufacturers, the Normale had a monoblock engine without a separate gearbox. The three-speed gearbox was operated by a lever positioned on the right-hand side of the fuel tank.

The Normale was produced until 1924. However, its basic design was very advanced for its time and it was used in the development of future models up to the early 1930s.

Model:	Normale
Year:	1921
Power:	8 bhp
Capacity:	498 cc
Type:	Horizontal ohv single-cylinder, 4-stroke

Moto Guzzi C2V

A new cylinder head, classic engine tuning and a new frame with a longer wheelbase distinguished the C2V racing bike from the Normale. The 'Corsa Due Valvole' had a top speed of 120 km/h (75 mph). As the machine was no longer competitive in the mid-1920s, Moto Guzzi's engineers developed the much more advanced C4V with a 4-valve cylinder head.

Model:	C2V
Year:	1923
Power:	17 bhp
Capacity:	498 cc
Type:	Single-cylinder, 4-stroke

Moto Guzzi C4V

The C4V or 'Quattro Valvole' was Moto Guzzi's first Grand Prix machine in 1924. From this model on, the 'C' denoted racing machines, while '4V' stood for the four-valve technology used. The C4V was light, weighing just 130 kg (287 lb), and capable of 150 km/h (93 mph), a speed which was not exceeded by any other motorcycle in this class for a long time.

Model:	C Quattro Valvole
Year:	1924
Power:	22 bhp
Capacity:	498 cc
Type:	Single-cylinder, 4-stroke

Moto Guzzi 500 S

The 500 S was also powered by a 4-valve horizontal single-cylinder engine, which in this model managed to develop a solid 18 bhp. The girder fork with two central springs provided a reasonable level of comfort. The 130-kg (287-lb) motorcycle was capable of a top speed of 100 km/h (62 mph).

Model:	500 S
Year:	1928
Power:	18 bhp
Capacity:	498 cc
Type:	Single-cylinder, 4-stroke

Moto Guzzi GT Norge

The name 'Norge' ('Norway') referred to the dangerous race to the Arctic Circle undertaken by Carlo Guzzi and his brother Giuseppe. The advantages of the motorcycle lay in ongoing improvement in the level of comfort. At the time, torsional strength seemed incompatible with rear suspension. Guzzi therefore developed a different system, finding space for four springs in the front part of the frame.

Model:	GT Norge
Year:	1928
Power:	18 bhp
Capacity:	498 cc
Type:	Single-cylinder, 4-stroke

Moto Guzzi Bicilindrica

On the basis of the successful 250-cc single-cylinder racing bike, Carlo Guzzi developed this 500-cc model with V-engine in 1933. The highly original 120° engine was chosen for its ignition sequence and the resulting high level of torque. This was the first racing bike with rear suspension and it won the Tourist Trophy in 1935.

Model:	Bicilindrica
Year:	1935
Power:	44 bhp
Capacity:	493 cc
Type:	2-cylinder, 4-stroke

Moto Guzzi Condor

With the Condor, at the end of the 1930s, Moto Guzzi offered a production racing bike that stood a real chance of winning races straight out of the factory. The petite 500-cc motorcycle was initially called the GTCL, before being named after the bird of prey. Technically, the racing bike was based on the GTV touring bike. By using magnesium and aluminium parts, the weight was reduced to 140 kg (309 lb). Equipped with lights, some of these exclusive racing bikes were used as escort vehicles for Mussolini.

Model:	Condor
Year:	1941
Power:	28 bhp
Capacity:	498 cc
Type:	Single-cylinder, 4-stroke

Moto Guzzi G.T.V.

Production of the V series of ohv engines with four-speed gearboxes began in 1933, marking an important turning point for Moto Guzzi. Both the road performance and the styling heralded a new era. Furthermore, it was one of the first motorcycles with the option of rear suspension. Apart from some improvements, the engine design was maintained for more than 30 years, being used for example in the Astore and the G.T.C.

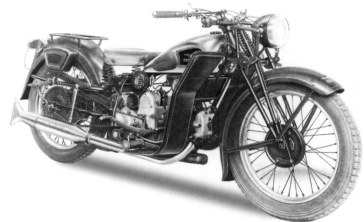

Model:	G.T.V.
Year:	1945
Power:	19 bhp
Capacity:	498 cc
Type:	Horizontal ohv single-cylinder, 4-stroke

Moto Guzzi Motoleggera

Lightweight motorcycles such as the Moto Guzzi Motoleggera played an important part in providing the Italian population with transport after the war. Its simple technology and the high level of reliability associated with the brand's sporting name made it one of the best-selling vehicles of its time. Given its high sales, the price was reduced between 1946 and 1954. The Cardellino, based on a similar concept, had slightly more up-market features.

Moto Guzzi Dondolino

A revamped version of the pre-war Condor, the Dondolino (meaning 'rocking chair') offered new rear suspension. Manufactured in small quantities in the racing department, it was used by many private riders in circuit and mountain races, but it stood out in particular in long-distance races such as the Milan-Taranto race, which it won four times in a row. Depending on the intended use, it was available with or without lights.

Moto Guzzi Superalce

The Superalce was the follow-on from the Alce, used in the Second World War, made with the V engine. It was a military motorcycle used by the Carabinieri, as a single-seater or two-seater with sidecar. One unique feature was the rear suspension, which could be adjusted by turning a wheel next to the engine. The Superalce was produced from 1946 to 1957.

Model:	Motoleggera 65	Model:	Dondolino	Model:	Superalce
Year:	1946	Year:	1946	Year:	1946
Power:	2 bhp	Power:	33 bhp	Power:	18.5 bhp
Capacity:	64 cc	Capacity:	498 cc	Capacity:	498 cc
Type:	Single-cylinder, 2-stroke	Type:	Single-cylinder, 4-stroke	Type:	Single-cylinder, 4-stroke

Moto Guzzi Airone

The Airone (meaning 'heron'), a derivative of the P.E., first appeared in 1939. In 1940 it was given a new chassis with rear suspension. The 250-cc model was the top-selling Italian motorcycle in its class for 15 years, suitable for both everyday use and racing. During production, improvements were made such as hydraulic steering dampers, aluminium cylinders and a new cylinder head. A sports version was launched in 1949.

Model:	Airone
Year:	1949
Power:	9.5 bhp
Capacity:	246 cc
Type:	Horizontal ohv single-cylinder, 4-stroke

Moto Guzzi Galletto

The Galletto (meaning 'cockerel') was designed by Carlo Guzzi himself. This successful attempt to combine the advantages of a high-wheel motorcycle with those of a scooter was launched in 1950. The rider benefited from a comfortable riding position and good weather protection, while the technology was easy to operate. The engine capacity grew from 160 cc to 175 cc and then to 192 cc, and it was eventually available with an electric starter.

Model:	Galletto
Year:	1950
Power:	6 bhp
Capacity:	192 cc
Type:	Horizontal ohv single-cylinder, 4-stroke

Moto Guzzi Falcone Sport

To this day, the name Falcone (meaning 'falcon') is synonymous with the Guzzi horizontal single-cylinder motorcycle. In the early 1950s, this reliable, high performance model was the most popular Guzzi motorcycle. From 1953, it was available in two versions – Turismo and Sport – but it faced difficulties due to the growing market for cars. Nevertheless, the Falcone 17 was produced for 17 years, notably at the request of government authorities, which began to convert slowly to the V7 in 1967.

Model:	Falcone Sport
Year:	1950
Power:	23 bhp
Capacity:	498 cc
Type:	Single-cylinder, 4-stroke

Moto Guzzi 350 Bialbero

From the engine to the frame, this was a completely new design. Some of the technical features are still in use, such as the double ignition and the steel space frame. With a top speed of 220 km/h (137 mph), the 350 Bialbero enjoyed success in international competitions. It also dominated the World Championships, with unbroken wins until 1957.

Model:	350 Bialbero
Year:	1954
Power:	37 bhp
Capacity:	350 cc
Type:	Single-cylinder, 4-stroke

Moto Guzzi Lodola

The Lodola (meaning 'lark') was the company's first 4-stroke motorcycle, marking Guzzi's final departure from the horizontal single-cylinder concept. It was initially intended to rival the ohc sports models of other Italian manufacturers such as Mondial in the popular 175-cc class. However, for reasons of cost, the bevel-gear-driven overhead camshafts of the Normale and Sport versions were replaced by push-rods and rocker levers in the Lodola Gran Turismo 235 cc.

Model:	Lodola 235
Year:	1956
Power:	11 bhp
Capacity:	235 cc
Type:	Single-cylinder, 4-stroke

Moto Guzzi Otto Cilindri

Moto Guzzi's V-8-powered racing bike was undoubtedly one of the most spectacular motorcycles in history. Engineer Giuliano C. Carcano's aim was to create the ultimate GP racer of the 1950s. The first prototypes were made in 1955, while the following year was devoted to the complicated preparation stages, during which indications of the bike's extraordinary potential could already be seen.

Model:	Otto Cilindri Gara
Year:	1956
Power:	68 bhp
Capacity:	498 cc
Type:	Dohc V-8, 4-stroke

Moto Guzzi Otto Cilindri

The 68 bhp achieved in the first series was increased to 78 bhp in 1957, giving a maximum speed of 275 km/h (171 mph). The final version of the 8-cylinder motorcycle broke a number of long-standing records in World Championship events. However, due to the economic situation in the motorcycle industry, Moto Guzzi withdrew from racing in 1957, so this sensational model was unable to demonstrate its capabilities for a full season.

Model:	Otto Cilindri Gara
Year:	1957
Power:	78 bhp
Capacity:	498 cc
Type:	Dohc V-8, 4-stroke

Moto Guzzi Zigolo

The Zigolo (meaning 'bunting'), with its 2-stroke engine, was the successful attempt to close the gap between the lightweight motorcycle and the Galletto scooter. It was initially a deliberately sparingly-equipped everyday 99-cc machine, which was later put on a level with the better-equipped Lusso. As one of the first motorcycles, it had a hard-chromed cylinder from 1958 and the capacity was increased to 110 cc a year later.

Model:	Zigolo
Year:	1960
Power:	4 bhp
Capacity:	110 cc
Type:	Horizontal Single-cylinder, 4-stroke

Moto Guzzi Stornello

As a reaction to the crisis in the motorcycle market in the late 1950s, the closed-down racing department was instructed to design a model which would be extremely economical and inexpensive to produce. The outstanding result was the Stornello (meaning 'little star'), which became one of the top-selling motorcycles in its class and helped the factory through those difficult years. Production of the final version began in 1976.

Model:	Stornello Sport
Year:	1960
Power:	10 bhp
Capacity:	123 cc
Type:	Ohv Single-cylinder, 4-stroke

Moto Guzzi V7 Corazzieri

The very first V7 model was delivered to the Corazzieri presidential guard in Rome. Various visual features disitnguished it from civil and public service models. In order to make these escort motorcycles particularly prestigious, Guzzi equipped the black 700-cc model with low-reaching mudguards, chromed toolboxes, oversized leg guards and a fixed luggage holder. These motorcycles were used to escort Italian state visitors.

Model:	V7-700
Year:	1967
Power:	35 bhp
Capacity:	703 cc
Type:	V-twin, 4-stroke

Moto Guzzi Nuovo Falcone

The Nuovo Falcone was created in 1968 as a result of the authorities' desire for a completely new interpretation of the horizontal single-cylinder concept, with traditional engine manufacture and a modern twin-cradle frame layout. A special feature of both the military and the later civilian version was the dynamo, which in the lightweight machine also functioned as an electric starter. It was produced using Carlo Guzzi's original design until 1976.

Model:	Nuovo Falcone Militare
Year:	1970
Power:	26 bhp
Capacity:	498 cc
Type:	Horizontal ohv single-cylinder, 4-stroke

Moto Guzzi V7 Special

Moto Guzzi began thinking of a large-volume V-engine in the late 1950s, both for military purposes and for possible use in small cars. A concept of this kind was applied to a new production motorcycle in 1965, the original 700-cc V7. This version, and the V7 Special shown here with greater cubic capacity, were quick to catch on and they continue to shape Moto Guzzi's image to this day.

Model:	V7 Special
Year:	1969
Power:	45 bhp
Capacity:	757 cc
Type:	Ohv V-twin, 4-stroke

Moto Guzzi V7 Ambassador

The Italian factory created the Ambassador specially for the US market. Along with the other versions, the Eldorado and the California, this motorcycle established Moto Guzzi's solid reputation on the other side of the Atlantic, enabling it to oust even domestic manufacturer Harley-Davidson with special versions for the US police.

Model:	V7 Ambassador
Year:	1969
Power:	45 bhp
Capacity:	757 cc
Type:	Ohv V-twin, 4-stroke

Moto Guzzi Le Mans CX 100

Motorcyclists in the United States have always had different tastes from Europeans. In the US, one of the most important factors is cubic capacity. Since the Le Mans II had an engine of just 850 cc, at the request of the US importer engineers fitted the 950-cc 1000 SP engine into the Le Mans chassis. Although the sporting 850-cc engine offered 13 bhp more than the larger touring engine, enabling the bike to accelerate much more quickly, Americans preferred the CX 100, which was only available in the US.

Model:	Le Mans CX 100
Year:	1981
Power:	61 bhp
Capacity:	948 cc
Type:	V-twin, 4-stroke

Moto Guzzi 850 Le Mans III

The V7 Sport was replaced by the first version of the Le Mans, named after the French race track, with which Moto Guzzi enjoyed some success. In further development, the lines in particular were modernised and the full fairing of the Le Mans II was made even closer-cut in the Le Mans III. Having been developed in its own wind tunnel, Moto Guzzi's fairings were more effective than those of many other machines.

Model:	850 Le Mans III
Year:	1981
Power:	76 bhp
Capacity:	844 cc
Type:	V-twin, 4-stroke

Moto Guzzi Mille GT

The Mille GT was developed with classic features such as a large amount of chrome, fine lines and optional spoked wheels. Initially planned as a limited edition, surprisingly strong demand led to the series production of the bike in Mandello and the development of accessories such as trunks and windshields.

Model:	Mille GT
Year:	1986
Power:	67 bhp
Capacity:	942 cc
Type:	V-twin, 4-stroke

Moto Guzzi 850 T5

With the T5, Moto Guzzi began its shift from traditional motorcycle design. The daring shape of this new touring bike was designed by De Tomaso in Modena. The small 16-inch wheels, square fibreglass shell and car cockpit reflected the ideas of the 1980s. The engine was also built with 'square' cylinders in a Guzzi tourer. The Italian authorities used the T5 with 18-inch wheels.

Model:	850 T5	Year:	1987	Power:	67 bhp
Capacity:	844 cc	Type:	V-twin, 4-stroke		

Moto Guzzi Le Mans 1000

From 1985, the Le Mans was produced with a full 1-litre capacity. Because of stricter emission and noise requirements, the Le Mans 1000 was not much faster than its predecessors. However, resourceful tuners found ways of adding another few bhp to the large V-twin engine. The chassis, which in the Le Mans IV had a controversial 16-inch front wheel, was also intelligently improved. The 1987 Le Mans 1000 had reliable 18-inch wheels.

Model:	Le Mans 1000
Year:	1987
Power:	82 bhp
Type:	V-twin, 4-stroke

Moto Guzzi Magni Sfida

Magni, the former racing engineer from MV Agusta, specialised in refining Moto Guzzi bikes. After producing chassis kits for the BMW R 100 and the Honda CB 900, Magni offered complete vehicles based on the large V-twin model from Mandello. A number of different versions of the sporting Magni Guzzis were available. A parallelogram swing-arm minimised the shaft-drive effect.

Model	Sfida	Year:	1990	Power:	82 bhp
Capacity:	948 cc	Type:	V-twin, 4-stroke		

Moto Guzzi Nevada

The Nevada made its debut in 1991. The small chopper with a 1980s look enjoyed respectable sales in Italy but failed to bowl people over elsewhere. The Nevada was powered by the 'small' V-twin engine, which was first produced in 1977 and over the years became available with capacities of 350 cc and 750 cc. The Nevada bore the typical Guzzi hallmarks of a 90° V-twin engine and final transmission with a low-maintenance shaft drive.

Model:	Nevada Club
Year:	1996
Power:	48 bhp
Capacity:	744 cc
Type:	V-twin, 4-stroke

Moto Guzzi Sport 1100

The Sport 1100 was launched in 1996 to succeed the Le Mans. In this model, the time-honoured two-valve engine was powered by fuel injection. However, with just 90 bhp, the shaft-driven V-twin had had its day. Despite the sporting chassis compared with the Le Mans and the pleasing design, this model failed to become a major success and production was brought to an end in 2001.

Model:	Sport 1100 Corsa
Year:	1998
Power:	90 bhp
Capacity:	1064 cc
Type:	V-twin, 4-stroke

Moto Guzzi Daytona

For racing enthusiasts, Moto Guzzi also offered an enhanced version of the Sport range: the Daytona. Thanks to its powerful four-valve engine producing over 100 bhp, it could also achieve impressive times on the race track. The sports components, including the brakes and suspension used in the Daytona, came from suppliers such as Brembo and White Power.

Model:	Daytona
Year:	1999
Power:	101 bhp
Capacity:	992 cc
Type:	V-twin, 4-stroke

Moto Guzzi Centauro

It may be hard to believe, but this ornate model was also based on the central tube frame structure of the Daytona and the Sport. The four-valve Daytona engine was given more torque and the maximum power was lowered to 95 bhp. The Centauro was also offered as Sport and GT models (with windshield and twin seat).

Model:	Centauro
Year:	1999
Power:	95 bhp
Capacity:	992 cc
Type:	V-twin, 4-stroke

Moto Guzzi V11 Sport

The V11 Sport was generally recognised as the successor to the glorious V7 Sport of the 1970s. Not only was its classic shape similar, but also its red frame. The powerful two-valve engine was finally given a more compact and precise six-speed gearbox. The Marzocchi inverted forks could be adjusted to match the desired use. The rear suspension worked on the cantilever principle and could be adjusted for spring preloading, compression and rebound.

Model:	V11 Sport
Year:	1999
Power:	90 bhp
Capacity:	1064 cc
Type:	V-twin, 4-stroke

Moto Guzzi Quota

Moto Guzzi was also involved in adventure bikes. In the early 1970s, this was demonstrated by its participation in six-day trials with the single-cylinder Lodola and Stornello. As enduro bikes evolved from pure adventure bikes into fast tourer models – or travel enduro bikes – the Quota was produced in Mandello. However, with just 68 bhp, its engine was much too feeble to compete with more powerful models and production was ended after three years.

Model:	Quota 1100 ES
Year:	1999
Power:	90 bhp
Capacity:	1064 cc
Type:	V-twin, 4-stroke

Moto Guzzi Jackal

It is impossible to think of the Moto Guzzi range without thinking of the California. In the Jackal, the equipment was reduced to the bare minimum with just a single front disc brake and no unnecessary aesthetic details. This enabled the model to be priced significantly lower than the other Californias.

Model:	California Jackal	Year:	2000	Power:	75 bhp
Capacity:	1064 cc	Type:	V-twin, 4-stroke		

Moto Guzzi V11 Rosso Mandello

Following on from this great tradition and to celebrate the company's 80th anniversary in 2001, Moto Guzzi launched the V11 Sport Rosso Mandello as a limited special edition. The typical racing elements made from carbon fibre emphasised the contrast between tradition and innovation. The streamlined fairing, which made the V11 Sport seem less bare, was also made from carbon fibre and the same material was used for the front wing and the cockpit. The carbon exhaust also made the Rosso a shade lighter and faster. The small but clearly visible anodised details, creating an impressive colour effect, gave it an air of exclusivity. The foot-peg supports and valve cap of the V-twin engine were anodised in a bright red colour.

Model:	V11 Sport Rosso Mandello	Year:	2001	Power:	90 bhp
Capacity:	1064 cc	Type:	V-twin, 4-stroke		

Moto Guzzi EV 80

To celebrate the company's 80th anniversary, the most traditional Moto Guzzi model also underwent a revamp. A luxury version of the California was created in collaboration with Italy's leading upholstery manufacturer, Poltrona Frau. This company, founded in 1912, is regarded as the originator of classic leather furniture and lent its full expertise to the California. The handlebar grips, seat and sissy pad were hand-made in the finest leather. The crowning touch was the luggage system designed especially for this model.

Model:	California EV 80
Year:	2001
Power:	75 bhp
Capacity:	1064 cc
Type:	V-twin, 4-stroke

Ghezzi & Brian Supertwin

Beppo Ghezzi and Brian Saturno make individual racing motorcycles based on Moto Guzzi models. The Supertwin did not offer unbridled performance because the Italian designers focused on their particular area of expertise, the chassis. The comparatively modest 80-bhp engine was fitted in their own box frame, together with their own double swing-arm. An under-seat exhaust and other weight-reducing measures brought the weight to just 210 kg (463 lb). Other eye-catching features such as the 420-mm brake discs appealed not only to technology freaks. The two luxury-bike designers also support the Moto Guzzi team in Maranello by lending their expertise in chassis design.

Model:	Ghezzi & Brian Supertwin	Year:	2003	Power:	80 bhp
Capacity:	1064 cc	Type:	V-twin, 4-stroke		

Moto Guzzi California EV

The California Armada flagship model was called the EV. This top model in the Italian easy rider range was built with a number of chrome elements such as the gearbox, instruments, seatposts, cylinder protection bars and exhaust. Various extras gave the EV authentic style. The rear luggage rack also served as a comfortable back rest for the passenger. Moto Guzzi also introduced an integral braking system to the California EV, with stronger braking power and a delay valve, in order to reduce the braking distance while also enhancing brake stability.

Model:	California EV
Year:	2002
Power:	75 bhp
Capacity:	1064 cc
Type:	V-twin, 4-stroke

Moto Guzzi – V11 Le Mans

The Le Mans tradition was revived once again by Moto Guzzi with this model in 2002. The elegant fairing provided the rider with a high level of protection against strong headwinds and ensured comfort on long journeys. In addition, the Le Mans was structurally identical to the unfaired V 11. The reworked engine with sound pipes and three-way catalytic converter now produced 91 bhp.

Model:	V11 Le Mans
Year:	2002
Power:	91 bhp
Capacity:	1064 cc
Type:	V-twin, 4-stroke

Moto Guzzi California Titanium

Titanium is both light and very strong. The California Titanium was certainly robust, but was it light? This sporting version weighed 270 kg (595 lb). It was also pleasing to the eye, with chrome wheels, a twin seat and stylish cockpit fairing, and reached a top speed of 200 km/h (124 mph). The new 90° V-twin engine with hydraulic tappets and catalysed exhaust give it all the character of a Moto Guzzi.

Model:	California Titanium
Year:	2003
Power:	75 bhp
Capacity:	1064 cc
Type:	V-twin, 4-stroke

Moto Guzzi Breva 750

With the Breva 750 Moto Guzzi could at last again offer a competitive machine in the mid-capacity sector. This stylishly-designed all-rounder admittedly had a power of only 50 bhp, but its power delivery at low revs was a pleasure. With its fuel injection, computer-controlled catalytic converter and low-maintenance shaft drive, the bike appealed to the economical and environmentally conscious biker who nonetheless did not want to ride a nondescript motorbike. In order to compete on price with Asian competition, the Breva relinquished the second front disc and excessively sophisticated telescopic forks, but this did not cause any deficiencies in the excellent riding qualities of the bike.

Model:	Breva 750 I.E.
Year:	2003
Power:	49 bhp
Capacity:	744 cc
Type:	V-twin, 4-stroke

Moto Guzzi California EV

The California is a legend, a motorbike which has created a style which has achieved a fame and renown which others have romanticised in the cruiser bike. This model is now a machine with every imaginable comfort and necessary indulgence for touring. The California has undergone numerous changes and alterations over the years. As well as the modified engine with hydraulic valve balancing, computer-controlled catalytic converter and improved suspension elements, the 2004 EV of the latest generation had an improved integral braking system with the floating 320-mm brake discs and high-quality Brembo four-piston callipers of the Serie Oro. Even this strapping bike could be slowed down safely with these powerful brakes.

Model:	California EV Touring
Year:	2004
Power:	75 bhp
Capacity:	1064 cc
Type:	V-twin, 4-stroke

Moto Guzzi Rosso Corsa

The design with the chequered flag in the tradional Moto Guzzi red is reminiscent of the victorious tradition of the bikes from Mandello del Lario, and the 90° V-twin engine is traditional as well. As usual this power unit has two valves operated by overhead rocker arms and light alloy push-rods. However the V11 Le Mans Rosso Corsa had the new 2003 engine with a higher compression ratio, interference tubes and computer-controlled catalytic converter. The suspension components too were of the finest: the inverted forks and rear swing-arm were from Öhlins, ensuring absolutely precise springing and damping. A detail that quickly proved its worth when driving at speed was the standard fitting of a twin-tube steering damper.

Model:	Rosso Corsa
Year:	2004
Power:	91 bhp
Capacity:	1064 cc
Type:	V-twin, 4-stroke

Moto Guzzi Breva 1100

After the Mandello company had put an up-to-date mid-capacity bike on the market in the form of the Breva 750, it set out to repeat the successful recipe in the next class up by developing a sister model of 1100 cc. However, in the meanttime the near-bankruptcy of Moto Guzzi's parent company Aprilia prevented the model being produced in the 2004 season. This was a pity, because the big Breva had everything that is now demanded of a large capacity touring bike, with a pepped-up V-twin engine, new gearbox, single swing-arm, shaft drive, fuel injection and computer-controlled catalytic converter. Since the design was also coolly modern yet solid, the Italians should be able repeat their earlier success in this category.

Model:	Breva 1100
Year:	2004
Power:	84 bhp
Capacity:	1064 cc
Type:	V-twin, 4-stroke

Moto Guzzi California Stone

Two wheels, one driver, a frame and an engine. The essentials of a motorbike must have something to do with the quest for the purist form. This is the philosophy of the Stone, to achieve the technical embodiment of freedom in a motorbike which incorporates all that is needed and excludes the superfluous. Just so: the Stone has all that is required for trips alone or with a passenger to near or far-off destinations, which shows that often less is more. So, when one decides on the minimalist version one gives up a rev counter. Such Spartan thoughts originated from the true chopper bikes of days gone by…

Model:	California Stone
Year:	2004
Power:	75 bhp
Capacity:	1064 cc
Type:	V-twin, 4-stroke

Moto Guzzi Nevada

After the Nevada had survived almost 15 years in the plain style of the 1980s, a fundamentally revised version eventually came out in 2005. The design was now representative of the new millennium and the engine was the V-twin from the Breva 750 with computer-controlled catalytic converter and fuel injection. It was an ideal bike for novices and returning riders who did not want to give up the sensation of riding a V-twin.

Model:	Nevada Classic I.E.
Year:	2005
Power:	49 bhp
Capacity:	744 cc
Type:	V-twin, 4-stroke

Moto Guzzi Griso

This beautiful muscle bike took its name from Griso, a character from the famous Italian novel *I Promessi Sposi* by Alessandro Manzoni, a story which is set on the shores of Lake Como. It was a Moto Guzzi motorbike pointing the direction in the new millennium. What the V-Rod has been to Harley-Davidson, the Griso could be to Moto Guzzi. It was a new and up-to-date interpretation of the chopper, or rather high-performance cruiser, to use the terminology of today. Nevertheless it was in traditional style with a four--valve V-twin engine and distinctive design. As power unit the Griso is fitted with a thoroughly modified Guzzi engine developing 88 bhp.

Model: Griso
Year: 2005
Power: 88 bhp
Capacity: 1064 cc
Type: V-twin, 4-stroke

Moto Guzzi Stone Touring

The Spartan California Stone was also available in the 'Touring' variant with a larger windshield and luggage system. It was a motorbike for riders who travel far rather than fast.

Model: California Stone
Year: 2005
Power: 75 bhp
Capacity: 1064 cc
Type: V-twin, 4-stroke

Moto Guzzi MGS 01

At last, here was a thoroughbred racing bike from Mandello once more, but the MGS/01 Corsa was not approved for use on public roads. The basis was the well-known four-valve engine from the Daytona and the Centauro. The engine had been modified and its 1256 cc developed 122 bhp at 8,000 rpm while the torque was 117 Nm at 6,400 rpm. The list of equipment read magnificently: aluminium swing-arm, Öhlins suspension elements, Brembo radial calliper brakes, OZ aluminium frame and carbon fibre parts. The overall weight was 192 kg (423 lb). The weight distribution was perfect, with 50% on each wheel.

Model: MGS 01
Year: 2005
Power: 122 bhp
Capacity: 1256 cc
Type: V-twin, 4-stroke

Moto Guzzi V11 Scura

In 2002 Moto Guzzi brought the 'Scura' to the market, the most sporty model of the V11 bike so far produced. Powered by the unaltered two-valve engine fitted to the VG11 naked bike, the Scura was fitted with Öhlins suspension elements giving it superb cornering, like the other V11 models. In addition, Moto Guzzi offered the Scura exclusively in matt black apart from two carbon-fibre silencers as well as the red anodised mountings for the foot rests. Admittedly these details do not make it go any faster, but they give its appearance even greater distinction.

Model:	Moto Guzzi V11 Sport Scura
Year:	2002
Power:	91 bhp
Capacity:	1064 cc
Type:	V-twin, 4-stroke

Motobécane – Still thriving thanks to the Mobylette

The French motorcycle company Motobécane presented its first motorbike in 1923. This simple motorbike was powered by a 175-cc 2-stroke engine and became a best-seller. To differentiate the larger motorbikes which the company planned to make from these simple bikes, the company's owners founded the marque Motoconfort in 1925. But over the years the motorbikes built by Motobécane and Motoconfort came to differ from each other hardly at all. During the 1920s Motobécane developed a 4-stroke motorbike fitted with 350 and 500-cc Blackburn engines. Then in 1930 the company developed its own 4-stroke side-valve engine with integrated three-speed gearbox. In the 1950s Motobécane returned to its roots and concentrated on simple 2-stroke motorbikes. Motobécane's greatest market success has always remained its mopeds. In the 1980s Motobécane limited its production to bikes of 50 cc, 80 cc and 125 cc, and in 1983 the marque was taken over by Yamaha.

Motobécane Madame

The first model from the French maker was a simple 2-stroke motorbike of 175 cc. The 'Madame' was the ladies' version of this everyday vehicle. The lowering of the crossbar and the tank of the men's model made it easier for ladies to mount and ride when wearing a skirt.

Model:	Madame
Year:	1923
Power:	1.75 bhp
Capacity:	175 cc
Type:	Single-cylinder, 2-stroke

Motobécane Monsieur

The counterpart ot the 'Madame' version was this men's model of the little 175-cc Motobécane. The taller frame was typical of a motorcyce and it was sturdy as well as responding to knee pressure on the fuel tank when cornering. This appealed to men with sporty inclinations. Not surprisingly, the sales of the 'Monsieur' always exceeded those of the ladies' version.

Model:	Monsieur
Year:	1923
Power:	1.75 bhp
Capacity:	175 cc
Type:	Single-cylinder, 2-stroke

Motobécane Speciale 50

Motobécane's first sports moped was the Speciale 50, which was based on the Mobylette. Because of its striking colour, it was also known as the 'Orange'. Beneath the sports fuel tank, it had the same pressed-steel frame as the Mobylette. Contrary to the fashion of the time, the Speciale had no gearbox, but a centrifugal coupling.

Model:	Speciale 50
Year:	1969
Power:	2.7 bhp
Capacity:	49 cc
Type:	Single-cylinder, 2-stroke

Motobécane 125 SP

From the lively 2-cylinder street machine, the 125 LT was also available in limited quantities as a racing bike for fledgling racing riders. These 125 SP bikes were fitted with all the equipment necessary for racing and were a persuasive entry bike for many well-known competition riders. Weighing under 80 kg (176 lb), it could reach a speed of 180 km/h (112 mph).

Model:	125 SP
Year:	1974
Power:	26 bhp
Capacity:	124 cc
Type:	2-cylinder, 2-stroke

Motobécane 350

In the early 1970s the French moped giant surprised everyone by independently producing a mid-range machine. As competition for the Japanese 2-stroke models, the 350 was developed with an air-cooled 3-cylinder 2-stroke engine. After Motobécane had sold only a few examples of this interesting machine, the company's management decided to terminate this project.

Model:	350
Year:	1974
Power:	38 bhp
Capacity:	349 cc
Type:	3-cylinder in-line, 2-stroke

Motobécane D 55 TT

Developed in response to the little Italian motorcycles which were very popular in France, the sporty D 55 appeared in 1975 with twin-cradle frame and disc brake at the front. However an enduro version of the D 55, the TT, did not result in satisfactory sales. The time of the sports moped was past.

Model:	D 55 TT
Year:	1976
Power:	2.7 bhp
Capacity:	49 cc
Type:	Single-cylinder, 2-stroke

Münch – 'The Mammoth man'

Friedel Münch was born on 6 February 1927 in Dorn-Assenheim in the Wetterau region of Germany. After completing his training as a motor-vehicle engineer, he set up his own own motorbike workshop specialising in Horex motorbikes. It did not take long before the young entrepreneur became famous throughout Germany as the most brilliant Horex specialist in the country. His 'Münch racing brakes' for the front wheel caused a real sensation. At a time when no one really believed in motorbikes, this brilliant engineer built the 'Mammut' (meaning 'Mammoth'). In 1966 this Big Bike, powered by a 55-bhp 1000-cc 4-cylinder NSU engine, was the most powerful bike in the world and the fastest. To help him produce the Mammut in commercial quantities Friedel Münch found a financially strong partner in the person of American motorcycle enthusiast and millionaire Floyd Clymer. Soon Münch's small company was employing 20 people and in the first three years of production 137 Münch-4 bikes were built. In 1970, for health reasons, Floyd Clymer sold his shares in the company to George Bell from Miami, Florida. Bell was not only mad about motorbikes but he was also extraordinarily rich. This resulted in a new Münch motorbike factory being built in Altenstadt near Friedberg at a cost of over two million deutschmarks, or one million euros. At the same time George Bell bought the URS racing team from Helmut Fath. The development of the Münch-4 soon led to the production of high-speed touring bikes. As a further support Friedel Münch acquired a new partner in the shape of the company. In 2000 Friedel Münch's dream was finally fulfilled when he launched his new generation of Münch motorbikes with the 'Mammut 2000'.

MÜNCH-4 TTS 1200
(sidecar frame)

When Friedel Münch brought out his 'Mammut' or 'Mammoth' in 1966, it was the first 'Big Bike' to coincide with the approach of the new motorbike boom. After the first machines with 1000 and 1100-cc engines, the maker used only the 1200-cc NSU power unit. The ingenious designer had modified the 4-cylinder engine to produce 88 bhp and the top speed of the Münch-4 was over 200 km/h (124 mph). At that time, there was no comparable machine, which with its rugged frame was also suitable for use with a sidecar. At the end of the 1960s, the Münch-4 was the most exclusive, the strongest, the fastest, and also the most expensive motorbike which could be purchased. The Mammut was the quintessential masculine dream machine.

Model:	4 TTS 1200
Year:	1969
Power:	88 bhp
Capacity:	1177 cc
Type:	4-cylinder, 4-stroke

MÜNCH-4 TTS 1200 (new frame)

The manufacture of the Münch-4 involved skilled, conscientious hand work. Each machine incorporated a few 'little improvements', and customers' wishes such as single or twin headlights, size and shape of fuel tank and single or twin seats were also taken into account. From the 1970 model year, Friedel Münch used a new chassis. Instead of the steel rear frame, a self-supporting rear section cast in electron metal was now used.

Model:	4 TTS 1200
Year:	1973
Power:	88 bhp
Capacity:	1177 cc
Type:	4-cylinder, 4-stroke

MÜNCH-4 TTS-E 1200

As 1972 turned into 1973, a new Big Bike promptly appeared: the Münch-4 TTS-E 1200. At one fell swoop Friedel Münch had thrown down the gauntlet to the rest of the world, and in particular to Kawasaki with its new 900-cc Z1. The 'E' of the TTS-E stood for 'Einspritzer', meaning 'fuel injection', and the power of 100 bhp gave a speed of 244 km/h 152 mph). No bike in the world was faster or more expensive.

Model:	4 TTS-E 1200
Year:	1974
Power:	100 bhp
Capacity:	1177 cc
Type:	4-cylinder, 4-stroke

MÜNCH-4 TTS-E 1200 Turbo

In 1974 Friedel Münch had sold his motorbike factory to Heinz W. Henke. From 1976 the 'Mammoth Man' was independent again with his new company Horex-Motorrad GmbH. The busy designer responded to customer demand with his Münch-4 TTS 1200 which later had fuel injection and a turbocharger. The Münch Turbo developed 125 bhp and reached almost 250 km/h (155 mph). With this performance, the Münch was the most powerful and fastest street bike available at the time.

Model:	4 TTS-E 1200 Turbo
Year:	1977
Power:	125 bhp
Capacity:	1177 cc
Type:	4-cylinder, 4-strok

Münch Mammut 2000

The Münch Mammut 2000 appeared as a technical sensation. With a capacity of 2000 cc, fuel injection and turbocharging, it developed a maximum torque of 295 Nm. Friedel Münch achieved his lifetime dream with this machine: 'I wanted to bring this legend to the street once more,' he said when it was launched in the year 2000. With a weight of 354 kg (780 lb), this Big Bike used the 2-litre 4-cylinder 4-stroke engine from the Opel Calibra Turbo. Münch Motorrad Technik GmbH ceased production of the Münch Mammut 2000 after 15 machines had been made because manufacturing it was not commercially justifiable. A limited series of 250 examples was planned.

Model:	Mammut 2000
Year:	2000
Power:	260 bhp
Capacity:	1998 cc
Type:	4-cylinder in-line, 4-stroke

MV Agusta – Italian aristocracy

The Sicilian Count Giovanni Agusta was a genuine aviation pioneer who designed his first aeroplane in 1907 and later founded the aircraft factory Costruzioni Aeronautiche Giovanni Agusta. But like all Italian companies specialising in this field, it was banned from any involvement in the production of armaments. Consequently Giovanni's son Domenico Agusta founded a new company, Meccanica Verghera, which launched its first motorbike in 1946. This was followed a year later by the 125 Bicilindrica, an exclusive mass-produced motorbike, and soon afterwards the company became involved in racing in order to make its bikes better known. Between 1948 and 1976 Agusta's works racing bikes had won 275 Grand Prix victories and 38 Drivers' World Championship titles. But the production bikes, in spite of initially selling well, were always in the shadow of the highly sophisticated racing bikes. It was Count Agusta himself who decided which model would be built; he also decided on engineering and styling points and appointed the riders and other members of the team himself. He was both father figure and dictator and his management style, similar to that of Enzo Ferrari, was unusual. But then this maker was also unique in the world of racing. It is significant that the MV Agusta company only survived its founder until 1980, stifled by bad budgeting, an ill-advised board of directors and bureaucracy. This fate was similar to that of Gilera and Moto Guzzi on the deaths of their founders. But while these two companies were taken over by other groups, the MV emblem disappeared completely from motorbike fuel tanks – until Claudio Castiglioni revived it with the F4. In spite of all these problems there is now a works Superbike team again.

MV Agusta 125

The 125-cc category of motorcycle races rapidly achieved widespread popularity and MV reacted by sending this slight machine with three-speed gearbox, largely based on the similar production bike, onto the track in 1948. It clocked up its first big victory in the same year at the Grand Prix in Faenza. A year later came a version with a four-speed gearbox; it was this bike that was the springboard for the career of racing rider Carlo Ubbiali.

Model:	125 Tre Marce
Year:	1948
Power:	9 bhp
Capacity:	123 cc
Type:	Single-cylinder, 2-stroke

MV Agusta 125 TEL

In 1949, on the heels of the commercial success of the first and very basic three-speed 125 models, came this visually and technically completely revamped four-speed machine. It could be had as a tourer, or as a more powerful sports version which could be recognised by its larger exhaust. In terms of quality, the TEL was the start of a new era at MV. It was also the beginning of MV's strange tradition of using baffling model designations.

Model:	125 TEL Sport
Year:	1949
Power:	6 bhp
Capacity:	123 cc
Type:	Single-cylinder, 2-stroke

MZ Skorpion Traveller

For bikers with a lust for travel MZ brought out a touring version of the Skorpion equipped with a cowling and side cases as standard. MZ offered a sports version for racier souls; this featured a half-fairing and a smaller seat.

Model:	Skorpion Traveller
Year:	1995
Power:	48 bhp
Capacity:	659 cc
Type:	Single-cylinder, 4-stroke

MZ Skorpion Replica

Evoking its glorious heyday in motor sport, MZ entered the Supermono European Cup, in which it consistently finished among the fastest. In 1995 MZ brought out a replica of its successful European Cup machine, which was actually more of a tuned-up sports version of the Skorpion than a true replica. The bike's tubular beam frame corresponded with other Skorpion models; White Power provided the suspension and Brembo the double 280-mm disc brakes. Thanks to the twin exhaust and a modified engine the bike delivered a hefty 50 bhp.

Model:	Skorpion Replica
Year:	1995
Power:	50 bhp
Capacity:	659 cc
Type:	Single-cylinder, 4-stroke

MZ Mastiff

MZ began offering a supermoto fun bike in 1997 in the shape of the Mastiff, recognisable by its tall silhouette. Like the Skorpion models it was powered by Yamaha's robust five-valve single-cylinder engine. It was not exactly a wild, high-powered machine, but its solid chassis and individual looks raised MZ's profile.

Model:	Mastiff
Year:	1997
Power:	50 bhp
Capacity:	659 cc
Type:	Single-cylinder, 4-stroke

MZ Baghira

The Baghira and Mastiff models were conceived as siblings in 1997. The Baghira was a very successful enduro variant which could handle even adventurous off-road expeditions and hold its own in performance challenges with the Japanese competition. The robust but ageing single-cylinder engine admittedly looked weak up against the new Yamaha single-cylinder generation. The picture shows the Black Panther, an all-in-black supermoto version.

Model:	Baghira Black Panther
Year:	2001
Power:	50 bhp
Capacity:	659 cc
Type:	Single-cylinder, 4-stroke

MZ RT 125

The 2000 RT 125 was not just a resurrection of Zschopau's legendary million-selling model, but also the first MZ of the modern era to feature one of MZ's own engines. The water-cooled 125-cc dohc 4-stroke power unit with four valves and balancing shafts delivered an enthusiastic 15 bhp. Steady export sales to numerous countries finally marked the return of better times for MZ.

Model:	RT 125
Year:	2000
Power:	15 bhp
Capacity:	124 cc
Type:	Single-cylinder, 4-stroke

MZ 125 SX

MZ had two other models in its range based on the successful RT 125 ready for the 2001 season. The SX version was another bike that had no problem making its presence felt thanks to its powerful, sophisticated 4-stroke engine. The characteristics of the chassis could match the competition from the Far East and the design was appealingly up-to-date.

Model:	125 SX
Year:	2002
Power:	15 bhp
Capacity:	124 cc
Type:	Single-cylinder, 4-stroke

MZ 125 SM

The supermoto version of the 125 enduro model answered to the designation 'SM' and with its 17-inch wheels it was easily distinguished from the off-road variant. It was not quite a drift queen, but this nippy little bike still invited its owners to overheat its tyres anytime they liked.

Model:	125 SM
Year:	2002
Power:	15 bhp
Capacity:	124 cc
Type:	Single-cylinder, 4-stroke

MZ 1000 S

By the 2004 season MZ was finally ready to bring out its own long-awaited sports tourer model. The bike had been over three years in development and the Malaysian parent company had invested about 15 million euros in the project to give MZ a fighting chance in the fiercely competitive motorcycle market. Despite the bike's sporty appearance, the MZ 1000 was billed as a touring bike, as was emphasised by its thorough wind protection and comfortable seating position. The chassis was robust and offered an ideal compromise between sportiness and comfort. Any criticism was mainly directed at the engine, which reacted somewhat abruptly to the rider's commands at under 4,000 revs. Several attempts were made to solve the problem by altering the fuel injection settings but the results were never completely satisfactory. On the other hand this Saxon beauty was at least environmentally sound; as well as fuel injection there were two catalytic converters.

Model:	1000 S
Year:	2004
Power:	115 bhp
Capacity:	998 cc
Type:	2-cylinder in-line, 4-stroke

MZ 1000 SF

MZ unveiled a streetfighter version of the 1000 S for the 2005 season, the 1000 SF. The original bike's full fairing was replaced by a design resembling the style used on its sister model's headlight casing. This market demanded a certain bad-boy quality of its machines and the SF really does not deliver, with its fairly harmless aura and chunkiness around the middle.

Model:	1000 SF
Year:	2005
Power:	112 bhp
Capacity:	998 cc
Type:	2-cylinder in-line, 4-stroke

NSU 351 SS

NSU's great run of motorcycle racing victories began with the acquisition of rider Walter William Moore from Norton. Moore developed the 501 SS and 351 SS racing machines. Besides the cunningly designed vertical shaft drive single-cylinder engine, the bike's low centre of gravity added to its marvellous handling characteristics.

Model:	NSU 351 SS (the affordable racing motorbike)
Year:	1936
Power:	25 bhp
Capacity:	346 cc
Type:	Single-cylinder, 4-stroke, vertical shaft drive

NSU OSL 601 combination

Like so many post-war motorcycles, this model was put together in the NSU factory from remaining stores of spare parts. Components from the pre-war OSL and the post-war Konsul, such as the seat covering, steering head and dashboard, front headlamp and silencer, were combined. Apart from the Bing carburettor, the engine and transmission unit were identical to the OSL 601. As was typical of the time, many parts were chrome-plated.

Model:	NSU OSL 601 combination (post-war)
Year:	1951
Power:	24 bhp
Capacity:	562 cc
Type:	Single-cylinder, 4-stroke

NSU Konsul

The Konsul was a modernised version of the pre-war OSL with four-speed gearbox transmission, rear wheel suspension and telescopic forks. Conceived as a robust touring machine and suitable for fitting a sidecar, the Konsul models were regarded as post-war showpieces. Oil-tight valves and a covered chain housing to the rear wheel were striking features. At first sight the engine was reminiscent of that of the SS series, but the Konsul's wide chrome tube did not in fact contain any vertical shafts; as with the OSL models, they contained the push rods for the ohv engine. NSU offered a sports kit for the 500 model which increased its power by 30 hp.

NSU Max

In the 1950s the Max was the most widely ridden bike of any class in Germany. Designer Albert Roder had created a motorbike head and shoulders above the competition, both at home and abroad. The Ultramax push-rod valvegear was revolutionary and delivered high revs. On its launch the relatively small Max was able to deliver almost the same amount of power as the Konsul I, despite the extra 100 cc of the latter.

NSU Rennmax ('Racing Max')

It was on this machine that Werner Haas rode to the German and World Championship title in 1953. Top speed: 210 km/h (130 mph), weight: 117 kg (258 lb). The bike's pressed sheet metal frame, rear wheel swing-arm and front forks were similar to the production Max model. The 2-cylinder Racing Max just could not be beaten. For NSU, 1953 was the most successful racing year since the foundation of the firm.

Model:	Konsul		Model:	Max Standard		Model:	Rennmax (works racer)
Year:	1951		Year:	1952		Year:	1953
Power:	17.5 bhp		Power:	17 bhp		Power:	36 bhp
Capacity:	349 cc		Capacity:	247 cc		Capacity:	248 cc
Type:	Single-cylinder, 4-stroke		Type:	Single-cylinder, 4-stroke		Type:	2-cylinder, 4-stroke

NSU Superlux

Experience garnered on the racing track also led to improvements in NSU's standard street models: an increase of power from 8.6 to 11 bhp, large aluminium full hub drum brakes and a noise-reducing Difusor silencer were strong selling points of the Superlux, which also set new standards of rider comfort at its introduction in 1951.

Model:	Superlux
Year:	1955
Power:	11 bhp
Capacity:	198 cc
Type:	Single-cylinder, 2-stroke

NSU Geländemax (off-road)

Production Max models were converted for off-road use. It is no exaggeration to say that no two off-road Max machines were identical, customised as they were for each individual rider. Factory machines and private conversions featured external shock absorbers. The machine pictured was the one that carried Erwin Schmider to ten German 350 cc championship titles between 1958 and 1967.

Model:	Geländemax (off-road)
Year:	1956
Power:	21 bhp
Capacity:	297 cc
Type:	Single-cylinder, 4-stroke

NSU Max-Gespann (sidecar)

This sidecar model was converted for off-road riding. The NSU advertising of the time was not shy in promoting the bike's sporting success: 'The 1956 German moto-cross championship presented competitors with formidable obstacles: only people who can really ride and have a machine praiseworthy beyond words can win this race – so when are you going to start on an NSU?'

Model:	Max-Gespann (sidecar)
Year:	1956
Power:	21 bhp
Capacity:	297 cc
Type:	Single-cylinder, 4-stroke

NSU 'Mini-Max' Fox

NSU motorbikes, and motorbike engines for installation in other chassis were sold all over the world. One Danish importer marketed Fox and Max bikes with 16-inch wheels as special models. This model with a Fox engine was on show at a 1956 exhibition in Copenhagen.

Model:	'Mini-Max' Fox
Year:	1956
Power:	5.2 bhp
Capacity:	98 cc
Type:	Single-cylinder, 4-stroke

NSU Quickly 'Cavallino'

This was NSU's sports moped with Italian lines. NSU advertised its Quickly bike with the slogans 'Lucky the riders that ride Quickly' and 'Stop walking, buy Quickly', although they were not striking enough for the teddy boys of the late 1950s. The Quickly Cavallino fulfilled the desire for a moped with an authentic motorcycle look. The name means 'colt' in Italian and came from Cavallino in Italy, where the 'NSU Lido' company campsite was located.

Model:	Quickly 'Cavallino'
Year:	1959
Power:	1.7 bhp
Capacity:	49 cc
Type:	Single-cylinder, 2-stroke

Opel – A car giant on two wheels

Opel and motorbikes? The eventful history of the Opel company started in 1862 with the production of sewing-machines. In 1886 Adam Opel decided to produce bicycles and in 1901 the first motorbike left the factory at Rüsselsheim. It was followed by single-cylinder range with a frame open at the bottom or an enclosed frame and in 1905 Opel developed a parallel-twin model. Later the company successfully marketed light motorcycles which increasingly had the appearance of real motorbikes. Opel was also active in the world of racing and it even had its own racing circuit in its home town. The high point was in 1929 when it had a trial run with a rocket-powered motorbike. When Opel took over Elite-Diamant AG in Reichenbrand in 1928, it manufactured the 500-cc motorbikes there. This was also the year when the most famous Opel model was launched, the Motoclub. But the imminent economic crisis hampered its success and production ceased in 1931.

Opel 3 1/2 horsepower

With this large touring motorbike with a 2-cylinder engine the pioneering Opel engineers diverged from the normal way of doing things. Unlike most of its rivals with a V-engine, they decided on an engine with two parallel upright cylinders side-by-side . But as was charactersitic of motorbikes of the time, the seat position was very far back and it the vehicle did without a front brake.

Model: 3 1/2 horsepower	Year: 1905	Power: 3.5 bhp
Capacity: 680 cc	Type: 2-cylinder, 4-stroke	

Opel rocket-powered motorbike

Fritz von Opel was fascinated by rocket technology. In the early 1920s he experimented with rocket cars, then with a rocket-powered tracked vehicle and a rocket-powered aircraft. Then in 1928 Opel began making a rocket-powered motorbike. The bike was based on a Motoclub 500 SS, but as well as the single-cylinder engine which was in series production, this first had six and later 14 rockets at the back. This bike was only shown in public on one occasion.

Model:	RAK
Year:	1928
Power:	22 bhp plus rockets
Capacity:	498 cc
Type:	Single-cylinder, 4-stroke, plus rocket power

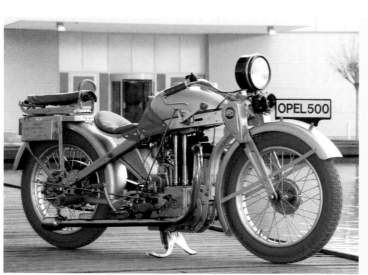

Opel Motoclub

With the Motoclub the Opel range included one of the most modern motorbikes of the time. Based on the revolutionary ideas of the constructor Ernst Neumann-Neander, this Opel was fitted with a single-cylinder engine and produced in series. The riveted pressed-steel frame, as well as the forks, the tank and the mudguards, were painted silver, while the saddle, handgrips, footrests and even the tyres were red. The touring version with side-valve engine developed 16 bhp while the ohv Supersport model developed 22 bhp.

Model:	Motoclub T
Year:	1929
Power:	16 bhp
Capacity:	498 cc
Type:	Single-cylinder, 4-stroke

Peugeot – A sturdy bike from France

The French maker Peugeot, which had specialised in the production of spring steel since 1887, was one of the pioneers in the development of powered two-wheeled vehicles. But the two Peugeot brothers separated in 1892 since Eugène wanted to make cars and Armand wanted to build motorbikes. By the turn of the century, Armand was already producing his first motorbikes in his Beaulieu factory. These had unsprung bicycle frames, fitted with a single-cylinder engine, and they soon proved successful on the race tracks. In 1905 Peugeot's 1.1-litre V-twin racer set an absolute speed record with a top speed of 123.2 km/h (77 mph). By 1933 Peugeot had developed a range of sturdy everyday and touring motorbikes but shortly after the Second World War the company restricted its production to 2-stroke motorbikes. In the 1950s, reflecting the trend towards mergers in the motor industry, the Peugeot group took over the Magnat Debon, Automoto and Terrot marques. At the same time it was already apparent that the demand for motorbikes was in strong decline. Peugeot was quick to react and specialised instead in the manufacturing of small low-powered 50-cc mopeds.

Peugeot Tricycle

The first motorbike built by Peugeot in Beaulieu was a tricycle. After the failure of attempts using a steam engine which was much too heavy, it was fitted with a 140-cc single-cylinder engine patented by Benz. With this engine, this petrol-fuelled tricycle was able to reach a speed of at least 40 km/h (25 mph), definitely enough for the unsprung, barely reinforced bicycle frame.

Model:	Tricycle	Year:	1898	Power:	1.5 bhp
Capacity:	140 cc	Type:	Single-cylinder, 4-stroke		

Peugeot P 107

Besides bikes for everyday use with 2-stroke engines, Peugeot also produced a range of 4-stroke engines. The small side-valve single-cylinder transferred the power through a three-speed gearbox attached to the rear wheel. The dynamo for lighting, driven by an open belt, was available only as an optional extra.

Model:	P 107	Year:	1932	Power:	5 bhp
Capacity:	247 cc	Type:	Single-cylinder, 4-stroke		

Peugeot 515 Records

In 1934 the racing team attempted to break a few records with the new Peugeot 515, presented at the October Salon in 1933. Three new records were set, which included the 750 and 1000-cc categories as well as 500 cc. With the rider lying flat, this speed bike, based on the production model, was able to reach a top speed of 140 km/h (87 mph).

Model:	515 Records	Year:	1934	Power:	20 bhp
Capacity:	495 cc	Type:	Single-cylinder, 4-stroke		

Peugeot 517

The top model in the 1930s, this luxury version had a sophisticated 500-cc engine. Although it was very successful in competition and combined high quality with excellent reliability, Peugeot experienced sales problems, as did many other bike manufacturers at the time.

Model:	517	Year:	1937	Power:	12 bhp
Capacity:	495 cc	Type:	Single-cylinder, 4-stroke		

Puch – Mountain goats with twin piston

The Austrian Johann Puch founded his company 'Erste Steiermärkische Fahrradfabrik AG' to produce bicycles, soon to be followed by motorbikes. The motorbikes built by Puch were distinguished by their particular engine construction: the single-cylinder 2-stroke twin-piston or split-single engine. This unusual technique remained Puch's speciality for 50 years. In 1934 the group formed by the merger of Steyr, Daimler and Puch created the largest motorbike factory in Austria. After the Second World War new models were developed which were fitted with an up-dated version of the split-single engine. However at the end of the 1960s the Austrians abandoned the expensive split-single technology in favour of sporty single-cylinder 2-stroke engines. By 1973 the company started taking part in moto-cross competition but pulled out from official involvement in 1977 in spite of having won a title in the World Championship. In 1987 the Italian company Piaggio took over the motorbike division.

Puch 220

The successful story of the split-single 2-stroke Puch engines began in 1923. The LM (meaning 'light motorbike') model had a 122-cc engine, originally designed by Garelli, which was then much improved by design engineer Giovanni Marcellino. It was followed by a 175 and then a 220-cc version with 2-speed gearbox and chain drive, of which 12,000 were sold between 1926 and 1928. Puch had read the market absolutely correctly.

Model: 220	Year: 1926	Power: 4.5 bhp
Capacity: 223 cc	Type: Split-single cylinder 2-stroke	

Puch 250 S4

In 1933 the Austrian Max Reisch went on a brave journey which took him all the way to India by the overland route. He was travelling on a standard 250-cc Puch. It was a thrilling adventure and at the same time he put the reliability of this small motorbike seriously to the test. This little bike with a twin-piston 2-stroke engine, carrying two people and lots of luggage, safely reached its destination without any serious problems. The only difference from the production model available on the market was that it had a larger fuel tank and several luggage racks.

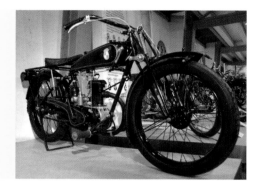

Model: 250 S4	Year: 1933	Power: 11 bhp
Capacity: 246 cc	Type: Split-single cylinder 2-stroke	

Puch 125 SL, 175 SL, 250 SL

In 1950 Puch presented new 125, 175 and 250-cc motorbikes with a pressed steel frame. Because the Austrian 2-stroke engine had high torque and a comparatively broad power band, they made powerful motorcycle combinations – supplied from the factory with a sidecar made by Felber – and they were capable of astounding performance on mountain roads.

Model: 125 SL	Year: 1950	Power: 7.5 bhp
Capacity: 124 cc	Type: Split-single cylinder 2-stroke	

Puch GS 175

Since 1969 former cross-country rider Luigi Frigerio and his brother had imported Puch bikes to Italy and improved them. With a lighter frame, suspension elements by Betor and Ceriani and a higher performance, they made the bikes internationally competitive. In 1972 the Frigerio brothers provided the Puch works team with suitably modified bikes. Because of their low-slung chrome-molybdenum frame the Frigerio-Puch bikes were known as 'Bassotto' and they were exported mainly to the United States. In 1973 Puch took part officially in the Moto-Cross World Championship and in 1975 Harry Evans won the world title in the 250-cc class.

Model: Bassotto 175 Sei Giorni	Year: 1973	Power: 24 bhp
Capacity: 169 cc	Type: Single-cylinder, 2-stroke	

Royal Enfield – Classic motorbikes from India

The cycle manufacturer Enfield Cycle Company made its first step towards motorisation in 1899 with three-wheelers powered by De Dion engines. The first motorbike, fitted with a Minerva engine, was launched in 1901. But the company did not build another motorbike until it produced one fitted with a Motosacoche 2-cylinder engine in 1910. It was followed by further V-twins with 770-cc JAP engines. The first models in the style of the present-day Royal Enfield bikes date back to 1931. Royal Enfield was at the technical forefront in the country because of its innovative chassis with its front forks and hydraulically damped telescopic arms on the rear swinging forks. Enfield was the first maker to use rear-wheel suspension even in scrambler bikes. When the plant in Redditch was modernised in 1955, the two single-cylinder bikes were also given a face-lift. The company was taken over by the Smith group in 1962 and the single-cylinder was abandoned. Then in 1967 the main plant at Redditch was closed and the marque finally disappeared in 1970. But since 1955 there has been a subsidiary plant in India which had operated completely independently. This was because the Madras Motor Company had been importing Royal Enfields since 1949 and when the Indian government chose the Bullet 350 as its official motorbike, the demand from India exceeded the English production capacity. This is how the Enfield India Ltd Incorporated came to be founded in Madras.

Enfield Bullet

The Bullet, designed by Ted Parode in the 1930s with 350 and 500-cc versions, was comprehensively revamped in 1948. With its rear-wheel swinging fork and hydraulically damped suspension strut and telescopic front forks with rebound and compression damping, the Royal Enfield was far ahead of its British competitors, which mostly still used rigid rear frames. Its suitability as a cross-country bike played a crucial part in its being chosen for military use.

Model:	Bullet 350
Year:	1953
Power:	16 bhp
Capacity:	346 cc
Type:	Single-cylinder, 4-stroke

Enfield Diesel

This Spartan version of the normal Enfield had an air-cooled diesel power unit actually designed as a stationary engine, with a nominal maximum of 3,000 rpm. So this bike of 180 kg (397 lb) was able to rattle along at a mere 80 km/h (50 mph), but on the other hand its fuel consumption was under 2 litres per 100 km (140 mpg) so it could travel 1,000 km (over 600 miles) on a full tank.

Model:	Bullet 325 Diesel
Year:	2000
Power:	7 bhp
Capacity:	325 cc
Type:	Single-cylinder, diesel

Enfield Scrambler

Various importers also offered nostalgic reproductions based on the Bullet. So, as well as a motorcycle with sidecar, the Swiss Fritz Egli had also built an interesting sports model with cylinder capacity increased to 625 cc and power to 40 bhp. The Scrambler shown here, built by the German Enfield dealer Jochen Sommer in Eppstein, was also fitted with a more powerful engine. Its engineering and visual appearance were clearly inspired by the 1950s models.

Model:	Bullet 535 Scrambler
Year:	2001
Power:	32 bhp
Capacity:	535 cc
Type:	Single-cylinder, 4-stroke

Enfield De Luxe

The 500 cc Enfield was produced in two versions, Standard and De Luxe, similar in their construction. The main difference was that the De Luxe version had more chrome-plated parts. In addition, an electric starter and new five-speed gearbox were also available to order. The large Bullet was built exclusively for export while in India only the 350-cc model was available.

Model:	Bullet 500
Year:	2001
Power:	24 bhp
Capacity:	499 cc
Type:	Single-cylinder, 4-stroke

Sachs – Innovation with tradition

Two names in particularly are linked with the name of the Sachs company: Karl Fichtel and Ernst Wilhelm Sachs. These two men founded the 'Schweinfurter Präzisions Kugellagerwerke' in 1885, the highly qualified precision engineer Wilhelm Sachs contributing his ideas and Fichtel the money. Their first great success came in 1903 with the torpedo hub for bicycles. In 1925 the company became a limited company but was sold to SKF of Sweden in the same year because of the world economic crisis. Then the enthusiastic cyclist Ernst Sachs had the idea of fitting an engine to a bicycle. Soon small-capacity engines from Schweinfurt were being used by motorbike manufacturers all over the world. After the death of his father (1932), Willy Sachs took over the management and expanded the company's range of products by producing clutches and shock-absorbers. But motorbikes sold under the Sachs name remained a rare exception because the company was first and foremost a supplier to motorbike manufacturers. In 1963 it took over the Hercules company of Nuremberg so that the Sachs group now had its own motorbike marque. So the true forerunner of the present-day Sachs Fahrzeug- und Motorentechnik GmbH was strictly speaking not Sachs but Hercules. When Fichtel & Sachs was bought by the Mannesmann group in 1995, the bicycle division of Fichtel & Sachs was sold to the Dutch ATAG group while the motorised division was hived off as as Sachs Fahrzeug- and Motorentechnik GmbH. Three years later it was sold to the Dutch Winning Wheels Group, but this pulled out at the end of 2000. At the beginning of 2001 the Nuremberg management and a few workers were able to save the company from bankruptcy through a management buy-out. The company is now independent again and produces over 25,000 two-wheelers a year, ranging from electric-powered bicycles to mopeds, scooters and high capacity motorbikes. It is now one of the largest manufacturers of powered two-wheeled vehicles in Germany.

Sachs K 75 GS

This small cross-country bike with air-cooled 2-stroke engine was marketed under the Sachs label. It was based on the little Hercules K 50 bike introduced in 1962 and was launched two years after it. It had a five-speed gearbox, 19-mm Bing carburetor and longer suspension travel. But in spite of all this, it was still unable to compete successfully in the German cross-country championships against bikes from makers such as Victoria and Zündapp.

Model:	K 75 GS
Year:	1964 to 1969
Power:	7 bhp/from 1967: 8.5 bhp
Capacity:	74 cc
Type:	Single-cylinder, 2-stroke

Sachs GS 250

GS or 'Geländesport' means cross-country which is why the whole GS range (125, 175, 250, 350 and 350 MC) had a seven-speed gearbox, telescopic front forks and rear swinging fork with two suspension struts so that riders could indulge in their passion for competition. Sadly this impressive sports package was also its undoing. Lack of new blood and new regulations for the protection of the environment gradually suppressed cross-country racing, and the GS was not really suited to be an enduro road bike.

Model:	GS 250
Year:	1976 to 1980
Power: 2	6 bhp
Capacity:	245 cc
Type:	Single-cylinder, 2-stroke

Sachs K 50 Ultra II LC

This legendary little bike was made for 16-year-old tearaways in the 1980s. Fitted with Marzocchi forks, Grimeca two-rotor disc brake system and liquid-cooled engine, it managed to reach a top speed of 100 km/h (61 mph). Bent over the handlebars behind a cockpit-style fairing, its young riders could imagine that they were the racing bikers of the future.

Model:	K 50 Ultra II LC
Year:	1979 to 1983
Power:	6.25 bhp
Capacity:	49 cc
Type:	Single-cylinder, 2-stroke

Sachs Beast

Sachs caused an absolute sensation at the 2000 Intermot Fair with its concept design for the 'Beast'. 'We wanted to show how we pictured the ultimate motorbike, although we accept that the Beast in this form has no chance of being approved for road use,' explained chief engineer Hartmut Hahn, thus dashing any expectations of an immediate realization of the concept. The firm wanted to test the public's reaction and then decide how to develop the concept. Judging by the extremely positive response in Munich, heads must then have started spinning in Nuremberg to try and bring this two-wheeled wonder onto the road. A brilliantly powerful V-twin bike had been developed, with every aspect displaying great originality. But unfortunately it could not be produced in this form – there are laws against this kind of technical permissiveness. And Sachs still had no suitable engine. The Folan V-twin power unit mounted on the prototype, used in the Swedish Highland hard-core off-road bike, has proved its structural strength on several rallies and with 90 bhp it had clearly increased its power. But the new powerful generations of V-twin from Rotax, KTM and Aprilia would also be possible for the Beast. We are still being kept in suspense…

Model:	Beast
Year:	2000
Power:	76 bhp
Capacity:	1000 cc
Type:	V-twin, 4-stroke

Sachs Roadster s-650

The bike had a pleasing streamlined appearance and the powerful 650-cc Suzuki engine was sturdy and sufficiently powerful. But in spite of a certain 'made in Germany' bonus and the still-illustrious name of a traditional maker, this small roadster has not been particularly successful in this age of streetfighters, supersport bikes and monster cruisers. This is true even of the exclusive version shown here with its titanium look, which is also available in an 800-cc roadster version.

Sachs Roadster 800

Just as unadorned as its smaller sibling, the 800-cc Roadster with the V-twin Bollerman engine with shaft drive drive, used in the Suzuki Intruder models, made its debut in 2002. The extremely comfortable chassis and excellent traction made this large roadster an ideal bike for touring, but on the other hand for people who are often in a hurry its performance would be thought somewhat uninspiring.

Sachs b-805

As a tribute to the much-admired Beast and for the Sachs enthusiasts who did not want to wait until the day when the Beast might eventually go into production, Sachs remodelled its 800-cc Roadster to include some of the design features of the concept bike. Nevertheless the result was not quite as thrilling as the Beast itself…

Model:	s-650 Roadster
Year:	2002
Power:	50 bhp
Capacity:	644 cc
Type:	Single-cylinder, 4-stroke

Model:	800 Roadster
Year:	2002
Power:	58 bhp
Capacity:	805 cc
Type:	V-twin, 4-stroke

Model:	b-805
Year:	2003
Power:	58 bhp
Capacity:	805 cc
Type:	V-twin, 4-stroke

Sachs MadAss

In 2004 Sachs launched the ultra-space-age MadAss, also inspired by the Beast, and this was extremely successful. This distinctive low-powered moped with 'underseat' exhaust system and robust 50-cc 4-stroke engine – a reproduction of the legendary Honda Dax bike – soon acquired cult status among the young. There had been nothing like it since the Kreidler Flory period. It was therefore not surprising that Sachs was already working on a 125 and even a 500-cc version both of which would inherit the spectacular design of the little MadAss. On the left is a prototype of the 500-cc version which was presented at the Intermot Fair in Munich in 2004.

Model:	MadAss
Year:	2004
Power:	3 bhp
Capacity:	49 cc
Type:	Single-cylinder, 4-stroke

SUZUKI – The bikes with the distinctive 'S'

The 'Suzuki Shokkuki Seisakusho' company was founded in 1909 in Hamamatsu by the 22-year-old Michio Suzuki. This technically gifted young entrepreneur was a carpenter by profession and built not motorbikes but weaving looms until the Second World War. The recovery of industry was speedy after the war but because there was very little demand for looms, the company switched to agricultural machinery. At the end of 1951 the mentally-alert head of the company made a clever business move and decided to build motorbikes. Admittedly the first Suzuki 'Power Free' only had a capacity of 36 cc and a power of 1 bhp but by the end of 1952 Suzuki had sold over 10,000 2-stroke mopeds. Things were going so well that the company then launched the A 100, T20 and T500 models. Suzuki was on the path of success in both Japan and the USA. The new GS 750 4-cylinder bike, launched in 1976, was a real sensation. It was the first time that Suzuki had had a 4-stroke in its range and the GS 750 was an immediate success. But in the early 1980s the 'extended Suzuki family' in parts of Europe slipped into crisis. The only way out was an intervention by the head office in Japan and by 1984 management was directly from Japan. At the same time Suzuki launched its next sensation: the GSX-R750. A racing bike for public roads! Suddenly everyone was talking about it. Suzuki has been going for over 50 years during which time it has fulfilled everyone's needs and desires.

Suzuki Power Free

Anyone who wanted to be mobile in post-war Japan had to ride a push-bike or be fortunate enough to own one with an auxiliary engine. Aware of the great demand for personal transport, Suzuki responded by launching the Power Free. It was in 1952 with this 36-cc bike that Michio Suzuki laid the foundation of his motorbike empire, soon becoming Japan's third-largest bike manufacturer.

Model:	Power Free
Year:	1952
Power:	1 bhp
Capacity:	36 cc
Type:	Single-cylinder, 2-stroke

Suzuki 125 ST6A

In 1954 Suzuki launched the Colleda range. In the meantime, however, Suzuki's 2-stroke bikes had grown into real motorbikes, well able to keep up with those of its rivals Yamaha and Honda. In 1959 the top model in the Colleda rangewas the ST6A with 125-cc engine delivering an impressive 8 bhp. It was then that the distinctive Suzuki 'S' appeared for the first time on the fuel tank.

Model:	125 ST6A
Year:	1959
Power:	8 bhp
Capacity:	124 cc
Type:	Single-cylinder, 2-stroke

Suzuki 250 T10

In the mid-1960s Suzuki was already well-established on the Japanese motorbike market and had started to export the first bikes to the United States. In 1963 the top model was the T10 with a 250-cc 2-cylinder 2-stroke engine, capable of developing 21 bhp. Suzuki described the T10 as a 'masterpiece'. The 'Suzuki Selmix' separate lubrication sysem ensured the reliable supply of oil to the 2-stroke engine.

Model:	250 T10
Year:	1963
Power:	21 bhp
Capacity:	248 cc
Type:	2-cylinder, 2-stroke

Suzuki A100

Suzuki also built great motorbikes in the smaller categories. The A 100 was such a bike. The lively single-cylinder 2-stroke engine had rotary valves and was capable of developing an impressive 9.5 bhp. Only a few of these sporty little numbers came to Europe.

Model:	A100
Year:	1967
Power:	9.5 bhp
Capacity:	98 cc
Type:	Single-cylinder, 2-stroke

Suzuki TC 305 Scrambler

In the early 1960s there was a real motorbike boom in the United States. The young motorbike generation was absolutely crazy about cross-country bikes. So, because the United States was the number 1 export country for Japanese motorbike manufacturers, every one of them had scramblers in their range. Suzuki's was the 37 bhp TC 305.

Model:	TC 305 Scrambler
Year:	1968
Power:	37 bhp
Capacity:	305 cc
Type:	2-cylinder, 2-stroke

Suzuki T 500 Titan

In 1967 Suzuki brought out the T 500, mainly geared to the US market. This powerful 2-cylinder 2-stroke bike was capable of developing an impressive 47 bhp and a top speed of almost 170 km/h (106 mph). In spite of the bike's sporty performance, impressive for the time, the Titan was sold in the States as a tourer-sports bike with shoulder-high handlebars.

Model:	T 500 Titan
Year:	1971
Power:	47 bhp
Capacity:	492 cc
Type:	2-cylinder, 2-stroke

Suzuki GT 550

At he beginning of the 1970s bike fans were still very much into 2-stroke motorbikes and it was for them that Suzuki created a series of models which ranged from 50 to 750 cc. In 1972 Suzuki launched the GT 550 with a 3-cylinder 2-stroke engine. This mid-range bike had a silky-smooth engine, capable of developing 48 bhp, both electric and kick starters and the RamAir system for optimal air-cooling of the engine.

Model:	GT 550
Year:	1972
Power:	48 bhp
Capacity:	543 cc
Type:	3-cylinder, 2-stroke

Suzuki GT 750 'Water Buffalo'

Suzuki has been famous as a 2-stroke specialist manufacturer since it started manufacturing two-wheelers in 1952. With the GT 750 it was starting a new chapter in the history of large 2-stroke road bikes. In spite of ever-stricter noise and exhaust regulations, the company remained faithful to the 2-stroke system. Technical solutions such as 'CCI' – clean oil injection – as well as a second 'SRIS' (Suzuki Recycle Injection System) lubrication circuit and the 'ECTS' exhaust system made the Suzuki 2-stroke engine a sturdy and reliable power unit.

Model:	GT 750
Year:	1972
Power:	62 bhp
Capacity:	739 cc
Type:	3-cylinder, 2-stroke

Suzuki GT 250

The GT 250 was often described as the beginner's bike in the GT range. But this light 250 cc bike was a crafty one. No other 250 cc was as fast as the agile 32-bhp sports bike with a six-speed gearbox worthy of a racing bike.

Model:	GT 250
Year:	1973
Power:	32 bhp
Capacity:	247 cc
Type:	2-cylinder, 2-stroke

Suzuki TR 750 III works racing bike

Suzuki built the TR 750 III, based on the GT 750, specially for 'Formula 750' (1973 to 1976). In its very first year the engaging English rider Barry Sheene, who was at the peak of his career in 1976 and 1977, won the series. Sheene went on to win the 500-cc World Championship on Suzuki's new RG 500, a 4-cylinder works bike.

Model:	TR 750 III
Year:	1973
Power:	110 bhp
Capacity:	749 cc
Type:	3-cylinder, 2-stroke

Suzuki RE5 Wankel

The new RE5 Wankel was a massive project for Suzuki. No other model had required such a long period of development or so much money, and by the end of it some 20 patents were pending. However Suzuki was confident that hi-tech-mad bikers would rush to the Suzuki dealers and snatch up this extraordinary bike. But the Wankel proved to be too heavy, not powerful enough and too slow. Speed freaks were not interested and stayed away. The RE5 remained a slow seller.

Model:	RE5 Wankel
Year:	1975
Power:	63 bhp
Chamber volume:	487 cc
Type:	Rotary-piston engine

Suzuki GT 500

Confirmed Suzuki 2-stroke enthusiasts had been aware of the Suzuki 500 for years through hearsay. But it wsa not until 1976 that this nimble 2-stroke was imported into Europe. The 40-bhp 500 GT had enormous traction power and amazing acceleration. The 500-cc twin was a perfect all-rounder which could be used both as a sports bike and also for leisure outings with a friend or to the ends of the earth.

Model:	GT 500
Year:	1976
Power:	40 bhp
Capacity:	492 cc
Type:	2-cylinder, 2-stroke

Suzuki GT 380

The 380 cc model could be described as the long-running success in the GT 3-cylinder 2-stroke range. It was launched in 1972 and remained in production until 1980. Visually it hardly differed from the GT 550 but it was easier to push and easier to handle when riding. In fact, it was an ideal beginner's bike.

Model:	GT 380
Year:	1977
Power:	33 bhp
Capacity:	371 cc
Type:	3-cylinder, 2-stroke

Suzuki GS 750

It had been clear since the early 1970s that the era of the 2-stroke bike was ending. Motorbike fans wanted 4-cylinder 4-stroke bikes like the Honda CB 750 Four. In response Suzuki launched the GS 4-stroke range. The GS 750 had its world premiere at IFMA in 1976. The specifications indicated 8,800 rpm but it could reach 10,000 rpm without difficulty, and the bike's maximum speed was 200 km/h (124 mph).

Model:	GS 750
Year:	1977
Power:	63 bhp
Capacity:	748 cc
Type:	4-cylinder, 4-stroke

Suzuki TS 250 ER

The TS 250 remained in the Suzuki catalogue for a good ten years, from 1972 till 1981. The nimble 2-stroke enduro was sturdy and reliable and was an ideal off-road bike for outings through hedges and ditches. In 1979 the Suzuki engineers fitted the single-cylinder 2-stroke engine with reed valves and the model designation changed to TS 250 ER.

Model:	TS 250 ER
Year:	1981
Power:	17 bhp
Capacity:	246 cc
Type:	Single-cylinder, 2-stroke

Suzuki GS 650 G Katana

The new Katana range, introduced in 1980, was a brave move on the part of Suzuki. The design was unusual and far from being to everyone's taste, at least as far as the 750 and 1100-cc models were concerned. The GS 650 G Katana had been specially conceived for the sport-loving touring rider. It was a lively, racy-looking bike but with shaft drive which fulfilled the requirements of all long-distance riders.

Model:	GSX 650 Katana
Year:	1981
Power:	74 bhp
Capacity:	673 cc
Type:	4-cylinder, 4-stroke

Suzuki GS 400 E

Like the GS 750, the GS 400, launched in 1976, was one of Suzuki's first generation of 4-stroke bikes. The robust 400-cc twin engine with six-speed gearbox was available in 27 or 34-bhp versions. The GS was a popular instruction bike and was also described as a beginner's bike.

Model:	GS 400 E
Year:	1982
Power:	27 bhp
Capacity:	395 cc
Type:	2-cylinder, 4-stroke

Suzuki DR 500 S

The trend whereby an enduro should be powered by a 2-stroke engine had come to an end once and for all in 1976 with the Yamaha TX 500. In 1981, some five years later, Suzuki brought out its first 500-cc off-road bike. In spite of its modern 4-valve engine and excellent cross-country performance, the DR 500 S was unable to make a breakthrough.

Model:	DR 500 S
Year:	1982
Power:	27 bhp
Capacity:	499 cc
Type:	2-cylinder, 4-stroke

Suzuki GSX 750 S Katana

In retrospect the Katana range developed by Hans A. Muth was not only extraordinarily brave but – initially unexpectedly – it became a milestone in the history of Suzuki. In 1980 opinions about it were much divided; there is after all no accounting for taste. Technically the new GSX 750 E was very much at the forefront of technology with its four-valve engine. The only problem was its appearance, since the bike looked much too unsophisticated. This was where star designer Muth stepped in and solved the problem, adding a half-fairing with corners and sides.

Model:	GSX 750 S Katana
Year:	1982
Power:	82 bhp
Capacity:	747 cc
Type:	4-cylinder, 4-stroke

Suzuki GSX 1100 S Katana

The flagship of the Katana range was the GSX 1100 S Katana. The only outward differences compared to the 750 cc Katana were the seat, with its colour arrangement, and the front mudguard. But it was worlds apart so far as performance was concerned. The new GSX 1100 four-valve engine developed a breathtaking 100 bhp, enabling this avant-garde sports bike to achieve a top speed of 220 km/h (137 mph).

Model:	GSX 1100 S Katana
Year:	1982
Power:	100 bhp
Capacity:	1075 cc
Type:	4-cylinder, 4-stroke

Suzuki GSX 1100 ES

In 1980 Suzuki presented the new GSX range, a logical development of the successful GS 2-valve range. The jewel in the crown of this refined 4-stroke engine was the patented TSCC twin-swirl combustion chamber shape, part of the new 4-valve technology. The top model of the range was the GSX 1100 E which in the course of time became available in countless variations including naked bike, half-fairing, full fairing and as the Katana. The GSX 1100 ES with half-fairing was a successful sports bike and touring bike rolled into one.

Model:	GSX 1100 ES
Year:	1983
Power:	100 bhp
Capacity:	1075 cc
Type:	4-cylinder, 4-stroke

Suzuki RG 250 W Gamma

In 1983, in keeping with the motto 'tradition demands', Suzuki surprised the fans of the 2-stroke engine with the completely newly developed RG 250 W Gamma. This sporty 250-cc bike was the first mass-produced bike with an aluminium frame. Weighing only 146 kg (322 lb), it was able to achieve a top speed of 180 km/h (112 mph). On narrow, winding minor roads the Gamma was the undisputed king.

Model:	RG 250 W Gamma
Year:	1985
Power:	45 bhp
Capacity:	247 cc
Type:	2-cylinder, 4-stroke

259

Suzuki GSX-R 750

The description could not be more accurate: 'from the race track to the road'. When the brand-new Suzuki GSX-R 750 was presented at the IFMA Fair in Cologne in 1984 it caused an absolute sensation and the superbike became the talk of the fair. No wonder. A 750-cc bike developing 100 bhp with an aluminium chassis, weighing barely 200 kg (441 lb), able to reach a top speed of 230 km/h (143 mph) and with the breathtaking appearance of a racing bike – this had never been seen before.

Model:	GSX-R 750
Year:	1985
Power:	100 bhp
Capacity:	748 cc
Type:	4-cylinder, 4-stroke

Suzuki DR 600 S Dakar

The Paris-Dakar Rally is the toughest off-road race of all. Suzuki has taken part in this legendary desert marathon with impressive results on several occasions. In 1986 Suzuki launched the DR 600 S Dakar for the enduro fans. Light, easy to handle, robust and an excellent off-road bike, it was also unbeatable on the narrow, winding roads on which the Suzuki Dakar was happiest.

Model:	DR 600 S Dakar
Year:	1986
Power:	44 bhp
Capacity:	585 cc
Type:	Single-cylinder, 4-stroke

Suzuki LS 650 Savage

The stereotype of the real chopper is not difficult to describe: very long front forks, high handlebars, foot-rests positioned far forward and a bullish V-twin engine – perhaps a Harley-Davidson. What do you do when someone wants a small chopper? Suzuki's answer was the LS 650. To avoid any confusion with the cult bikes from Milwaukee, the Suzuki engineers fitted the frame with the modified single-cylinder engine of the DR 600.

Model:	LS 650 Savage
Year:	1986
Power:	27 bhp
Capacity:	647 cc
Type:	Single-cylinder, 4-stroke

Suzuki VS 750 GL Intruder

The first Japanese 'Easy Rider' bikes were jokingly known as 'soft choppers' because they were subsequently-modified production bikes. But that was not the case with the VS 750 GL Intruder. It could rightly be described as the first true chopper 'made in Japan' with its 45° V-twin water-cooled engine with overhead camshafts, four valves and shaft drive. The Intruder looked really cool.

Model:	VS 750 GL Intruder
Year:	1986
Power:	50 bhp
Capacity:	738 cc
Type:	V-twin, 4-stroke

Suzuki GSX 1100 E

Long before unfaired bikes were called 'naked bikes', they were merely described as heavy bikes. Because these very heavy monsters needed a name, the expression 'macho-bike' was invented. Enormously powerful, extremely heavy and breathtakingly fast, these were definitely bikes for grown men.

Model:	GSX 1100 E
Year:	1986
Power:	100 bhp
Capacity:	1075 cc
Type:	4-cylinder, 4-stroke

Suzuki GS 1100 G

The era of the GS 2-valve engine had actually come to an end by 1980. But to the great joy of the fans of the classic big bikes, in 1986 Suzuki brought out the GS 1100 G and production continued until 1988. This big bike with its powerful engine and shaft drive was the ideal means of transport for touring riders who love to feel the wind rush by.

Model:	GS 1100 G
Year:	1986
Power:	95 bhp
Capacity:	1074 cc
Type:	4-cylinder, 4-stroke

Suzuki GSX-R 1100

Barely a year after launching the sensational GSX-R 750, Suzuki presented the GSX-R 1100. An improvement had seemed hardly possible. But in keeping with the motto 'do what is feasible', it developed the 1100-cc which immediately became the flagship of Suzuki's production. The bike was fitted with the Hyper Sports 130-bhp engine.

Model:	GSX-R 1100
Year:	1986
Power:	130 bhp
Capacity:	1052 cc
Type:	4-cylinder, 4-stroke

Suzuki RG 500 Gamma

Racing has always been important for Suzuki. It had competed in the 500-cc category with a 4-cylinder 2-stroke racing-bike with rotary valves since 1974. The special feature of this engine was the square cylinder arrangement. In 1976 and 1977 Barry Sheene won the World 500-cc Championship on this works racer. Marco Luchinelli repeated the feat in 1981 and Franco Uncini in 1982. After these successes, in 1984 Suzuki decided to launch the RG 500 on the market as a road sports bike. The RG 500 weighed 181 kg (399 lb) and had a top speed of 230 km/h (143 mph).

Model:	RG 500 Gamma
Year:	1987
Power:	95 bhp
Capacity:	495 cc
Type:	4-cylinder, 2-stroke

Suzuki GSX 600 F

In the 1980s Honda had launched a new tourer sports model in the mid-range category, the Honda CBR 600 F. Suzuki was not long in responding. In 1987 it launched the GSX 600 on the market. The fully-faired all-rounder was available with a choice of 27, 34, 50 and 86-bhp engines. The GSX 600 F was a long-running success and remained in the Suzuki catalogue until 1998.

Model:	GSX 600 F
Year:	1988
Power:	86 bhp
Capacity:	594 cc
Type:	4-cylinder, 4-stroke

Suzuki RGV 250

In 1990 Suzuki presented the RGV 250 at IFMA in Cologne, to the great surprise of all 2-stroke fans. The racing replica had a 52-bhp V-twin 2-stroke engine with reed valves and catalytic converter. The aluminium chassis was adjustable and gave the 190-km/h (118-mph) racing bike impeccable roadholding.

Model:	RGV 250
Year:	1991
Power:	52 bhp
Capacity:	249 cc
Type:	V-twin, 2-stroke

Suzuki DR 800 S Big

In 1987 Suzuki launched the DR 750 S which was the largest single-cylinder enduro on the market. It was followed in 1990 by the DR 800 S Big. The enormous 4-valve engine was capable of developing 50 bhp and gave this maxi-enduro a maximum speed of 160 km/h (99 mph). The Big was an ideal travel-enduro and those who felt confident enough could rely on this long-legged off-road bike to carry them safely across the fields.

Model:	DR 800 S Big
Year:	1991
Power:	50 bhp
Capacity:	779 cc
Type:	Single-cylinder, 4-stroke

Suzuki DR 350 S

Real off-road freaks have their own ideas about what an enduro should be like. It should be light, easy to handle, hard-wearing and indestructible. Every smidgeon of bike weight counted. A weight of 140 kg (309 lb) and a 30-bhp engine was a good compromise. For cross-country acrobats who thought the jumps were not long enough, the ditches not deep enough and sandy stretches not extensive enough, Suzuki developed the DR 350 S. The off-road fun came free with the bike.

Model:	DR 350 S
Year:	1993
Power:	30 bhp
Capacity:	349 cc
Type:	Single-cylinder, 4-stroke

Suzuki DR 650 RS

Enduros were in fact conceived as cross-country bikes but they were also excellent travel bikes. Sitting upright with the face in the wind, the rider could go and enjoy nature and the countryside. Because of the wide handlebars and light weight, the bike was extraordinarily easy to handle and unbeatable on narrow, winding roads and even on mountain passes. Because riding cross-country is largely prohibited, enduro riders now mostly keep to country roads.

Model:	DR 650 RS
Year:	1994
Power:	46 bhp
Capacity:	641 cc
Type:	Single-cylinder, 4-stroke

Suzuki VS 1400 Intruder

The big fat 'Truder', as the 1400-cc is often called by its fans, had already been developed in almost identical form in the late 1980s. The unadorned chopper was powered by an air and oil-cooled 45° V-twin engine with transmission through a shaft drive. The Intruder was often used as a basis for spectacular customizations.

Model:	VS 1400 Intruder
Year:	1998
Power:	61 bhp
Capacity:	1360 cc
Type:	V-twin, 4-stroke

Suzuki TL 1000 S

The TL 1000 S had a short life. After its debut in 1997, this 2-cylinder sports bike was plagued by engine problems and difficulties with the handlebars which Suzuki eventually managed to resolve. But its reputation had been irreversibly damaged so that – at least in Germany – the TL 1000 S ceased to be available from 2001 onwards.

Model:	TL 1000 S
Year:	1999
Power:	98 bhp
Capacity:	996 cc
Type:	V-twin, 4-stroke

Suzuki TL 1000 R

The R-version of the 1000cc TL was launched in 1998 and was certainly not the most beautiful of supersports bikes. The aerodynamic fairing looked like a bulging addition and detracted from its sporty look. This was in contrast to the trim, agile V-twin engine, which could develop 125 bhp. By 2000 the TL was already being phased out.

Model:	TL 1000 R
Year:	1999
Power:	125 bhp
Capacity:	996 cc
Type:	V-twin, 4-stroke

Suzuki VL 250 Intruder

In spite of its modern 65° V-twin engine and very attractive design, this smaller Intruder led a shadowy existence in Germany. A 250-cc engine and cruising did not go well together, so the little Intruder was removed from the market after only two years.

Model:	VL 250 Intruder
Year:	2000
Power:	24 bhp
Capacity:	248 cc
Type:	V-twin, 4-stroke

Suzuki GSF 600 Bandit

The GSF 600 was launched in 1994 and for many years it remained a best-seller in the Suzuki range. The snappy appearance of the Bandit was reflected in its lively 4-cylinder engine which gave this 'naked bike' a power of some 78 bhp and a maximum speed of 200 km/h (124 mph).

Model:	GSF 600 Bandit
Year:	2000
Power:	78 bhp
Capacity:	600 cc
Type:	4-cylinder in-line, 4-stroke

Suzuki GSF 600 S Bandit

The Bandit was comprehensively revamped in 2000 and given among other things a new frame, firmer suspension elements, sharper brakes and a modified engine. The S-version shown here now had a larger half-fairing with a windshield which was clearly much better than that of its predecessor.

Model:	GSF 600 S Bandit
Year:	2000
Power:	78 bhp
Capacity:	600 cc
Type:	4-cylinders in-line, 4-stroke

Suzuki GSX-R 750

When Suzuki presented the new 750 cc GSX-R for the 2000 season, the fans breathed a great sigh of relief. After the various technical design mistakes of the previous model, such as the shapeless rear end, all was right with the world again. The new model was the sinewy supersports bike which racing enthusiasts had been waiting for. The lightweight construction reduced the unladen weight to 166 kg (366 lb), while at the same time the power was increased to 140 bhp. The picture was completed by a first-class chassis and a very attractive appearance.

Model:	GSX-R 750
Year:	2000
Power:	140 bhp
Capacity:	749 cc
Type:	4-cylinder in-line, 4-stroke

Suzuki DR-Z 400

The DR 350 by then being rather long in the tooth, in 2000 Suzuki finally brought out a successor to the very popular mid-range enduro. The sports version of the 400-cc single-cylinder (shown here) was capable of developing a lively 49 bhp. The toned-down S-version with secondary air-system emission control was still capable of developing 42 bhp and the engine was now brought to life by an electric starter. The water-cooled 4-valve single-cylinder engine was extremely compact and boasted sophisticated technical features such as a cylinder barrel coated with a nickel-silicon-phosphorus compound which increased its resistance to wear.

Model:	DR-Z 400
Year:	2000
Power:	49 bhp
Capacity:	398 cc
Type:	Single-cylinder, 4-stroke

Suzuki GS 500 E

The GS 500 had been included in the Suzuki range since the end of the 1980s as a very reliable bread-and-butter design. Generations of learners have learned to ride on this model. Its light weight, low seat, enjoyable handling, low-maintenance technology and reasonable price all contributed to make the GS 500 E one of the most popular motorbikes for beginners.

Model:	GS 500 E
Year:	2001
Power:	45 bhp
Capacity:	487 cc
Type:	2-cylinder in-line, 4-stroke

Suzuki SV 650

The SV 650, first presented to the public in 1998, succeeded in making a beginner's bike more fun to ride. This nimble little bike with a lively V-twin engine of 70 bhp was a pleasure to ride.

Model: SV 650
Year: 2001
Power: 70 bhp
Capacity: 645 cc
Type: V-twin, 4-stroke

Suzuki XF 650 Freewind

Those who rarely stray from main roads do not need a hard enduro bike. The rather tame Freewind was conceived as an unpretentious, undemanding everyday bike which could also deal with gravel terrain if the need arose. This 650-cc bike was derived from the DR 650 and was extremely sturdy.

Model: XF 650 Freewind
Year: 2001
Power: 48 bhp
Capacity: 644 cc
Type: Single-cylinder, 4-stroke

Suzuki SV 650 S

It was not only its reasonable price and lively engine which made this small SV so very successful. Its modern streamlined appearance was also extremely attractive, especially with the elegant half-fairing which appealed to many buyers. It provided an adequate windshield while allowing the tubular space frame to show itself off to best advantage.

Model: SV 650 S
Year: 2001
Power: 70 bhp
Capacity: 645 cc
Type: V-twin, 4-stroke

Suzuki GSX-R 600

As the years went by, Suzuki has expanded the GSX-R range upwards with a 1000-cc version and downwards with a 600-cc one. But things became more serious with the second generation of small GSX-R bikes. Compared to their somewhat chubby predecessor, the new model launched in 2001 had lost about 11 kg (24 lb) in weight. The power was increased to 116 bhp so that the GSX-R 600 had considerably more power than its legendary ancestor, the original GSX-R launched in 1985. And it was considerably lighter too.

Model: GSX-R 600
Year: 2001
Power: 116 bhp
Capacity: 600 cc
Type: 4-cylinder in-line, 4-stroke

Suzuki GSX 750

If there is one motorbike that can be described as 'unadorned', it is certainly the GSX 750. The reliable, air and oil-cooled 4-cylinder in-line engine was mounted on a classic steel tube chassis with a timeless fairing. It had got everything right; even the price was attractive.

Model:	GSX 750
Year:	2001
Power:	86 bhp
Capacity:	750 cc
Type:	4-cylinder in-line, 4-stroke

Suzuki GSX 750 F

While the 750-cc power unit in the naked GSX was entirely geared to torque, in the F-version it concentrated slightly more on performance. An increase of 6 bhp in the 'F' gave it a lively 92 bhp which was quite enough to keep this honest tourer-sports bike moving at a good speed.

Model:	GSX 750 F
Year:	2001
Power:	92 bhp
Capacity:	750 cc
Type:	4-cylinder in-line, 4-stroke

Suzuki VL 800 Intruder LC Volusia

The 800-cc Intruder with the name Volusia made its debut in 2001. It was a picture-book cruiser, extremely stylish, powered by a water-cooled 45° V-twin engine. The drive shaft power transmission also made it a low-maintenance bike.

Model:	VL 800 Intruder LC Volusia
Year:	2001
Power:	53 bhp
Capacity:	805 cc
Type:	V-twin, 4-stroke

Suzuki GSX 1300 R Hayabusa

This was the first production bike to break the 300 km/h (196 mph) barrier. The powerful 1300-cc 4-cylinder in-line engine was capable of developing a breathtak-ing 175 bhp. From 2002 exhaust emissions were controlled by a catalytic converter. In view of its incredible power output, it is surprising how supple and relaxed the Hayabusa was in its handling. The firm chassis was not a supersports type but it was a successful compromise between comfort and agility which made the GSX suitable for both country roads and motorways.

Model:	GSX 1300 R Hayabusa
Year:	2001
Power:	175 bhp
Capacity:	1298 cc
Type:	4-cylinder in-line, 4-stroke

Suzuki GSX-R 1000

Because Honda's Fireblade and Yamaha's R 1 both had large 1000-cc 4-cylinder engines, Suzuki naturally also had to give its 750-cc GSX-R a bigger sibling. The figures alone – 160 bhp for a dry weight of only 170 kg (375 lb) – suggested that Suzuki's new big bike would be an absolute sensation. The GSX-R 1000 immediately took the lead in the league of supersport bikes.

Model:	GSX-R 1000
Year:	2001
Power:	160 bhp
Capacity:	988 cc
Type:	4-cylinder in-line, 4-stroke

Suzuki GSF 1200 S Bandit

The half-faired S-version of the Bandit was also revamped. As well as the improvements which were also made to the 'naked' GSF, it was fitted with a larger fuel tank and new fairing.

Model:	GSF 1200 S Bandit
Year:	2001
Power:	98 bhp
Capacity:	1157 cc
Type:	4-cylinder in-line, 4-stroke

Suzuki GSF 1200 Bandit

The 'large' Bandit was also comprehensively revamped in 2001. Although the timeless design of the elegant 1200-cc Bandit remained largely unchanged, it was given a new frame with straight upper tubes. It had an improved six-piston brake calliper and a much more efficient transmission, especially in the middle speed range, thus ensuring that the GSF 1200 remained in the forefront of technology.

Model:	GSF 1200 Bandit
Year:	2001
Power:	98 bhp
Capacity:	1157 cc
Type:	4-cylinder in-line, 4-stroke

Suzuki VL 125 LC Intruder

Suzkli also introduced an Intruder in the 125-cc category. The frame and chassis were derived from the 250-cc Intruder which is why the smallest of them all had a decidedly grown-up appearance. The 125 Intruder with its compact V-twin engine and power of less than 14 bhp could certainly be described as a sheep in wolf's clothing.

Model:	VL 125 LC Intruder
Year:	2002
Power:	13.5 bhp
Capacity:	124 cc
Type:	V-twin, 4-stroke

Suzuki GSX 600 F

The fully-faired GSX 600 F, an all-rounder bike suitable for touring, was one of the long-running successes in the Suzuki catalogue. Not really beautiful but fast and economical, a bike for all occasions and reasonably priced, it was an excellent proposition. The 4-cylinder in-line engine, also used in the 600-cc Bandit, would undoubtedly appeal to the rider who would derive much pleasure from it.

Model:	GSX 600 F
Year:	2002
Power:	78 bhp
Capacity:	1157 cc
Type:	4-cylinder in-line, 4-stroke

Suzuki GSX 1400

The GSX 1400, the successor to the GSX 1200, made its debut on the German market in 2002. The massive torque of 126 Nm at only 5,000 rpm is still impressive today. For fans of traditional motorbike construction, it was an absolute delight, even though the 1400 cc GSX included some modern technological features such as a fuel injection system.

Model:	GSX 1400
Year:	2002
Power:	106 bhp
Capacity:	1402 cc
Type:	4-cylinder in-line, 4-stroke

Suzuki RV 125 Van Van

Retro bikes such as the Suzuki Van Van were extremely popular on the Asian market. This handy, urban sports bike was very reminiscent of the Suzuki RV models of the late 1970s but its low-pressure tyres nevertheless gave it its own distinctive look. At the same time it had a sophisticated 4-stroke power unit rather than a screeching 2-stroke engine.

Model:	RV 125 Van Van
Year:	2003
Power:	12 bhp
Capacity:	125 cc
Type:	Single-cylinder, 4-stroke

Suzuki RM 250

The French rider Mickaël Pichon won several World Championship titles for Suzuki with this works moto-cross bike. At the beginning of its career the 250-cc RM was slightly overweight but through constant improvements it developed into a powerful hardcore moto-cross bike which could successfully hold its own at the top of the league.

Model:	RM 250
Year:	2003
Power:	54 bhp
Capacity:	249 cc
Type:	Single-cylinder, 2-stroke

Suzuki VL 1500 LC Intruder

At the end of the 1990s Suzuki returned and jumped on the cruiser band-wagon with the VL Intruder. The unadorned bike was visually very reminiscent of Harley's Fat Boy, the mother of all cruisers. Over 2.5 metres (8 feet) long and with a generous dry weight of 300 kg (661 lb), the fat Intruder was one of the most imposing motorbikes ever made. The cylinder capacity of the V-twin engine, derived from the original 1400-cc Intruder engine, was increased by 100 cc in the LC ('Legendary Classic'), giving it a little more torque and slightly more bhp. In contrast to Harley-Davidson, Suzuki used a low-maintenance shaft drive for its heavy-weight cruiser.

Model:	VL 1500 LC Intruder
Year:	2002
Power:	67 bhp
Capacity:	1462 cc
Type:	V-twin, 4-stroke

Suzuki B-King

This purist muscle-bike with ultra-radical appearance was presented as a concept by Suzuki in 2003. The 4-cylinder engine of the Hayabusa, souped-up with a turbocharger, could develop about 250 bhp. Its appearance was marked by the presence of many costly materials such as carbon fibre, stainless steel, polished aluminium and leather. Techno freaks were enraptured by the plasma-welded aluminium swinging forks and Brembo four-piston brake callipers. It also included modern gimmicks such as rider-recognition through fingerprints and an interactive telematic system. The B-King concept bike even included internet access.

Model:	B-King
Year:	2003
Power:	250 bhp
Capacity:	1299 cc
Type:	4-cylinder in-line, 4-stroke, turbocharged

Suzuki SV 650

The Suzuki SV 650 has been an amazing best-seller ever since it was launched in 1998. No other bike in this category was so much fun. To ensure that it remained so the SV underwent a comprehensive modification in 2003. The new bridge-type frame of cast aluminium had a striking rectangular profile which further increased its stiffness compared to the already very sturdy frame of its predecessor.

Model:	SV 650
Year:	2003
Power:	71 bhp
Capacity:	645 cc
Type:	V-twin, 4-stroke

Suzuki SV 650 S

The S-version of the 650 cc SV was also given a new aluminium frame and benefited from all the same innovations as its unfaired sister. Fuel tank, seat and headlights were redesigned in both models and the fairing of the S-version was now much more distinctive. The 650 V-twin was fitted with a fuel injection system for petrol engines and catalytic converter without lambda probe. The power was increased by 1 bhp and the fuel consumption was reduced by almost 1 litre per 100 km (14 mpg).

Model:	SV 650 S
Year:	2003
Power:	71 bhp
Capacity:	645 cc
Type:	V-twin, 4-stroke

Suzuki SV 1000

In the 2003 season the two very successful 650-cc SV models greeted the arrival of two larger siblings. Each was fitted with the lively V-twin power unit of the respected TL 1000. Both models had a distinctive aluminium frame and were quite similar in appearance to the 650-cc bikes.

Model:	SV 1000
Year:	2003
Power:	115 bhp
Capacity:	996 cc
Type:	V-twin, 4-stroke

Suzuki SV 1000 S

In the 'big' SV models the 1000-cc engine was capable of developing some 115 bhp. It was because of this extremely powerful engine that the half-fairing in the S-version was so important: the bike reached a speed of 200 km/h (124 mph). At this speed the respectable windshield of the SV 1000 S provided a certain degree of protection – at least when the rider bent forward.

Model:	SV 1000 S
Year:	2003
Power:	115 bhp
Capacity:	996 cc
Type:	V-twin, 4-stroke

Suzuki DL 1000 V-Strom

The Suzuki DL 1000 V-Strom could hardly be described as an enduro any longer because its preferred stamping ground was undoubtedly the road. Mounting the famously powerful Suzuki V-twin engine on a kind of large supermoto bike had already been done by Cagiva with the Navigator. Hand-protectors and tyres with coarse treads could not disguise the fact that the Suzuki was more a country-road roamer than a Land Rover equivalent. The cast wheels and the spring travel of only 160 mm betrayed the fact that the bike had no serious ambitions anoff-roader. But the dynamic streamlining of the enduro was very useful when riding along narrow, winding roads. That these features did not make it a slow bike was clearly emphasised by the impressive engine. With 98 bhp, over 100 Nm torque and a six-speed gearbox, the bike could easily reach a top speed of 200 km/h (124 mph). At the same time the engine could be turning at less than 2,000 rpm, then a violent thrust could set in which would not stop until the needle reached the red line at 9,500 rpm.

Model:	DL 1000 V-Strom
Year:	2003
Power:	98 bhp
Capacity:	996 cc
Type:	V-twin, 4-stroke

Suzuki GS 500 F

In 2004, after 15 years, the Suzuki GS 500 range was joined by a fully-faired sibling, the GS 500 F. Both models were similar in construction and only their fairings differed. With its light weight, low seat and enjoyable handling the F-version also appealed to the new rider who would enjoy learning on this reasonably-priced, low-maintenance, everyday bike with good weather protection.

Model:	GS 500 F
Year:	2004
Power:	34 bhp
Capacity:	487 cc
Type:	2-cylinder in-line, 4-stroke

Suzuki DL 650 V-Strom

In the same way that the 650 cc SV was later expanded upwarda by the addition of two 1000-cc models, this successful recipe was also applied downwards, from the larger bike to a smaller one. The very successful travel-enduro V-Strom was joined in 2004 by a sibling, fitted with the reliable V-twin power unit of the 650 cc SV models. In doing this Suzuki was making excellent use of its 'modular construction set', creating six different models with only two engines.

Model:	DL 650 V-Strom
Year:	2004
Power:	67 bhp
Capacity:	645 cc
Type:	V-twin, 4-stroke

Suzuki GSX-R 600

The arms race in the 600-cc supersport category resulted in a completely revamped GSX-R with high-tech power unit capable of developing 120 bhp. Hollow camshafts, titanium valves and magnesium cylinder head reflected the engineers' efforts to make the most of every single bhp and to reduce weight as much as possible. A top speed of 260 km/h (161 mph) for a 660-cc bike was quite something.

Model:	GSX-R 600
Year:	2004
Power:	120 bhp
Capacity:	599 cc
Type:	4-cylinder in-line, 4-stroke

Suzuki GSX-R 750

In 2004, barely 20 years after the first GSX-R made its debut, the 750 cc was comprehensively modified. As a result, the mother of all supersport bikes became lighter, more powerful and faster. Visually the three GSX-R models launched in 2004 were identical. It was also remarkable that Suzuki was the last Japanese manufacturer still to include 750-cc models in its range. Honda, Kawasaki and Yamaha only had 600 and 1000-cc supersport bikes in their catalogues. Who would have thought ten years ago that the 750-cc supersport category would have become a niche market ?

Model:	GSX-R 750
Year:	2001
Power:	148 bhp
Capacity:	749 cc
Type:	4-cylinder in-line, 4-stroke

Suzuki Marauder 1600

To survive the increasingly tough competition, to be able to develop new projects and to manufacture at reasonable prices, Japan's number three and number four makers – Kawasaki and Suzuki – have concluded a far-reaching agreement to cooperate. The Marauder 1600, whose construction is very similar to that of a Kawasaki, is a result of this cooperation. Thanks to the 1600-cc V-twin power unit and excellent chassis the Marauder is also an excellent sports bike.

Model: Marauder 1600
Year: 2004
Power: 73 bhp
Capacity: 1553 cc
Type: V-twin, 4-stroke

Suzuki GSF 650 Bandit

Suzuki's very successful Bandit model was getting on in years but it was still far from lagging behind. To remain at the forefront of technology, it was completely revamped in 2005. One of the most important changes was the increase in capacity, which was raised to 656 cc. This did not increase the top speed but it raised the torque . There were few visible changes and the Bandit was now available with optional ABS. Naturally there was also a half-faired version.

Model: GSF 650 Bandit
Year: 2005
Power: 78 bhp
Capacity: 656 cc
Type: 4-cylinder in-line, 4-stroke

Suzuki Intruder M 800

In 2005 Suzuki introduced an 800-cc Intruder with the requisite power-cruiser look. Its aim was to produce a contemporary 'low rider' in the mid-range category. The famous V-twin was now fitted with a petrol injection system and the power transmission of the 53 bhp was through a drive shaft.

Model: Intruder M 800
Year: 2005
Power: 53 bhp
Capacity: 805 cc
Type: V-twin, 4-stroke

Suzuki Intruder C 1500

Rarely has a Japanese manufacturer succeeded in producing a cruiser bike as comparable to the original Harley-Davidson as Suzuki with its 1500-cc Intruder. It was long, flat and, with a weight of over 300 kg (661 lb), rather heavy. The large V-twin power unit was based on the reliable air and oil-cooled 1400-cc engine of the original Intruder but it was bored out by about 100 cc and fitted with a fuel injection system. Optional accessories such as a large windshield and a top case made this Intruder a real snappy dresser.

Model: Intruder C 1500
Year: 2005
Power: 67 bhp
Capacity: 1462 cc
Type: V-twin, 4-stroke

Suzuki GSX-R 1000

The half-life of a Japanese supersport bike is two years at the most. Then the impossible must be made possible again: more power and less weight. This is what the most recent version of the GSX-R1000 has achieved once more with maximum performance better than ever. The Suzuki engineers have succeeded in extracting an incredible 178 bhp from the 1000-cc engine. This was enough to push the needle on the speedometer to a dizzying 290 km/h (180 mph).

Model:	GSX-R 1000
Year:	2005
Power:	178 bhp
Capacity:	999 cc
Type:	4-cylinder in-line, 4-stroke

Triumph Daytona 955i

The Daytona 955i was the first model from the second generation of Hinckley Triumphs not to use the successful unit construction system which had re-established Triumph as a serious player in the motorcycle market. This bike had all the qualities it needed to carve out a niche for itself in the fiercely competitive big-cylinder supersport bike category: a powerful engine with easily changed gears, an immaculate chassis which did not fail to impress even on the toughest race track, and incredibly efficient brakes. This made it all the more surprising that Triumph's original concept with the Daytona 955i was for a road bike rather than a pure racer.

Model:	Daytona 955i
Year:	2000
Power:	128 bhp
Capacity:	955 cc
Type:	3-cylinder in-line, 4-stroke

Triumph Adventurer

The Adventurer was a successful mix of popular chopper styling and classic Triumph design. With this model Hinckley had primarily had the American market in mind, but the nippy machine seems to have been insufficiently chunky for the Americans and its engine capacity too low, even though the production 3-cylinder engine boasted strong torque and great flexibility. Effective brakes and a rigid chassis all added up to high-class riding experience.

Model:	Adventurer	Year: 1999	Power: 69 bhp
Capacity: 885 cc		Type: 3-cylinder in-line, 4-stroke	

Triumph Thunderbird Sport

Inspired by early classic flat-track machines, the Thunderbird Sport was a bike with traditional styling but the dynamic features of a modern superbike. Unlike the Thunderbird, the Thunderbird Sport possessed completely adjustable suspension and twin-disc front brakes. The T-Bird Sport's characterful 3-cylinder engine propelled its sporty 17-inch wheels with an equally sporty 78 bhp.

Model:	Thunderbird Sport	Year: 1999	Power: 78 bhp
Capacity: 885 cc		Type: 3-cylinder in-line, 4-stroke	

Triumph Tiger 855

The Tiger was less an enduro than a sports tourer in enduro style. The elongated suspension offered first-class protection from the very worst driving conditions and married with a practical tubular beam frame, it all added up to superior handling qualities and a stable ride. The upright riding position made for a lot of fun during quick combinations of left and right corners. The Tiger was powered by the proven 885-cc 3-cylinder fuel-injected engine and had a three-way catalytic converter.

Model:	Tiger 885	Year: 1999	Power: 83 bhp
Capacity: 885 cc		Type: 3-cylinder in-line, 4-stroke	

Triumph Legend TT

The Legend TT was based on the Adventurer. With its slim profile, low riding position and low-lying centre of gravity it was designed as a user-friendly bike suitable for beginners; an easily manoeuvred and stable ride whether on city streets or country roads. It combined classic design elements such as spoked wheels, metallic paint and a teardrop fuel tank with powerful brakes and a potent 3-cylinder engine, even in the de-tuned version.

Model:	Legend TT	Year: 2000	Power: 69 bhp
Capacity: 885 cc		Type: 3-cylinder in-line, 4-stroke	

Triumph Speed Triple

The second generation Speed Triple was a huge hit. Its daring looks and lean, aggressive styling lent it the ultimate streetfighter aura. The 108-bhp version of the Daytona 3-cylinder was designed for strong torque and gave the bike unbelievable acceleration as well as an inimitable growl that would bring any motorbike fan out in goose bumps.

Model:	Speed Triple
Year:	2000
Power:	108 bhp
Capacity:	955 cc
Type:	3-cylinder in-line, 4-stroke

Triumph Thunderbird

The Thunderbird married the trappings of a glorious past with up-to-date engine and frame technology and became the best-selling model among Triumph's modern classically-styled cruisers. It had polished aluminium and gleaming chrome elements combined with smart multi-layered metallic paint to revive the spirit of the old masterpieces while meeting contemporary standards of chassis and performance. The 3-cylinder engine delivered strong torque at low rpm allowing for a relaxed ride.

Model:	Thunderbird
Year:	2000
Power:	69 bhp
Capacity:	885 cc
Type:	3-cylinder in-line, 4-stroke

Triumph Sprint ST

The Sprint ST arrived in 1999 and immediately started beating well-established Japanese sport tourers in performance tests. It united the power and handling of a sports bike with the comfort of a tourer. The liquid-cooled 3-cylinder engine originated in the Daytona 955i but was redesigned to perform using a wider range of rpm. The engine's enormous reserves of power were held in check by durable, responsive four-piston twin-disc brakes.

Model:	Sprint ST
Year:	2000
Power:	105 bhp
Capacity:	995 cc
Type:	3-cylinder in-line, 4-stroke

Triumph Daytona 955i

The flagship of the Triumph range was given a complete overhaul half-way through the 2001 season. It was powered by the second generation of the large capacity 3-cylinder engine which impressed with its strong torque and characteristic sound. A catalytic converter was included as was a secondary air-injection system. The already pleasing chassis was further improved. The bike's handling characteristics were determined by a shorter wheelbase, the now double swing-arms, the light 17-inch front wheel and the adjustable suspension and shock absorbers.

Model:	Daytona 955i
Year:	2001
Power:	147 bhp
Capacity:	955 cc
Type:	3-cylinder in-line, 4-stroke

Triumph Sprint RS

Promptly at the turn of the millennium, Triumph came out with a sportier sibling for the Sprint ST: the Sprint RS. A fat 105 bhp was delivered by the electronically fuel injected engine with its catalytic converter. The engine was painted in two-tone black and graphite grey and has been left visible by the slim half-fairing which housed the Triumph trademark oval headlamps.

Model:	Sprint RS
Year:	2001
Power:	105 bhp
Capacity:	955 cc
Type:	3-cylinder in-line, 4-stroke

Triumph Trophy 900

Even the sacred Trophy was eventually altered with the addition of the 885-cc 3-cylinder engine which had won so much praise from so many quarters, and a massive 91 bhp was coaxed out of it in a bid to pep up the heavy tourer. The resulting performance was respectable, but by no means outstanding.

Model:	Trophy 900
Year:	2001
Power:	91 bhp
Capacity:	885 cc
Type:	3-cylinder in-line, 4-stroke

Triumph TT 600

The 600 supersport bike class was firmly in the hands of Japanese manufacturers. At least every two years the Japanese had been bringing out a new generation of highly-refined 4-cylinder production sport bikes, pushing back the boundaries of the possible with ever cleverer technology. In the 2001 season Triumph dared to launch itself into this bitterly competitive market with the TT 600, a bike that was intended to set new standards. Its chassis was solid and its brakes were bitingly effective. However it did not win all-round acclaim: its design was too reminiscent of Honda's latest CBR generation and the engine could not deliver the promised performance. Despite extravagant technological highlights such as suction injection and the Ram-Air system, the greedy low-volume engine lacked that last measure of power and verve. It was enough to disappoint performance-hungry potential customers and the unsuccessful TT 600 was soon replaced by its successor, the Daytona 600, after only 2 years.

Model:	TT 600
Year:	2001
Power:	110 bhp
Capacity:	599 cc
Type:	3-cylinder in-line, 4-stroke

Triumph Bonneville

The name was the same and the formula – a high-torque 2-cylinder, a nimble chassis and slim, classic styling – was unchanged. The return of the Bonneville saw Triumph reawaken the look, feel and timelessness of its most famous parallel twin for the 2001 season by bringing it up to the cutting edge of technology. The model's once earthy vibrations were largely eliminated by balancing shafts, the exhaust was cleaned by a catalytic converter and the engine's sound was – unfortunately – made to comply with modern regulations.

Model:	Bonneville
Year:	2002
Power:	62 bhp
Capacity:	790 cc
Type:	2-cylinder in-line, 4-stroke

Triumph Bonneville America

With its long elongated forks, low seating position and handlebars that reached far back, the Bonneville America was an archetypal cruiser primarily designed for the US market. It was powered by the same dependable 2-cylinder engine used in the standard Bonneville model. The 270° firing interval (as opposed to 360°) allowed for a satisfying exhaust noise from the two stylish silencers. Overall the America made a successful entrance. This was thanks not just to the stretched silhouette but also the tank-mounted cockpit with its speedometer with large numbers and the luxurious two-tone paint job reminiscent of the Thunderbird models of the 1950s. Forward-sited chrome foot-pegs were just as much standard fixtures (for US models) as the long handlebars mounted high up on the fork brace.

Model:	Bonneville America
Year:	2002
Power:	61 bhp
Capacity:	790 cc
Type:	2-cylinder in-line, 4-stroke

Triumph Bonneville Speedmaster

In 2003 Triumph opened another chapter in the Bonneville story when it introduced the Speedmaster. The bike's cast spoke wheels, wide handlebars and a second front-wheel brake disc made it the sportiest Bonnie in the Triumph range. It can be visually distinguished from its siblings by its single-section saddle and shorter mudguards.

Model:	Bonneville Speedmaster
Year:	2003
Power:	61 bhp
Capacity:	790 cc
Type:	2-cylinder in-line, 4-stroke

Triumph Speed Four

The Speed Four won worldwide acclaim at its debut in early 2002, but then a fire in the Hinckley factory brought production to an abrupt halt. In the same way that the large Daytona was overhauled to make the Speed Triple, so the Speed Four was a stripped-down version of the TT 600 supersport bike. The torque produced by the TT 600's 4-cylinder production engine was modified and its maximum power somewhat tuned down.

Model:	Speed Four
Year:	2003
Power:	98 bhp
Capacity:	599 cc
Type:	4-cylinder in-line, 4-stroke

Triumph T100

More than any other bike, the Bonneville embodied the essence of traditional motorcycling. The T100 was a special model brought out as part of the company's celebrations for its 100th anniversary. The T100 was all about attention to detail; the Bonneville's timeless lines, the solid rubber pads on the two-tone tank and the glittering chrome for that modern café racer touch.

Model:	T100
Year:	2003
Power:	61 bhp
Capacity:	790 cc
Type:	2-cylinder in-line, 4-stroke

Triumph Daytona 600

The Daytona 600 was another attempt by Triumph to steal the show from the Japanese. It looked more its own bike than the TT and the engine, above all, was much improved. The 16-valve dohc production engine was given new Keihin throttle valves and a zippy 32-bit processor so the bike would react immediately to the accelerator. Even with these enhancements the engine still could not quite match the performance of a Yamaha R6, but Triumph was very nearly there at last.

Model:	Daytona 600
Year:	2003
Power:	112 bhp
Capacity:	599 cc
Type:	4-cylinder in-line, 4-stroke

Triumph Tiger 955i

That much-loved big enduro model, the Tiger, also received the powerful 955 3-cylinder fuel-injected engine for the 2001 season. In 2004 the chassis was reworked with lowered suspension, a shorter caster and cast wheels to enhance the handling of the heavy machine weighing 245 kg (540 lb). The Brits also improved the bike's performance again. The Tiger's traditional strengths were unchanged. The effective cockpit fairing offered excellent weather protection and the large 24-litre (5.3-gallon) tank made refuelling stops a rare event, even on long trips.

Model:	Tiger 955i
Year:	2004
Power:	106 bhp
Capacity:	995 cc
Type:	3-cylinder in-line, 4-stroke

Triumph Thruxton 900

Today Thruxton is an almost forgotten racetrack in Hampshire which was famous in its day for the speeds promoted by the course's layout. In 1969 it gave its name to a very special racing bike from Triumph, the T120R Bonneville. During the legendary Thruxton 500, a race over 500 miles, riders on T120Rs achieved the stunning feat of snatching first, second and third places. The Thruxton 900 models with their souped-up engines were racing bikes. The air-cooled 790 cc parallel-twin engine was expanded to 865 cc for the new Thruxton 900, part of a performance-enhancing package which also included superior camshafts, a new exhaust and a megaphone silencer.

Model:	Thruxton 900
Year:	2004
Power:	70 bhp
Capacity:	865 cc
Type:	2-cylinder in-line, 4-stroke

Triumph Rocket III

'The Rocket III is a power unto itself, a mechanised cyclone of unyielding metal.' Thus did Triumph celebrate its monster cruiser. Its unique twelve-valve 3-cylinder in-line production engine boasted the largest engine capacity in the world. The Rocket III pumped out more torque than nearly every other bike, a massive 200 Nm at 2,500 rpm.

Model:	Rocket III
Year:	2004
Power:	140 bhp
Capacity:	2294 cc
Type:	3-cylinder in-line, 4-stroke

Triumph Daytona 955i

In order to keep up with the lightning pace of development set by the Japanese supersport bikes, Triumph overhauled its sports flagship once again for the 2004 season. Triumph's designers laboured long and hard over the details, from the new front with its stylish double head-lamps to the elegant twin seats and its rising tail. But what was really alluring about the Daytona was not its external flair but its hot-blooded 3-cylinder engine.

Model:	Daytona 955i
Year:	2004
Power:	147 bhp
Capacity:	995 cc
Type:	3-cylinder in-line, 4-stroke

Triumph Daytona 650

For the 2005 season Triumph made yet another attempt to match the Japanese at their own game in the 600 supersport class. Since it had already succeeded in the area of appearance and chassis with the 600 Daytona, the engine was the only stumbling block in its way. So the Triumph engineers subjected the liquid-cooled dohc 4-cylinder power unit to a thorough modernisation which included new quadruple valve technology and fuel injection. The stroke was lengthened by 3.1 mm to 44.5 mm, increasing the engine capacity by 47 to 646 cc and so delivering much more torque at mid-range rpm.

Model:	Daytona 650
Year:	2005
Power:	114 bhp
Capacity:	646 cc
Type:	4-cylinder in-line, 4-stroke

Triumph Sprint ST

In 2005 a thoroughly redesigned Sprint ST appeared. Its new 3-cylinder motor with 1050 cc and fuel injection now offered a huge 125 bhp. The beam frame was overhauled to give a shorter wheelbase of 1.454 m (4 ft 9 in) and therefore more agile handling. Classy new details, such as the wing-mirror-mounted indicators, gave the ST a distinctive personality. The bike's different design elements were perfectly harmonious, with the triple headlights on the front being beautifully echoed by the triple exhaust and LED tail light unit at the rear.

Model:	Sprint ST
Year:	2005
Power:	125 bhp
Capacity:	1050 cc
Type:	4-cylinder in-line, 4-stroke

Triumph Speed Triple

Over ten years ago the Speed Triple pulled off a feat which is by no means easy in the motorcycle world: it gained cult status. In 2005 the legend was reborn. Fresh from the drawing board, the bike's high-torque engine now of 1050 cc was fed by electronic fuel injection, delivering mid-range power and head-turning performance. The engine was mounted in a new aluminium frame while the rear profile was dominated by the two silencers mounted high on the machine.

Model:	Speed Triple
Year:	2005
Power:	130 bhp
Capacity:	1050 cc
Type:	4-cylinder in-line, 4-stroke

Victory – Serious competition for Harley-Davidson

In 1989 Polaris Industries started its own motorbike production under the name 'Victory'. Polaris are the world market leaders in the production of snowmobiles. Unlike many US derivatives which supply as well as make use of the so-called Harley clone engines from the after-market, Polaris Industries was, because of its outstanding technical knowledge, in a position to fit its Victory models with an engine developed by itself. This was – how could it be otherwise in the USA? – a large V-twin, known as the 'Freedom 92'. The figure '92' stood for the engine capacity of 92 cubic inches. But in contrast to the relatively out-dated engines used in Harley-Davidsons, the Victory V-twin was fitted from the start with overhead camshafts and four valves per cylinder. The 50° V-twin was a slightly long-stroke engine and was fitted with a modern fuel injection system.

Victory 'SportCruiser'

'Sport Cruiser' – two designations which, according to the standards of European motorcyclists at least, are mutually exclusive. A bike is either a 'sport' or a 'cruiser'. But in America, as always, things are a little different. Take the so-called 'sport' bikes from Harley which have never had anything to do with sportiness. Whatever the perspective, Victory's SportCruiser certainly possessed sporty tyres (front 120/70-17, rear 180/55-17) with Brembo double disc brakes at the front. But then there was also the bike's distinctly unsporty wheelbase of 1.615 m (5 ft 3½ in) and unladen weight of 285 kg (628 lb).

Model:	Victory V92C 'SportCruiser'
Year:	2001
Power:	80 SAE hp
Capacity:	1507 cc
Type:	V-twin, 4-stroke

Victory Cruiser

The 'Cruiser' was equipped with fat 16-inch tyres, expansive mudguards, a comfortable saddle and a staggered 2-into-2 exhaust. In line with its cruiser designation, the front wheel was fitted with only a single disc brake system. The bike also had many more chrome parts than the SportCruiser. The steering head was designed for touring and on longer journeys the rider's feet could rest comfortably on the footboards provided.

Model:	V92C 'Cruiser'
Year:	2001
Power:	80 SAE hp
Capacity:	1507 cc
Type:	V-twin, 4-stroke

Victory Deluxe

The Deluxe was a typical American fat bike. The series came with two-tone colour as standard and the broad mudguards, touring windshield, studded leather cases and small sissy bar (for the passenger to rest the back against) would satisfy even the most pampered touring rider. The Victory engineers demonstrated their sound sense of style by fitting their flagship with beautiful spoked wheels, but their mania for extras resulted in an unladen weight of 300 kg (661 lb).

Model:	V92C 'Deluxe'
Year:	2002
Power:	80 SAE hp
Capacity:	1507 cc
Type:	V-twin, 4-stroke

Victory 'Nessbike'

From the moment that Victory appeared as a new motorcycle manufacturer it cooperated with Arlen Ness, the so-called 'king of customising'. Ness is to the custom bike world what Muhammad Ali is to boxing: the greatest. From its early days Arlen Ness was advising Victory's designers and styling various custom bikes for the company on contract, such as the tourer pictured here with fixed handlebar fairing and hard cases.

Model:	V92C 'Nessbike'
Year:	2002
Power:	80 SAE hp
Capacity:	1507 cc
Type:	V-twin, 4-stroke

Victory Vegas

The Victory model known as 'Vegas' appeared on the market in 2002. It was Victory's first factory custom bike. Veteran master craftsman Arlen Ness helped with the design and blended elegance, beautiful shape and the kind of attention to detail which is otherwise found only on pure-bred custom motorcycles. The whole bike was lavished with chrome and a striking exhaust. With its unladen weight of 281 kg (619 lb), the Vegas was Victory's lightest bike.

Model:	'Vegas'
Year:	2005
Power:	80 SAE hp
Capacity:	1507 cc
Type:	V-twin, 4-stroke

Victory 8-Ball

The spanking new '8-Ball' model was essentially a 'Vegas' fitted out in black all over. With this bike Victory was copying the 'Night Train' from Harley-Davidson which already had its own dedicated customer base. The fork, steering column, handlebars, engine and painted elements – all were black. The sparkling aluminium wheels provided the single, and beautiful, visual contrast. Technically, the 8-Ball was identical to the Vegas.

Model:	8-Ball
Year:	2005
Power:	80 SAE hp
Capacity:	1507 cc
Type:	V-twin, 4-stroke

Victory Kingpin

The Kingpin was the result of crossing the elegant Vegas with a touring bike. Its inverted forks were uncharacteristic of a cruiser, but in all other respects it had everything a custom cruiser needed: an attractive teardrop tank sited well to the rear, broad mudguards extending low, a noble aluminium cradle chassis, aluminium wheels finely cut by CNC (computerised numerically-controlled) machine tools and a range of different custom paint schemes.

Model:	Kingpin
Year:	2005
Power:	80 SAE hp
Capacity:	1507 cc
Type:	V-twin, 4-stroke

Victory Touring Cruiser

The 2005 Touring Cruiser still closely resembled the 'Deluxe' of 2001. While the leather carriers had been replaced by hard cases and the saddle position and wind protection had been improved, Victory's tourer still rolled along on slim 16-inch wheels, something that greatly benefited the handling of this heavy bike weighing 327 kg (721 lb).

Model:	Touring Cruiser
Year:	2005
Power:	80 SAE hp
Capacity:	1507 cc
Type:	V-twin, 4-stroke

VINCENT-HRD – Faster than your shadow

The co-founder Philip C. Vincent was born in Fulham in London on 14 March 1908. The young Vincent was fascinated by all things mechanical and was soon bitten by the 'motorbike bug'. When still only 16, he bought himself a BSA. The bright engineering student improved the road-holding qualities of his BSA with a triangular rear swinging fork. With this system Vincent had invented the forerunner of the cantilever swing-arm which Yamaha subsequently presented as a newly-developed system.

In 1925 Vincent became acquainted with Howard R. Davies whose HRD motorbikes had an excellent reputation, and Davies became Vincent's idol. Determined to transform his hobby into a profession, the young man joined HRD. The company in Stevenage was called 'The Vincent-HRD Company Ltd'. Business was good and in 1933 Vincent was able to employ the Australian engine designer Phil Irving. Together they developed the first 500-cc ohv single-cylinder 4-stroke engine. The next milestone was the launch of the first 1000-cc Vincent-HRD in 1937. After the Second World War Vincent launched completely new 500 and 1000-cc bikes on the market. They were excellent but expensive bikes. The production process was very costly and in spite of their high price, each bike cost Vincent money. By 1950 his company was in debt. The very last Vincent-HRD motorbike left the factory in Stevenage on 18 December 1955.

Vincent-HRD 1000 A-Twin

The first 1000 Vincent HRD was a motorcycle which commanded the respect of even the most daring rider. This sports bike was the world's first series model to hit a recorded speed of 176km/h (109 mph). Essentially Vincent's designer, Irving, created this sensational sports motorcycle by combining two 500-cc single cylinders into one 1000-cc V-twin engine. Because of the engine's many external oil lines the bike came to be called the 'plumber's nightmare'.

Model:	1000 A-Twin
Year:	1937
Power:	45 bhp
Capacity:	998 cc
Type:	V-twin, 4-stroke

Vincent-HRD 1000 Black Shadow

In 1946, shortly after the end of the Second World War, Philip C. Vincent and Phil Irving decided to resume building motorcycles together. A well thought-out unit construction system was to be the basis of their 500 and 1000-cc models. The bike had five-gear transmission and its tubular frame served a second role as an oil tank. It had a Brampton trapeze fork at the front and the black-painted 1000 V-twin engine was a monoblock unit. Another marvel of the Vincent-HRD 1000 Black Shadow was the huge range of its speedo which went up to 250 km/h (155 mph).

Model:	1000 Black Shadow
Year:	1948
Power:	55 bhp
Capacity:	988 cc
Type:	V-twin, 4-stroke

Vincent 500 Comet

To avoid confusion between Harley-Davidson (HD) and Vincent-HRD, just the name 'Vincent' was used from 1949. Many parts of the 500 and 1000-cc models were interchangeable, although in contrast to the 1000's V-twin monoblock engine, the 500-cc single-cylinder followed 'classic English' principles of construction, the four-gear transmission being attached to the engine. The top model, the 500 Comet, could reach a good 150 km/h (93 mph).

Model:	500 Comet
Year:	1950
Power:	28 bhp
Capacity:	499 cc
Type:	Single-cylinder, 4-stroke

Vincent 500 Grey Flash

As well as numerous racing victories with the 1000 Black Lightning, Vincent also built the 'Grey Flash', a racing model for the 500-cc class. This pure-bred racer delivered 35 bhp and hit almost 200 km/h (124 mph). Famous riders such as John Surtees, Ted Davis, George Brown, Rene Milhoux and John Hodgkin notched up countless wins on the Grey Flash.

Model:	500 Grey Flash
Year:	1950
Power:	35 bhp
Capacity:	499 cc
Type:	Single-cylinder, 4-stroke

Vincent 1000 Black Lightning

13 September 1948 went down in Vincent legend. Dressed only in swimming trunks, sandals and a half-shell helmet, Rolli Free tore across the Great Salt Lake in Bonneville, Utah on a 1000-cc Vincent. At 240 km/h (149 mph) he succeeded in breaking the world record. Only 16 of these 80 bhp 1000 Black Lightning prototype racers were built. But Vincent did not want to boast about the world speed record and the brochure simply carried the remark: 'not yet tested'.

Model:	1000 Black Lightning
Year:	1950
Power:	80 bhp
Capacity:	998 cc
Type:	V-twin, 4-stroke

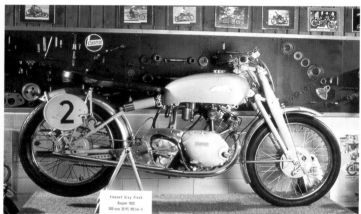

Vincent 1000 Rapide

Vincent offered something for every taste in the 1000-cc class. There was the 45-bhp Rapide for tourers and the 55-bhp Black Shadow for sports riders. Visually it was possible to tell the Rapide apart from the Black Shadow by its unpainted engine. Both models featured Vincent's 'Girdraulic' trapeze fork, first developed by the company in 1949.

Model:	1000 Rapide
Year:	1950
Power:	45 bhp
Capacity:	998 cc
Type:	V-twin 4-stroke

Vincent 1000 Black Shadow

Until the factory shut in 1955, the top of the Vincent range was the 1000 Black Shadow. A comfortable saddle and improved rear suspension ensured a pleasurable ride. In a departure from earlier models, the 'D series' engine was no longer painted black. The Shadow remained the most powerful and fastest bike then available.

Model:	1000 Black Shadow
Year:	1955
Power:	55 bhp
Capacity:	998 cc
Type:	V-twin, 4-stroke

Vincent 1000 Black Prince

Philip C. Vincent was always ahead of his time, and his 1000 Black Prince was no different. In early 1955 it became the first production bike to be encased in a glass-reinforced plastic shell. The casing was supposed to protect the bike from dirt in rainy conditions and protect the rider from punishing winds as he pushed the bike to its top speed of over 200 km/h (124 mph). The factory even delivered the bike with side cases. It was the perfect bike for sports touring and long-distance journeys. But all the effort was in vain. In the mid-1950s the motorcycle industry was in recession and by the end of 1955 this famous English maker was forced to close its factory gates forever.

Model:	1000 Black Prince
Year:	1955
Power:	55 bhp
Capacity:	998 cc
Type:	V-twin, 4-stroke

Egli-Vincent 1000

Between 1968 and 1971 Vincent motorcycles became available once more, but this time they were not English but Swiss, manufactured by Fritz W. Egli. He had tuned the V-twin engine to develop as much as 60 bhp and built a new frame around it. His 'Egli frame' made his reputation as one of world's most famous motorcycle tuners.

Model:	1000
Year:	1969
Power:	60 bhp
Capacity:	998 cc
Type:	V-twin, 4-stroke

Voxan – A French motorbike with charm and power

Seldom has a newcomer to motorbike making received so much praise for its productions as the exclusive French company Voxan, which in the late 1990s decided to win the hearts of motorbike fans. This it did in no time. Unfortunately, this brilliant beginning came to an abrupt end after only three years. The number of employees in the ultra-modern Voxan plant at Issoire, near Clermont-Ferrand, was slowly reduced from 150 to 10. In the middle of 2003 production was resumed on a small scale. About 190 suppliers contributed the roughly 2,000 parts used to

build a Voxan. The fact that the maker never really got back on its feet again after its temporary closure was certainly not due to the product – indeed the quality was always impeccable and it was described as similar to that of Honda. Even the V-twin engine developed by its own in-house engineers and the unusual design of the bike filled motorbike enthusiasts with enthusiasm and excitement.

Voxan VB1 Evo

This supersports model was developed by Thierry Henriette and his Boxer Design studio in Toulon, France, and it was first shown to the public at the Paris Salon in 1999. The VB1 was greeted with such great enthusiasm by the people responsible for Voxan that it was decided to build this sports bike in the Issoire plant as an independent model. However the financial situation of Voxan prevented it going into series production. This was unfortunate because the sports version of the uprated Voxan V-twin engine would have given the VB1 Evo a very good chance of success. Consequently the model remained more or less just an attractive design study.

Model:	VB1 Evo
Year:	1999
Power:	125 bhp
Capacity:	996 cc
Type:	V-twin, 4-stroke

Voxan Roadster

There must have been people who, after their first ride on a Roadster 1000, Voxan's top model, were filled with awe because the purist V-twin design reflected their faith in the true nature of motorcycling. Perhaps the appeal was the mechanical cleanness and free-running qualities of the V-twin engine, the eager, extremely well balanced chassis and suspension, the absolutely rock-solid braking equipment or the faultless workmanship: the enthusiasm for the purist Voxan design was manifold. For whatever reason, the first Roadster series only gave a vague foretaste of the strongly characteristic design of the model which would succeed it.

Model:	Roadster
Year:	2000
Power:	100 bhp
Capacity:	996 cc
Type:	V-twin, 4-stroke

Voxan Café Racer

The Voxan Café Racer raised a real storm of enthusiasm among design fans when it appeared. It was independent, French and charming; a real stunner with a graceful beauty which is not often see on the road. In spite of its relatively comfortable running chassis and suspension, the café racer was equally keen to chase down twisting lanes. With its lively 2-cylinder power unit, it was an excellent bike for enjoying a great time after working hours.

Model:	Café Racer
Year:	2001
Power:	100 bhp
Capacity:	996 cc
Type:	V-twin, 4-stroke

Voxan Scrambler

With the Scrambler, Voxan revived a type of motorcycle which had apparently been forgotten. Nevertheless, the motorcycle type with the same name somehow appeared at the wrong time. Scrambling could be seen as a country-lane version compatible with the supermotos booming today. However with the Scrambler it was quite possible to go genuinely off-road – provided no wild jumps were envisaged. The V-twin of this model delivered only 82 bhp which give poor performance compared with its sibling with substantially more power. But the acceleration from low revs gave lasting pleasure.

Model:	Scrambler
Year:	2002
Power:	82 bhp
Capacity:	996 cc
Type:	V-twin, 4-stroke

Voxan Street Scrambler

The Street Scrambler was as one might say the supermoto edition of its sibling model the Scrambler. Fitted with more powerful braking equipment, shorter spring travel and a smaller front wheel, this lively beauty would give a lot of pleasure in undulating terrain. This can be imagined simpy by looking at it on its stand, since the street look of the Street Scrambler was excellent. It was an advantage that for use on the track the more powerful version of the V-twin power unit was fitted. The 98 bhp that it developed meant that there was no shortage of power.

Model:	Street Scrambler
Year:	2004
Power:	98 bhp
Capacity:	996 cc
Type:	V-twin, 4-stroke

Voxan New Roadster

The second generation of the Roadster did away with the lamp fairing and went back to the classic naked-bike look. In this model the space saving 72° V-twin engine was mounted in the bridge frame that was typical of Voxan. The modern power unit had four valves and two sparking plugs per cylinder as well as an electronic petrol-injection system which resulted in modest fuel consumption and good power figures. A low centre of gravity was achieved by mounting the shock absorbers under the engine and fitting the tank fitted under the seat. This made the Roadster agile and flexible.

Model:	New Roadster
Year:	2004
Power:	98 bhp
Capacity:	996 cc
Type:	V-twin, 4-stroke

Voxan Black Magic

It is unbelievable what magic can be achieved with the Voxan building-block system. The Black Magic was completely different and touched the heart of all two-wheel purists. The classical citations of British motor cycle icons combined with the powerful Voxan look went well together. Previously this thunderbolt could only be admired at shows but it is possible that a small series may now be built after sufficient orders have been obtained via the internet.

Model:	Black Magic
Year:	2004
Power:	98 bhp
Capacity:	996 cc
Type:	V-twin, 4-stroke

Wanderer – Quality from Saxony

Like other manufacturers, the founders of the Wanderer company Johann Baptist Winkelhofer and Richard Adolf Jaenicke started their career in 1885 by manufacturing bicycles. In 1902 Wanderer started to produce motorbikes at Schonau near Chemnitz. After the First World War Wanderer was able to resume its successful business activities. In 1927 Wanderer tried to launch a reasonably-priced motorbike on the market. But in 1929 the factory was forced to cease motorbike production.

Wanderer 350

The call for a solid mid-range machine led to the design of the 350 series which was built from 1919. The side-valve single-cylinder 4-stroke engine was a monoblock and developed 6 bhp. The machine had a three-speed gearbox.

Wanderer 400

Besides the robust 200-series single-cylinder machine, the 400 with the V-twin power unit was the top model in the Wanderer range from 1908 to 1914.

Wanderer 500

The further-developed V-twin Wanderer was one of the genuinely mass-produced motor bikes after 1915. With its side-valve engine it reach a speed of 70 km/h (43 mph).

Model:	400		Model:	500		Model:	350
Year:	1911		Year:	1915		Year:	1921
Power:	3 bhp		Power:	4 bhp		Power:	6 bhp
Capacity:	408 cc		Capacity:	498 cc		Capacity:	327 cc
Type:	V-twin, 4-stroke		Type:	V-twin, 4-stroke		Type:	Single-cylinder, 4-stroke

Wanderer G200

The Wanderer G200 introduced in 1924 earned the description 'A guy who really stirs things up'. The Wanderer engineers installed the latest design of the 4-valve single-cylinder engine with a swept volume of 184 cc which developed 4.5 bhp. It was mounted horizontally, a design feature which gave a low centre of gravity and consequently impeccable handling. If the throttle lever of the G200 was opened right up to the stop it was possible for the machine to reach a speed of 80 km/h (50 mph).

Model:	G200	Year:	1924	Power:	4.5 bhp
Capacity:	184 cc	Type:	Single-cylinder, 4-stroke		

Wanderer K500

Frequently, the Wanderer was ahead of its time due to its high-quality technology. This was certainly reflected in the price. Wanderer machines were expensive and they were considered luxurious. But the K500 introduced in 1927 was intended to be a low-priced machine for everyday use. The design seemed to be right with a 16-bhp 50-cc single-cylinder engine and cardan shaft drive in a solid pressed steel frame. However the K500 was insufficiently developed and suffered from teething troubles. It was the last Wanderer machine because in 1929 the works ceased making motorcycles.

Model:	K500	Year:	1928	Power:	16 bhp
Capacity:	498 cc	Type:	Single-cylinder, 4-stroke		

Yamaha – Music for motorbike enthusiasts

The new company set up by the Nippon-Kakki Group in 1955 was named 'Yamaha Motor Co.' Ltd' in honour of the group's founder Torakusu Yamaha. It emphasised the family links with the manufacturing of musical instruments in its logo with the three crossed tuning forks. State subsidies enabled the director Genichi Kawakami to rebuild the production plant in Hamamatsu which had been damaged during the war. Like others, he decided to reproduce the successful DKW RT 125. The young company won two Japanese motorbike races at its first attempt and as a result was able to convince customers of the quality of its single-cylinder motorbikes. But the Japanese were also capable of more than copying. By the time the YD 1 was launched, it was obvious that the Hamamatsu company was a motorbike

manufacturer which should be taken seriously. But it was only at the end of the 1970s that it used 4-stroke technology and created a genuine legend with the XT 500 bike. By the 1980s the company was offering a wide range of models and launched the FZ range to dazzle the competition. In the mid-1980s, with its 100 bhp developed by a mere 750 cc, the bike was a real Supersport sensation. Apart from a few brief interruptions, the company was always involved in competition. Yamaha can boast 120 World Championship titles. Names such as Giacomo Agostini, Eddie Lawson and Phil Read have contributed to the reputation of Yamaha as it has become the second-largest motorbike manufacturer in the world.

Yamaha YA 1

The 'Red Dragonfly' was the first machine with the three crossed tuning forks on the tank. It was based on the DKW RT 125. With oil-damped forks at the front and direct springing for the rear wheel, the reddish-brown coloured lightweight bike offered a comfortable ride. Because of its high price it did not initially sell well, but this was changed by its success on the race track. In the first three years Yamaha sold over 11,000 machines.

Model:	YA 1
Year:	1955
Power:	5.6 bhp
Capacity:	123 cc
Type:	Single-cylinder, 2-stroke

Yamaha YC 1

The second model was introduced on the market in 1956 and like the previous YA 1 model the development of this machine did not cost much. It was also based on a German design, the DKW RT 175. Only the carburettor made in-house distinguished the greyish-brown machine from its parent model.

Model:	YC 1
Year:	1956
Power:	10.3 bhp
Capacity:	174 cc
Type:	Single-cylinder, 2-stroke

Yamaha YD 1

It was recognised in Hamamatsu at an early stage that the future of motor bikes lay in multi-cylinder machines. Yamaha's long history of 2-cylinder machines began with the 250-cc YD 1. This time DKW did not have a suitable model to copy so the engineers cast their eyes on an Adler MB 250. The manager of the development department at the time, Mr Watase, was not happy with this and succeeded in persuading the firm's management to set up its own design team. The success of the team showed that he was right since the YD 1 was a commercial success. In the style of the time the 2-cylinder motorbike with its bulbous tank, the strangest mudguards, the enclosed chain case and the wide double seat looked bizarre, but like the YA 1 it was a great success.

Model:	YD 1
Year:	1957 to 1958
Power:	14.7 bhp
Capacity:	247 cc
Type:	2-cylinder, 2-stroke

Yamaha YF 1

The inexpensive little YF 1 motorcycle was very popular in Japan in the years it was built. Propelled by a single-cylinder 2-stroke engine mounted in the pressed steel frame and with suspension consisting of a pressed steel link and two telescopic struts, the machine gave the driver a comfortable ride. The engine 'suspended' under the frame was only bolted to the chassis at the crankcase. A rotary disc valve looked after the fuel while the lubrication was carried out by the autolube system developed in Hamamatsu, which provided a separate oil supply for its 2-stroke engines.

Model:	YF 1
Year:	1965 to 1967
Power:	4 bhp
Capacity:	58 cc
Type:	Single-cylinder, 2-stroke

Yamaha TD 2

Further development of the running gear produced the first real production racer for private riders. The 250-cc production engine was fitted into the frame of a works RD 56 – a copy of the Norton 'featherbed' frame. The engine was based on the YDS 2 road model.

Model:	TD 2
Year:	1969
Power:	44 bhp
Capacity:	250 cc
Type:	2-cylinder, 2-stroke

Yamaha RT

The RT model series which was introduced in 1979 could at first sight be taken for a 'small 250', but it had a newly developed power unit. The machine had powerful acceleration and good roadholding qualities at 120 km/h (75 mph). The problem of kickback was solved by a decompression lever. Yamaha equipped the RT 2 with a membrane valve system, which provided an additional 2 bhp. The DT 360, Type RT 3, was the legitimate successor.

Model:	RT 1 / RT 2 / RT 3
Year:	1970
Power:	30/32/20 bhp
Capacity:	360 cc
Type:	Single-cylinder, 2-stroke

Yamaha TR 2

The design had already been tested in the TD 2. In the TR 2, a tuned R3 engine was transplanted into the chassis of the works RD 56. Consequently Yamaha had a 350-cc model, which could reach a speed of 240 km/h (149 mph). A modification in the regulations which specified that only 2-cylinder machines could compete in the 350-cc class was ideal for the production racer.

Model:	TR 2
Year:	1970
Power:	about 55 bhp
Capacity:	350 cc
Type:	2-cylinder, 2-stroke

Yamaha XS 1

At the Motor Show in Tokyo in 1969 Yamaha presented its first 650 4-stroke motorcycle and went on the offensive against its Japanese competitors, Honda and Kawasaki. Visually the parallel twin looked like an English model, but in its heart it was pure Japanese. The European market was not of much interest to Yamaha at the time and this fast 4-stroke was intended to be sold in the United States. Research had found that the 4-stroke engine note was more popular there than the 2-stroke, and the imminence of emission regulations to control smog on the West Coast was sa further reason for developing the cleaner 4-stroke.

Model:	XS 1
Year:	1970
Power:	53 bhp
Capacity:	650 cc
Type:	2-cylinder, 4-stroke

Yamaha DT 2

The DT 1 was the first enduro that Yamaha brought on the market. Its slender cradle-type frame and first-quality chassis made it a very popular bike. With a dry weight of only 105 kg (231 lb) it was not only easy to handle but also very beautiful. The DT 2, launched in 1971, had a reed valve induction system, which was the first time such a system had ever been used.

Model:	DT 2
Year:	1971
Power:	24 bhp
Capacity:	250 cc
Type:	Single-cylinder, 2-stroke

Yamaha XS 2 / XS 650 E

Just a year after Yamaha launched its first 4-stroke bike it brought out a second model, the XS 2. Although the parallel twin engine was fitted with an electric starter as well as a kick starter, it sold less well than had been expected and it only remained in the catalogue for two years.

Model:	XS2 / XS 650 E
Year:	1971 to 1973
Power:	35 bhp
Capacity:	650 cc
Type:	2-cylinder, 4-stroke

Yamaha TX 750

Yamaha launched its second 4-stroke bike, the TX 750, to compete with Honda and BMW Paroli. The ohc 4-stroke bike appealed particularly to those sporty riders who enjoyed cornering. With its excellent traction, easy handling and a rich, pure exhaust note, the Yamaha engineers were confident that the TX 750 would become a best-seller. Unfortunately the engine left a lot to be desired and the uncompetitive price and rather high maintenance costs prevented it from becoming a best-seller.

Model:	TX 750
Year:	1972 to 1975
Power:	63 bhp
Capacity:	742 cc
Type:	2-cylinder, 4-stroke

Yamaha RD 250

The confusing abbreviation of the Yamaha models came to an end in the late 1970s. The designation 'RD' was introduced for 2-stroke road bikes with tubular frame, still marketed in Japan as 2-cylinder AX or DX bikes. The air-cooled 2-stroke bike now had a reed valve induction system and the inlet cycle (exhaust and refill) was based on a new seven-port cylinder-scavenging system. It was constantly modified and improved technically and stylistically until the introduction of the RD 250 LC.

Model:	DX 2
Year:	1973 to 1980
Power:	30 bhp
Capacity:	247 cc
Type:	2-cylinder, 2-stroke

Yamaha RD 350

Rarely had Yamaha produced a model that required so little maintenance as the successor of the R5. Like the previous model, it had a reed valve induction system and a seven-port cylinder-scavenging system which reduced fuel consumption and improved the exhaust emission behaviour. It had a top speed of 165 km/h (103 mph) and disc brakes on the 18-inch front wheel. The RD 350 remained unchanged visually apart from the painting of the fuel tank and side panel.

Model:	RD 3
Year:	1973 to 1975
Power:	39 bhp
Capacity:	347 cc
Type:	2-cylinder, 2-stroke

Yamaha XS 500 / TX 500

The XS 500 was the first Yamaha bike with a dohv 4-valve power unit, which at the beginning was plagued with problems. These difficulties were only solved in 1977 when the valve seats were modified and lubrication improved. The XS also had interesting features such as automatic tensioning of the camshaft timing chain and two chain-driven counterbalancing shafts in the engine – this was the beginning of the Yamaha high-tech motorbikes. In spite of its 200 kg (441 lb), it was easy to handle and also comfortable on long-distance journeys. Its range was limited by a fuel consumption of up to 10 litres per 100 km (28 mpg).

Model:	XS 500
Year:	1973 to 1979
Power:	50 bhp
Capacity:	498 cc
Type:	2-cylinder, 4-stroke

Yamaha AT 2

Yamaha launched its first 125-cc enduro on the market in 1968. It was powered by a divided 2-cylinder engine, as used in the DS road bike. In 1972 this was replaced by a 2-stroke single cylinder engine and the AT 2 was fitted with a new reed valve induction system. The 11-bhp bikes had a top speed of 105 km/h (65 mph).

Model:	AT 2
Year:	1974
Power:	11 bhp
Capacity:	123 cc
Type:	Single-cylinder, 2-stroke

Yamaha XS 650

The most successful big-twin engine of the 1970s replaced the TX 750 which had proved unsatisfactory because of thermal problems. It was fitted in the improved American TX 650 chassis. With longer connecting rods, shorter pistons, modified engine timing, improved lubrication and a different carburettor and clutch, the power was increased to 51 bhp. Constant modifications such as the reduction of the power to 50 bhp (1976), which was more favourable for insurance purposes, new floating brake callipers (1977), and smoother valve gear (1979) ensured that the fans remained faithful to this 4-stroke bike for many years.

Model:	XS 650	Year:	1975 to 1984	Power:	51 bhp
Capacity:	653 cc	Type:	2-cylinder, 4-stroke		

Yamaha XT 500

With 127,000 sold worldwide, the XT could be seen on roads all over the world. Being an economical everyday bike, it was popular with globe-trotters and students alike. This short-stroke ohc 2-cylinder engine was extremely reliable. But just as legendary as its sturdiness was its obstinate behaviour when starting the engine. An indicator placed near the compression release device was supposed to help find top dead centre but in practice it did not always achieve the expected result. It was fatal for the shins if the decompression lever was not pulled when kick-starting.

Model:	XT 500
Year:	1976 to 1992
Power:	33 bhp
Capacity:	500 cc
Type:	Single-cylinder, 4-stroke

Yamaha XS 1100

The first big bike produced by Yamaha, the XS 1100 was Yamaha's entry in the competition to produce the biggest, most powerful and heaviest mass-produced motorbike. The Japanese competition was famous for their powerful 6-cylinder bikes and the booming motorbike market was clamouring for muscular beasts. This high-capacity mass-produced bike was certainly no slender maiden, weighing 282 kg (622 lb) with a full tank. Maintenance and upkeep were also demanding: it could use 10 litres per 100 km (28 mpg) when riding at a brisk speed and new rear brake pads were usually needed after 2,500 km (1,550 miles) – not surprising since it was the 'king of the road' with a top speed of 200 km/h (124 mph).

Model:	XS 1100
Year:	1978 to 1981
Power:	95 bhp
Capacity:	1001 cc
Type:	4-cylinder, 4-stroke

Yamaha XS 650 Special

At the end of the 197's Yamaha presented its first soft chopper. The boom of the 'Easy Riders' was already in full swing in America and Britain. The XS 650 base remained completely unchanged from a technical point of view; the teardrop-shaped tank, the slightly stepped seat, the chrome handle for the passenger, the thick rear-wheel tyre and the strongly cranked high handlebars turned this road bike into a chopper which became very popular.

Model:	XS 650 Special U.S. Custom
Year:	1978 to 1979
Power:	50 bhp
Capacity:	653 cc
Type:	2-cylinder, 4-stroke

Yamaha XJ 650

The XJ 650 which had been fitted with a shaft drive was a sporty bike. Its clean lines further emphasised the nature of the engine: an air-cooled, transverse 4-cylinder power unit. Bucket tappets with compensating shims controlled the valves. The rider was already aware of a powerful acceleration at low revolutions; then the revs would rise to 9,000 rpm, catapulting the bike to a remarkable speed of 195 km/h (121 mph).

Model:	XJ 650
Year:	1980 to 1985
Power:	71 bhp
Capacity:	653 cc
Type:	4-cylinder, 4-stroke

Yamaha RD 500 LC

The most powerful 500-cc motorbike with road approval was launched in the spring of 1984. It was a replica of the works V4 Grand Prix bike. Even in first gear, this 2-cylinder parallel twin bike reached an impressive 90 km/h (56 mph) and in sixth gear a breathtaking 225 km/h (140 mph). The chassis consisted of square steel tubes which led to the very steep steering head.

Model:	RD 500 LC
Year:	1984 to 1985
Power:	88 bhp
Capacity:	499 cc
Type:	V-4, 2-stroke

Yamaha XT 600

The XT 600, presented in 1983, only weighed 151 kg (333 lb), had a short wheelbase and steep steering head rake which promised much fun for the off-road fans. Fitted with disc brakes front and rear and with a mono-shock suspension system which had already been introduced in the XT 600 Z, it also combined the advantages of the XT 600 Z Téneré but without its weight and thermal problems. The greatest disadvantage of this light-weight bike was its guzzling habit which could rise to 8 litres per 100 km (35 pmg). So the range of its 11.5-litre (2.5-gallon) tank was limited. It was stylistically revamped in 1987 and its power increased to 45 bhp.

Model:	XT 600
Year:	1984 to 1989
Power:	44 bhp
Capacity:	600 cc
Type:	Single-cylinder, 4-stroke

Yamaha VMX Vmax

The Vmax, presented in 1985, had been developed independently by Yamaha. The specifications of this liquid-cooled dohc V4 16-valve engine left no room for doubt that it was a remarkably powerful machine: 145 bhp at 9,000 rpm with a maximum torque of 122 Nm at 7,800 rpm. It reached 160 km/h (100 mph) in 8 seconds and its top speed was 240 km/h (149 mph).

Model:	VMX Vmax
Year:	1985
Power:	145 bhp
Capacity:	1198 cc
Type:	V-4, 4-stroke

Yamaha FZR 1000

The 1000-cc top model was almost the culmination of the creation of the 5-valve dohc 4-cylinder power unit presented the year before: the FZR 1000 Genesis. The engine which had been used in the FZ 750 was comprehensively modified. With its Deltabox chassis, developed for racing, and the generous use of light metal, at 229 kg (505 lb) it was relatively light compared to its competitors.

Model:	FZR 1000
Year:	1986
Power:	135 bhp
Capacity:	989 cc
Type:	4-cylinder, 4-stroke

Yamaha FJ 1200

The metamorphosis of 'big bike' to sports tourer was reflected in the FJ 1100, which in 1986 came off the production line as the FJ 1200. Two years after its introduction, it was substantially revamped with new hollow light metal rims and replacement of the anti-dive system by forks with improved shock-absorber tuning. At the front was a twin-rotor disc brake with four-piston brake callipers.

Model:	FJ 1200
Year:	1986 to 1995
Power:	100 bhp
Capacity:	1188 cc
Type:	4-cylinder, 4-stroke

Yamaha FZX 750 Fazer

At first glance the Fazer looked like a Vmax with its muscular appearance and added dummy air box. Yamaha developed a sturdy chassis specially for the Fazer with a steel frame, completed by a telescopic fork with a travel of 140 mm (5½ in) and light metal swing-arm with two fully enclosed suspension struts. The riding position was unusual: with bent knees and stretched out arms it was a cross between a racing bike and a tourer. This pose was not univeraslly popular but it was a selling point in some markets.

Model:	FZX 750
Year:	1986 to 1989
Power:	94 bhp
Capacity:	599 cc
Type:	4-cylinder, 4-stroke

Yamaha SRX 600

The designers of the SRX 600 liked to think of their creation as 'a modern art bike'. The visible square tubes, the twin cradle-type frame which was both welded and bolted to the bottom tube, the box-shaped swinging fork with conventional suspension struts, very short silencers and original tank design gave the bike a very distinctive character.

Model:	SRX 600 1JK
Year:	1986 to 1989
Power:	45 bhp
Capacity:	608 cc
Type:	Single-cylinder, 4-stroke

Yamaha TZR 250

From the race track to the road: Yamaha's 2-stroke twin clearly showed how powerful and competitive a modern 2-stroke bike could look. The liquid-cooled 2-cylinder in-line engine with reed valve induction system and optimised Power Valve enabled this bike of 144 kg (317 lb) to reach a top speed of 183 km/h (114 mph). But in everyday road traffic it ran surprisingly smoothly in a very civilised manner.

Model:	TZR 250
Year:	1987 to 1989
Power:	45 bhp
Capacity:	249 cc
Type:	2-cylinder, 2-stroke

Yamaha XV 535 Virago

The Virago XV 535 with shaft drive was a success and one of the most popular Yamaha models of all time. Besides the XV 500 and XV 1000, there was also a mid-range 500-cc 70° V-twin chopper. The teardrop-shaped tank, the two dummy chrome-plated air-filter bowls and the silencers with bevelled edges in side-pipe style, spoked wheels, omnipresent chrome and polished aluminium emphasised the chopper look.

Model:	XV 535 Virago
Year:	1987 to 2000
Power:	46 bhp
Capacity:	598 cc
Type:	V-twin, 4-stroke

Yamaha FZR 600 Genesis

Genesis was not popular everywhere! What the 600-cc bike needed more than anything was a light metal chassis and a five-valve 4-cylinder engine. But the designers had convincing reasons for using four valves per cylinder. Tests had revealed that the five-valve technology only benefited larger capacities. The 600 Genesis fulfilled the requirements as a road bike and racing bike. In contrast to what might have been expected from the bike's appearance the Deltabox frame was not made from aluminium but painted steel tubes, the lower tubes being bolted on. This 600 appealed to the sport-loving rider.

Model:	FZR 600 Genesis
Year:	1988 to 1989
Power:	91 bhp
Capacity:	599 cc
Type:	4-cylinder, 4-stroke

Yamaha XT 500 S

Yamaha remained faithful to the XT concept throughout the years. Minor chages were made to the front wheel forks. Particularly striking were the gold-coloured anodised rims. A larger intake valve and spring travel increased from 110 to 128 mm (4.3 to 5 in) completed the 'minor' rejuvenating treatment of the aged lady.

Model:	XT 500 S
Year:	1988
Power:	33 bhp
Capacity:	500 cc
Type:	Single-cylinder, 4-stroke

Yamaha SR 500

Only two years after the successful introduction of the XT 500 with 4-stroke single-cylinder engine, the enduro was joined by a road bike. It included innovations such as hydraulic disc brakes at the front, electrics using a 12-volt system from the outset and maintenance-free transistorised ignition. This beautiful bike with teardrop-shaped tank was produced for 20 years and constantly improved. The photograph shows a later model dating from 1988.

Model:	SR 500
Year:	1978 to 1999
Power:	32 bhp
Capacity:	499 cc
Type:	Single-cylinder, 4-stroke

Yamaha XTZ 750 Super Ténéré

Yamaha's response to the powerful travel-enduros produced by BMW and Honda was called the Super Ténéré and the reference to success in desert rallies was no coincidence. The heart of the bike was a newly developed 2-cylinder in-line engine. Thanks to its excellent liquid-cooling system the Ténéré was a brilliant cross-country bike, but it also felt at home on the open road with a maximum speed of 180 km/h (112 mph). With 69 bhp and 7,500 rpm, it was the most powerful enduro of its time. With a seat height of 865 mm (34 in) it was easy to mount and its low centre of gravity made it easy to handle.

Model:	XTZ 750 Super Ténéré
Year:	1989 to 1999
Power:	69 bhp
Capacity:	749 cc
Type:	Single-cylinder, 4-stroke

Yamaha XT 600 E

E for electric starter – this was an improvement which to the regret of many also led to the downfall of the kick-starter. The chassis with longer wheelbase also improved directional stability. Floating calliper disc brakes and dual-piston callipers as well as low-profile tyres were all included on the first model. Five years later the XT was revamped: the rear of the chassis became self-supporting again, but although the gearbox was modified it did not bring about the expected increase in power.

Model:	XT 600 E
Year:	1990 to 2003
Power:	45 bhp
Capacity:	595 cc
Type:	Single-cylinder, 4-stroke

Yamaha XTZ 660

The new interpretation of the classic Ténéré, with frame-mounted fairing and long spring travel of 220 mm (8.7 in), was Yamaha's way of attracting the touring rider's attention. The other features had already been seen in the Paris-Dakar Rally, such as the liquid-cooled five-valve engine. This short-stroke engine was not made for the off-road fan. In 1994 the half-fairing with trapezoid headlight was replaced by a new fairing with twin headlights.

Model:	XTZ 660 Ténéré
Year:	1990 to 1998
Power:	48 bhp
Capacity:	660 cc
Type:	Single-cylinder, 4-stroke

Yamaha TDM 850

An enduro dressed like road bike or a road bike disguised as an enduro? It was difficult to classify this 5-valve bike in a particular category. The water-cooled dohc five-valve engine, derived from the XTZ 750 Super Ténéré, revealed its enduro identity. The Deltabox chassis was reminiscent of the Genesis engine of the FZR models. With its telescopic forks, steel box swing-arm and the fastest twin engine of its time, capable of driving it at 200 km/h (124 lb), it had an almost enduro-like suspension travel. This jack of all trades but master of none was very popular with the public.

Model:	TDM 850
Year:	1990 to 1995
Power:	78 bhp
Capacity:	849 cc
Type:	2-cylinder, 4-stroke

Yamaha XJ 600 S Diversion

A lot of bike for little money. In the early 1990s this model was unrivalled as far as price was concerned. It also delivered what its name suggested: entertainment and distraction with a bike which was perfect for everyday use and for travelling. It was very popular with motorbike-riding schools which often used this 4-cylinder bike because of its excellent chassis.

Model:	XJ 600 S Diversion
Year:	1991 to 2002
Power:	45 bhp
Capacity:	598 cc
Type:	4-cylinder, 4-stroke

Yamaha YZF 750 R

The replacement of the Genesis in the Supersport category was the YZF 750 R. It was fitted with the 5-valve engine of the FZ/FZR range and with a down-draught carburettor its 35° inclination to the front made a shorter wheelbase possible. The crankshaft was improved to ensure a more lively engine and the combustion chamber and cylinder were redesigned. The Deltabox lightweight metal frame was also modified. The original painting pattern and fox-eye front end contributed to the aggressive look of the bike but the handling remained good. Unfortunately at full throttle on the straight the handlebars suffered slight vibration.

Model:	YZF 750 R
Year:	1992
Power:	115 bhp
Capacity:	749 cc
Type:	4-cylinder, 4-stroke

Yamaha GTS 1000

This touring sports bike was the first production motorbike to have axle-pivot steering fitted and it was a milestone in the history of motorcycle manufacturing. The new 'Omega' chassis took Yamaha onto new paths in the field of frame construction and its name was inspired by the shape of the light alloy profiles located on each side of the engine block. There was no longer a frame upper bar so the 5-valve 4-cylinder engine had a low overall centre of gravity. The advantages of axle-pivot steering did not convince the test riders.

Model:	GTS 1000
Year:	1992 to 1998
Power:	100 bhp
Capacity:	1003 cc
Type:	4-cylinder, 4-stroke

Yamaha M1

In 2003 the Grand Prix regulations allowed the use of 4-stroke motorbikes with a maximum cylinder capacity of 990 cc. After decades of 2-stroke motorbike races, manufacturers suddenly found themselves having to deal with completely new levels of performance which could hardly be applicable to asphalt – not even on the most modern racing tracks in the world. The first official announcement of the YZR-M1 Grand Prix racing bike with 4-stroke technology followed in 2001. The designation of the bike's type was derived from the Yamaha racing bikes' customary abbreviation YZR with the addition of M1 for 'mission one'. Yamaha chose a 4-cylinder in-line engine which was fitted with Yamaha's usual 5-valve technology. The chassis, directly inspired by the chassis of the 2-stroke works bike, had the Deltabox frame with which the Japanese had won the Constructors' World Championship in 2000. The most difficult task facing the Yamaha engineers was to adjust the YZR-M1 engine with its power of over 200 bhp in such a way that the delivery of power was as even as possible, thus ensuring the best possible control of its output. In 2004, when the bike was still only in the third season of its development, Valentino Rossi rode it to victory in the MotoGP World Championship.

Model:	YZR-M1
Year:	2002
Power:	over 200 bhp
Capacity:	990 cc
Type:	4-cylinder in-line, 4-stroke

Yamaha YZF-R7

The R7 presented in 1999 was Yamaha's attempt to secure a title in the Superbike World Championship. Admittedly, it did not quite succeed but Haga from Japan managed to be runner-up in the 2000 World Championship on the R7. And for performance-hungry fans Yamaha built the road-approved model with 106 bhp. The bike was revamped twice with the power being increased first to 163 bhp and then to 177 bhp.

Model:	YZF-R7
Year:	1999
Power:	up to 177 bhp
Capacity:	749 cc
Type:	4-cylinder in-line, 4-stroke

Yamaha FZS 600 Fazer

A completely new mid-range all-rounder made its debut in 1998: the Yamaha FZS 600 Fazer. The Japanese equipped it with the lively 600-cc 4-cylinder in-line engine, used in the Thundercat, but with improved torque, on a simple tubular steel frame. With its excellent brakes and enjoyable handling, the Fazer quickly became a best-selling model.

Model:	FZS 600 Fazer
Year:	2000
Power:	95 bhp
Capacity:	599 cc
Type:	4-cylinder in-line, 4-stroke

Yamaha YZF-R1

In 1997 Yamaha presented the YZF-R1 at the Milan EICMA fair as a successor to the 1000-cc Thunderace. The YZF-R1 was to become one of the icons of modern supersport bikers. With 150 bhp for a dry weight of 177 kg (390 lb), packaged in a super-sharp design – Yamaha had suddenly raised the bar for its competitors by a couple of notches.

Model:	YZF-R1
Year:	2000
Power:	150 bhp
Capacity:	998 cc
Type:	4-cylinder in-line, 4-stroke

Yamaha WR 400 F

During the 1990s it became clear that the era of the 2-stroke engine was coming to an end, both for road racing and off-road-bikes. Consqeuently, in 1998 Yamaha launched a new generation of 4-stroke competition bikes. The WR 400 F enduro variant was also available with road approval whereby the power of this very modern five-valve single-cylinder engine was reduced from 45 to 37 bhp.

Model:	WR 400 F
Year:	2000
Power:	37 bhp
Capacity:	399 cc
Type:	Single-cylinder, 4-stroke

Yamaha YZ 426 F

Conceived as pure competition bikes, the YZ 4-stroke models created a real sensation. In the bike's very first season, Andrea Bartolini won the Motocross World Championship title on the YZ 400 F. But the Japanese manufacturers did not rest on their laurels and completely revamped the World Championship bike in readiness for the 2000 season. The cylinder capacity was raised to 426 cc by increasing the bore, which was reflected in the new name of the bike. The Yamaha engineers got down to serious work as usual and fitted the YZ among other things with lighter spring elements, a new exhaust system, a stronger clutch and a new carburettor as well as a closer ratio between the first two gears.

Model:	YZ 426 F
Year:	2001
Power:	58 bhp
Capacity:	426 cc
Type:	Single-cylinder, 4-stroke

YAMAHA

Yamaha FJR 1300

In 2000 Yamaha presented a new sports tourer at Intermot which seriously worried its competitors. As a successor to the FJ range it had all the prerequisites to become top of the class in the category of sports tourer bikes: a compact aluminium bridge-type frame, a powerful 4-cylinder in-line engine, fuel injection and three-way catalytic converter as well as a low-maintenance shaft drive. Because it was relatively light with a dry weight of just 240 kg (529 lb), the FJR was also very aerodynamic.

Model:	FJR 1300
Year:	2001
Power:	145 bhp
Capacity:	1298 cc
Type:	4-cylinder in-line, 4-stroke

Yamaha XVS 250 Drag Star

At the end of the 1990s Yamaha no longer called its chopper and cruiser models Virago but Drag Star. The 250-cc model in the Drag Star range, presented in 2001, had inherited the Virago's V-twin engine but the frame and appearance were completely new.

Model:	XVS 250 Drag Star
Year:	2001
Power:	21 bhp
Capacity:	249 cc
Type:	V-twin, 4-stroke

Yamaha XVS 650 Drag Star

The 650-cc Drag Star models were the successors to the extremely successful 535 Virago. The very stylish Drag Star 650 made its debut in 1997 and was followed a year later by a second model, the Drag Star Classic which with its low-reaching mudguards looked more like a cruiser.

Model:	XVS 650 Drag Star Classic
Year:	2001
Power:	40 bhp
Capacity:	649 cc
Type:	V-twin, 4-stroke

Yamaha FZS 1000 Fazer

After scoring a bull's eye with the 600-cc Fazer, Yamaha repeated this successful formula in the shape of the 1000-cc Fazer but a couple of rungs higher. The engine was the brilliant 4-cylinder in-line of the R1 but with less power and more torque. And the 143 bhp for this not too extreme road sports bike were not chicken feed. Thanks to its wide handlebars and half-fairing providing effective protection against airflow, the 1000 Fazer was an ideal bike for long and short tours of a sporty nature.

Model:	FZS 1000 Fazer
Year:	2001
Power:	143 bhp
Capacity:	998 cc
Type:	4-cylinder in-line, 4-stroke

Yamaha BT 1100 Bulldog

With the BT 1100 Bulldog, Yamaha in 2001 presented an unusual mixture of a cruiser and sports tourer, but with the emphasis clearly on the cruiser. This was largely because of the tame V-twin engine. This was in the same form as when it was used in the Virago and Drag Star models, to be precise. With 65 bhp the air-cooled 2-valve V-twin was not particularly sporty and the shaft drive also indicated that the Bulldog had little to do with racing.

Model: BT 1100 Bulldog	Year: 2001	Power: 65 bhp
Capacity: 1063 cc	Type: V-twin, 4-stroke	

Yamaha FZS 600 Fazer

In 2002 the little 600 Fazer was given the same stylish fairing as its larger sibling, which had already adopted the new Yamaha look at the show a year earlier. But this was not all; for the new season Yamaha had modifed many details of its successful model according to the customer's wishes, including the cockpit, fuel tank, seat and exhaust system.

Model:	FZS 600 Fazer
Year:	2002
Power:	95 bhp
Capacity:	599 cc
Type:	4-cylinder in-line, 4-stroke

Yamaha TDM 900

With the original TDM of 1990, Yamaha had already created a legendary all-purpose motorbike. Neither an enduro nor a tourer, it was intended to be an international all-rounder. In 2002 a completely new TDM generation was launched, with an aggressive appearance following its predecessors. The engine capacity was 50 cc greater, its power was up by 4 bhp, fuel injection and computer-controlled catalytic converter were fitted for cleaner exhaust emissions, and with its aluminium bridge frame and tighter suspension the new generation of TDM was not only more powerful but also more sporty in performance.

Model: TDM 900	Year: 2002	Power: 86 bhp
Capacity: 897 cc	Type: 2-cylinder in-line, 4-stroke	

Yamaha WR 250 F

In 2001 Yamaha produced a smaller 250-cc model to go alongside the 400 FS. In appearance and technically, both models were very similar. Also the single-cylinder power unit of the 250 had five titanium valves, which contributed to the enjoyable performance of the little engine.

Model:	WR 250 F
Year:	2002
Power:	41 bhp
Capacity:	249 cc
Type:	Single-cylinder, 4-stroke

Yamaha XJ 600 N

2002 was the penultimate season in which the XJ 600 was available. After more than ten years, the dependable mid-range all-rounder went into retirement in 2003. The 'N' version illustrated here differed from the type in the absence of half-fairing.

Model:	XJ 600 N
Year:	2002
Power:	61 bhp
Capacity:	599 cc
Type:	4-cylinder in-line, 4-stroke

Yamaha YZ 450 F

Towards the end of 2002, Yamaha gave its moto-cross racer an increase in capacity to 450 cc, which gave the single-cylinder engine an impressive power of 60 bhp. In spite of the use of an electric starter, the dry weight of 100 kg (220 lb) was unchanged as a result of weight-saving measures such as the new titanium exhaust which compensated for the weight of the electric starter.

Model:	YZ 450 F	Year: 2002	Power: 60 bhp
Capacity:	449 cc	Type: Single cylinde,r 4-stroke	

Yamaha YZF-R1

In the year 2002 the second generation of the R1 with numerous improvements was brought to the market. The 4-cylinder in-line engine with fuel injection system and catalytic converter had its power slightly increased by 2 bhp to 152 bhp. A new Deltabox frame improved the rigidity of the chassis by no less than 30%, which had a noticeable effect on the directness of the handling. As well as countless other detail improvements to the engine and chassis, the new appearance of the R1 above all aroused great enthusiasm. It was not fundamentally different but it was more crisply defined.

Model:	YZF-R1	Year: 2002	Power: 152 bhp
Capacity:	998 cc	Type: 4-cylinder in-line, 4-stroke	

Yamaha YZF-R6

Since 1998 Yamaha with the YZF-R6 has offered a sharp racing bike in the 600-cc Supersport category. The World Supersport Champion of Jörg Teuchert in 2000 was an impressive demonstration of the machine's potential. In the 2003 season the R6 underwent an extensive renovation. The new design, the complete reworking of the engine, now fitted with fuel injection, a Deltabox III frame constructed of die-cast light metal, modified chassis suspension geometry and many other details contributed to keeping the R6 in the lead.

Model:	YZF-R6
Year:	2003
Power:	123 bhp
Capacity:	599 cc
Type:	4-cylinder in-line, 4-stroke

Yamaha Road Star Warrior

In order to have a competitive model in the 'power cruiser' niche segment, in 2002 Yamaha launched the – considerably bored-out – V-twin engine of the 'normal' 1600 Wild fitted in a twin-cradle flat bar frame made of light metal. With a capacity of 1670 cc, the twin developed a power of 85 bhp. Unlike the Road Star models, the power was transmitted not through a drive shaft but by a toothed belt as normally employed by Harley-Davidson's Big Twins.

Model:	Road Star Warrior
Year:	2003
Power:	86 bhp
Capacity:	1670 cc
Type:	V-twin, 4-stroke

Yamaha BT 1100 V.Metal

Yamaha had designed this exhibition model in order to show off the customising possibilities of the Bulldog. Fitted with the K&N air filter kit specially designed for this model with laser-finished exhaust system, a new model was created. The principle followed was to use only prefabricated parts of the highest quality, so the front and rear suspension elements were supplied by Öhlins. This combination of prefabricated parts reinforced the effect of the compact, short rear part of the bike and allowed the wider tyre (180/55 x 17) of the rear wheel to be shown off to best advantage.

Model:	BT 1100 Bulldog V.Metal	Year:	2003	Power:	65 bhp
Capacity:	1063 cc	Type:	V-twin, 4-stroke		

Yamaha FZ6

The legacy of the successful Fazer 600 quickly gave rise to two different models: the naked FZ6 and the half-faired FZ6 Fazer. While there was no unfaired version of the first Fazer generation, in 2004 the new FZ6 successfully began to encroach on the preserve of the naked Honda Hornet. Both versions used the R6 engine restricted to 98 bhp and, following the current trend, the exhaust sysem with computerised catalytic converter controlling exhaust emissions stuck out beneath the stylish rear end in period style.

Model:	FZ6	Year:	2004	Power:	98 bhp
Capacity:	599 cc	Type:	4-cylinder in-line, 4-stroke		

Yamaha FZ6 Fazer

Made using the new aluminium die-casting technique, the frame of the two FZ6 models consisted of only two parts bolted together. Consequently the weight of welding together the individual frame members was saved and at the same time the stiffness of the frame was increased. The design technique of this process also enabled new methods of chassis shaping to be used, so the FZ6 Fazer looks much more modern and dynamic than its predecessor.

Model:	FZ6 Fazer
Year:	2004
Power:	98 bhp
Capacity:	599 cc
Type:	4-cylinder in-line, 4-stroke

Yamaha XT 660 R

After almost 15 years of production, the XT 600 finally gave way to an entirely newly designed successor in 2004. The engine was now water-cooled and had a larger capacity, with better performance and fuel injection. The 48 bhp it delivered was not particularly exciting, but it was clearly better than the meagre 40 bhp that the old XT had been reduced to by ever-stricter exhaust emission standards. With the new engine the Yamaha turned away from the five-valve XT cylinder head and reverted to four-valve technology.

Model:	XT 660 R
Year:	2004
Power:	48 bhp
Capacity:	659 cc
Type:	Single-cylinder, 4-stroke

Yamaha XT 660 X

Yamaha wanted to play a part in the increasingly popular supermoto sector and gave the new XT a smaller 17-inch front wheel, stiffer suspension elements and road tyres with better grip. The 'X' version also had powerful disc brakes with a 320-mm disc at the front.

Model:	XT 660 X
Year:	2004
Power:	48 bhp
Capacity:	659 cc
Type:	Single-cylinder, 4-stroke

Yamaha MT-03

Yamaha's MT-03 concept design pointed the way forward. That this study was not so very futuristic was indicated by the components. The single-cylinder engine with fuel injection was already in service with the new XT 660. The diode lighting technology of the headlight and tail light already exists in car manufacture. The belt drive, the exhaust system mounted under the rear part of the bike and the wave disc brakes are not actually sensational technical highlights. However, the working position of the telescopic suspension unit which lies at the right of the bike at the level of the rider's calf is unusual. One hopes that this concept bike will enter production as quickly as possible.

Model:	MT-03
Year:	2004
Power:	48 bhp
Capacity:	659 cc
Type:	Single-cylinder, 4-stroke

Yamaha XV 1600 Wild Star

2004 was for the time being the last year in which Yamaha imported its cruiser flagship, the XV 1600 Wild Star, into Europe. In spite of its many qualities, fewer and fewer buyers were being found for this mighty V-twin cruiser bike, an indication of the declining interest being shown in chopper and cruiser bikes as a whole.

Model:	XV 1600 A Wild Star
Year:	2004
Power:	63 bhp
Capacity:	1602 cc
Type:	V-twin, 4-stroke

Yamaha YZF-R1

Although the increase in performance of the previous new generation of the R1 was quite low at 2 bhp, the Yamaha engineers put this right for the 2004 version. The power was increased by a full 20 bhp with the capacity unchanged, and with a further 8 bhp resulting from the pressure build-up of the Ram-Air system the engine delivered an unbelievable 180 bhp. This was applied to the 2004 R1's dry weight of 172 kg (379 lb), a result among other things of its extra-slim Deltabox V frame. With a power-weight ratio of 1 bhp per kg (even without the Ram-Air effect), Yamaha's high-performance flagship set the new standard in motorbike construction.

Model:	YZF-R1
Year:	2004
Power:	172 bhp
Capacity:	998 cc
Type:	4 cyl. in-line, 4-stroke

Yamaha WR 450 F

The larger of the two WR versions had also been revised almost annually since its debut in 1998. After the first increase of capacity from 399 to 426 cc, in 2003 a 449-cc engine was on the way. The power of this hard enduro bike with this enlarged capacity went from 45 to 53 bhp. In the YZ 450 moto-cross version, this relatively small-capacity single cylinder power unit developed a full 60 bhp.

Model:	WR 450 F
Year:	2004
Power:	53 bhp
Capacity:	449 cc
Type:	Single-cylinder, 4-stroke

Yamaha FJR 1300 ABS

Travelling long distances at speed and in comfort was the domain of the FJR 1300. And if it had to, it would provide a reasonable sports ride on winding roads. At the end of the day, the great strength of the FJR was that it had no real weaknesses. It would tackle all demands without complaint and give pleasure with its many carefully-considered details. This was particularly the case since in the modifications of 2003 many miscellaneous niggles had been removed and final weaknesses ironed out. So now there was not only a powerful braking system at the front with 320-mm discs, but also ABS was fitted as standard.

Model:	FJR 1300 ABS
Year:	2004
Power:	144 bhp
Capacity:	1298 cc
Type:	4-cylinder in-line, 4-stroke

Yamaha XJR 1300

This muscular motorbike had been in the Yamaha range since 1994. It first appeared with a 1200-cc engine and in 1998 the XJR's capacity was increased to 1300 cc. Originally the engine came from the 1200-cc FJ but it was substantially modified for use in the XJR. The power output of 106 bhp from the air-cooled four-valve engine was more than enough for a traditional un-faired road bike and gave it a maximum speed of 210 km/h (130 mph).

Model:	XJR 1300
Year:	2005
Power:	106 bhp
Capacity:	1251 cc
Type:	4-cylinder in-line, 4-stroke

Yamaha BT 1100 Bulldog

The Bulldog was discreetly revised for the 2005 model year. The new seat design gave the rider more freedom of movement, the braking equipment from the R1 provided extreme stopping power and the shortened handlebars gave a more comfortable riding position while the catalytic converter provided better control of exhaust emissions. But Yamaha did nothing to increase the engine's relatively modest power output of 65 bhp.

Model:	BT 1100 Bulldog
Year:	2005
Power:	65 bhp
Capacity:	1063 cc
Type:	V-twin, 4-stroke

Yamaha YZF-R46

After Valentino Rossi finished the 2004 season by winning the World MotoGP Championship title for Yamaha, the popular Italian rider was honoured with a special model of the 2005 R6. The '46' referred to Rossi's number with which he had won all his titles so far. Apart from a hefty increase in price, the R46 with Rossi's paint job was a 2005 R6 Series with optimised handling and performance, and it was also fitted with radial-mounted brake callipers.

Model:	YZF-R46
Year:	2005
Power:	120 bhp
Capacity:	599 cc
Type:	4-cylinder in-line, 4-stroke

Yamaha Tricker Pro

With the Tricker Pro Yamaha has conjured from its sleeve the equivalent of a powered BMX bike. With its freestyle technology it was reasonably well-adapted to anything. The Tricker was ultra-light with a dry weight of 94 kg (207 lb) and it was extremely simple to operate. The combination of a high-torque single-cylinder 4-stroke engine and light suspension promised undiluted enjoyment of daring driving manoeuvres.

Model:	Tricker Pro
Year:	2005
Power:	n.a.
Capacity:	249 cc
Type:	Single-cylinder, 4-stroke

Yamaha MT-01

The undisputed scene-stealer of the 2004 Intermot show was the MT-01: a distinctive muscle bike with the 1700-cc V-twin engine of the Road Star Warrior. In contrast to the Warrior, the MT-01 was not a cruiser but a hefty, relaxed sports bike with a long stroke V-twin engine. Erik Buell had demonstrated how stimulating the combination of a nimble chassis and a smooth, powerful engine could be with his charismatic Harley Sportster bikes. Such was the composure of the Yamaha V-twin with its sheer power at low revs that even below 4,000 rpm it could deliver 150 Nm of magnificent torque. A dream indeed…

Model:	MT-01
Year:	2005
Power:	90 bhp
Capacity:	1670 cc
Type:	V-twin, 4-stroke

Yamaha YZ 250 F

With the introduction of the new regulations for the moto-cross GP125 category in the year 2002, the triumphal march of the 4-stroke machines in moto-cross events could no longer be continued. Yamaha's answer to the new regulations was the powerful, lightweight YZ 250 F. Already in the very first moto-cross event of 2003 with the RZ team rider Andrea Bartolini it gave proof of its powerful capabilities by making the fastest lap. With its short-stroke interpretation of the high-torque liquid-cooled 249-cc dohc 5-valve engine it had the remarkable power of 42 bhp and ample torque at low and middle revs. Since the more even performance of the 4-stroke engines made better lap times possible, 2-stroke moto-cross bikes have made a relatively slower showing in the meantime.

Model:	YZ 250 F
Year:	2004
Power:	42 bhp
Capacity:	249 cc
Type:	Single-cylinder, 4-stroke

Zündapp – 'The Green Elephant'

The 'Zünder- und Apparatebau GmbH-Nürnberg' company, founded by Fritz Neumeyer in 1917, produced armaments. The company began trading under the name 'Zündapp' in 1919 and it had a collaboration agreement with the English motorbike manufacturer Levis. Zündapp launched its own 'Z22' 2-stroke motorbike on the market on a Levis chassis. The EM 250, launched in 1925, became a best-seller. Zündapp bikes were sturdy and reliable and the Nuremberg company soon became Germany's second-largest motorbike manufacturer. Besides 2-stroke models, the company launched 4-stroke motorbikes for the first time in 1930. But the real sensation was the new 'K' series, presented by Zündapp in 1933. The 'K' stood for Kardan (cardan shaft drive) and for Kastenrahmen ('box frame'). The KS-600 2-cylinder boxer motorbike launched in 1938 became a legend. The bike had been specially developed for sidecars and it was the ancestor of the KS 601 'Green Elephant' which became so very popular after the Second World War. Zündapp resumed production after the war in 1947 with tried and tested 2-stroke bikes. The KS 601 became available from dealers in 1950 and Zündapp was soon offering a wide range of models. The company was also involved in cross-country races. In the 1960s and 1970s the company produced mopeds and light motorcycles. It ceased production in the 1980s when the market collapsed and the company was sold to China in 1984.

Zündapp EM 250 single-cylinder model

The Zündapp advertising slogan was simple and catchy: 'reliable'. And it was not a vain promise. The 2-stroke bikes were sturdy, long-lasting and required little maintenance. They were everyday motorbikes which could be relied upon. To advertise its bikes Zündapp put its faith in cross-country reliability trials and racing events. Here the customers could witness the victory of 'their bikes' and then ride home on a similar model.

Model:	EM 250 'single-cylinder model'	Year:	1927	Power:	4.5 bhp
Capacity: 249 cc		Type:	Single-cylinder, 2-stroke		

Zündapp Z 300

The Zündapp Z 300 was launched in 1928 as a successor to the EN 300. It was solid single-cylinder 2-stroke bike on which the sports loving Julius von Krohn crossed France in the 'Tour de France' for motorbikes without incurring any penalty points.

Model:	Z 300	Year:	1930	Power:	9 bhp
Capacity: 297 cc		Type:	Single cylinder	2-stroke	

Zündapp K 800

A healthy economic situation enabled Zündapp to launch the new K-range in 1933. The K 800 was a show-piece bike with a 4-cylinder boxer engine. The 2-bhp 4-stroke engine had extraordinary smoothness combined with powerful traction. This horizontal engine was mounted on a sturdy pressed-steel frame with a trapezoid forks for the front wheel, but the Zündapp engineers had not thought of introducing rear-wheel suspension.

Model:	K 800	Year:	1938	Power:	20 bhp
Capacity: 791 cc		Type:	4-cylinder boxer, 4-stroke		

Zündapp K 800 Gespann (combination)

In 1935 the power of the K 800 was increased from 20 to 22 bhp as part of some routine improvements. The 4-cylinder motorbike was available from the factory already fitted with a Zündapp-Stoye sport or tourer sidecar.

Model: K 800 Stoye sidecar
Year: 1935
Power: 22 bhp
Capacity: 791 cc
Type: 4-cylinder boxer, 4-stroke

Zündapp KS 601 Gespann 'Grüner Elefant' ('Green Elephant')

The Nuremberg Zündapp company launched the newly developed Zündapp KS 601 in 1950. The 28-bhp bike could be ordered from the factory as single motorbike or with a sidecar. The KS-601 bike with sidecar was extremely popular with inveterate bikers and was reverently referred to as the 'Green Elephant'. As an expression of their strong sense of belonging together, 'elephant herders' would meet up during the winter. This 'elephant-meeting' still exists today.

Model: KS 601 Gespann   Year: 1950   Power: 28 bhp
Capacity: 597 cc   Type: 2-cylinder boxer, 4-stroke

Zündapp KS 601 Sport

In 1953 Zündapp expanded the KS-601 range and brought out the KS 601 Sport for its more sport-orientated customers. The power was increased from 28 to 34 bhp while the maximum speed went up from 120 to 150 km/h (75 to 93 mph). The Sport was also available with a raised exhaust system to special order.

Model: KS 601 Sport   Year: 1957   Power: 34 bhp
Capacity: 597 cc   Type: 2-cylinder boxer, 4-stroke

Zündapp 250 S Trophy

Cross-country was always an important concept at Zündapp. Throughout the years the company had always been very successful in the prestigious 'International Six Day Trial event. In 1957 the Zündapp works team won the Six Day Trophy in Czechoslovakia. The experience gained in these competitions was applied to the production bikes and in 1958 the Zündapp 250 S Trophy was available from dealers. The sturdy single-cylinder 2-stroke engine was capable of developing 14.5 bhp and reached a top speed of 110 km/h (68 mph).

Model: 250 S Trophy   Year: 1958   Power: 14.5 bhp
Capacity: 245 cc   Type: Single-cylinder, 2-stroke

Zündapp GS 50 Geländesport

Lightweight bikes went through an amazing boom in the 1960s and 1970s. They were manufactured by well-known names such as Kreidler, Hercules, Sachs, DKW, Maico, Puch and Zündapp. The Zündapp K 50 went like greased lightning and was therefore extremely popular with the moped-crazy young. Zündapp continued to be very much involved in competition. The GS 50 won many victories and won the international Six Day Trial several times.

Model: GS 50
Year: 1966
Power: 5.25 bhp
Capacity: 49 cc
Type: Single-cylinder, 2-stroke

F-Rod

Fred Kodlin is one of the most famous customisers in the world. He has won several trophies at Daytona Bike Week, the custom bike show, and was voted Bike Builder of the Year in 2005. No wonder he was one of the first to create a radical customised bike powered by the new Harley-Davidson V-Rod engine. The chassis was completely different from that of the original. The frame was his own creation and it was this that made the radical styling of the F-Rod possible. The shape of the dummy tank seemed like a natural extension of the fairing. Dummy tank? Yes, that is correct, because in the production Harley-Davidson V-Rod the fuel tank was not where it might be expected to be, but under the seat to achieve the best possible centre of gravity position. The dummy petrol tank, on the other hand, contained the electrics and Ram-Air inlet duct which supplied the V-Rod power unit with sufficient air to operate at its best. The F-Rod was fitted with a jerk damper to ensure a smoother start; in this case it was fitted to the front wheel and not to the rear wheel as it was in mass-produced bikes.

Model:	F-Rod
Year:	2003
Power:	115 bhp
Capacity:	1130 cc
Type:	V-twin, 4-stroke

Author: Carsten Heil

With the assistance of: Dr. Michael Ahlsdorf, Diana Becker, Dr. Heinrich Christmann, Horst Heiler,
Dirk Mangartz, Winni Scheibe, Stephan H. Schneider, Jens Müller.

Picture sources/Photographers: Carsten Heil, Dirk Mangartz, Winni Scheibe, Stephan H. Schneider

Special thanks to the importers and manufacturers who have helped with picture material and technical information:
Aprilia Motorrad GmbH, Betamotor Deutschland GmbH, BMW Motorrad, Ducati Motor Deutschland GmbH, Harley-Davidson GmbH,
Honda Motor Europe (North) GmbH, Kawasaki Motors Deutschland N.V., KTM Sportmotorcycle GmbH, Piaggio Deutschland GmbH, März-
Motorrad-handel GmbH (Benelli), Motonobili Tommy Wagner (Bimota, Mondial), MSA GmbH (Hyosung), MV Agusta Motor Deutschland GmbH,
MZ Motorrad- und Zweiradwerk GmbH, Adam Opel AG, Polaris Industries Inc. (Victory), Sachs Fahrzeug- und Motorentechnik GmbH,
Stein-Dinse GmbH (Laverda), Suzuki International Europe GmbH, Triumph Motorrad Deutschland GmbH, Walz Hardcore Cycles (Jordan F1-Bike),
ZTK Erlebniswelt (Bimota) as well as the Deutschen Zweirad-Museum Neckarsulm, Jawa Club Wien, Volker Rost (pages 18/19),
KTM Action-Photos: Heil, Hofer, Mairitsch, Peuker, Fred Kodin Motorcycles (Borken), Walz Hardcore Cycles (Hockenheim),
Jochen Sommer Motorradtechnik (Eppstein-Vockenhausen)